THE WORLD CITIES

PETER HALL

THE WORLD CITIES

Second Edition

McGraw-Hill Book Company

*New York   St. Louis   San Francisco   Bogotá
Düsseldorf   Madrid   Mexico   Montreal
Panama   Paris   São Paulo   Tokyo   Toronto*

Reprinted by arrangement with
Weidenfeld and Nicolson,
London

First McGraw-Hill Paperback
edition, 1979

1234567890 MUMU 7832109

Library of Congress Cataloging in Publication Data
Hall, Peter Geoffrey.
    The world cities.

    Reprint of the ed. published by
Weidenfeld and Nicolson, London.
    Bibliography: p.
    Includes index.
    1. Metropolitan areas. I. Title.
[HT330.H3 1979]   301.36′4′0722   78-26071
ISBN 0-07-025607-1

Contents

Acknowledgments

For help during the writing of the first edition of this book, my grateful thanks are due to: Professor W. Gordon East and Professor Michael J. Wise, in London; Dr G.B.W. Huizinga, in Ommen, Netherlands; Mr Kunihiro Omori, in Tokyo; Messrs Stanley J. Tankel, Ernst Hacker and Joseph Leper, in New York; and Mr Rodric Braithwaite. I want especially to thank Birkbeck College for their generous grant which made it possible to study New York at first hand. Miss Ursula Stoksa typed the manuscript with great speed and efficiency. For the second edition of the book I am equally indebted to Professor Claude Chaline, on Paris; Mr Stephen Hamnett, on the Randstad; Dr Norman Perry, on Rhine–Ruhr; Dr Ian Hamilton, on Moscow; Mr Boris Pushkarev, on New York; and Professor William Robson, on Tokyo. My secretaries – Mrs Monika Wheeler, Mrs Linda Hoskins and Miss Linda Tarrant – also deserve my best thanks.

My thanks are due to Mrs Kathleen King who designed the maps, and to the following sources for providing material: Standing Conference on London Regional Planning; Her Majesty's Stationery Office; PADOG; IAURP; J. Winsemius; Het Rijksdienst voor het nationale Plan; Siedlungsverband Ruhrkohlenbezirk; Regional Plan Association, New York; Tokyo Metropolitan Government.

THE WORLD CITIES

1 The metropolitan explosion

There are certain great cities, in which a quite disproportionate part of the world's most important business is conducted. In 1915 the pioneer thinker and writer on city and regional planning, Patrick Geddes, christened them *the world cities*. This book is about their growth and problems.

By what characteristics do we distinguish the world cities from other great centres of population and wealth? In the first place, they are usually the major centres of political power. They are the seats of the most powerful national governments and sometimes of international authorities too; of government agencies of all kinds. Round these gather a host of institutions, whose main business is with government: the big professional organisations, the trades unions, the employers' federations, the headquarters of major industrial concerns.

These cities are the national centres not merely of government but also of trade. Characteristically they are great ports, which distribute imported goods to all parts of their countries, and in return receive goods for export to the other nations of the world. Within each country, roads and railways focus on the metropolitan city. The world cities are the sites of the great international airports: Heathrow, Kennedy, Orly, Schiphol, Shermetyevo. Traditionally, the world cities are the leading banking and finance centres of the countries in which they stand. Here are housed the central banks, the headquarters of the trading banks, the offices of the big insurance organisations and a whole series of specialised financial and insurance agencies.

Government and trade were invariably the original *raisons d'être* of the world cities. But these places early became the centres where professional talents of all kinds congregated. Each of the world cities has its great hospitals, its distinct medical quarter, its legal profession gathered around the national courts of justice. Students and teachers are drawn to the world cities; they commonly contain great universities, as well as a host of specialised institutions for teaching and research in the sciences, the technologies and the arts. The great national libraries and museums are here. Inevitably, the world cities have become the places where information is gathered and disseminated: the book publishers are found here; so are the publishers of newspapers and periodicals, and with them their journalists and regular contributors. In this century also the world cities have naturally become headquarters of the great national radio and television networks.

Not only are the world cities great centres of population: their populations, as a rule, contain a significant proportion of the richest members of the community. That early led to the development of luxury industries and shops; and in a more affluent age these have been joined by new types of more democratic trading: by the great department stores and the host of specialised shops which cater for every demand. Around them, too, the range of industry has widened: for the traditional luxury articles, forged by craftsmen in the world cities of old, have become articles of popular consumption, and their manufacture now takes place on the assembly lines of vast factories in the suburbs of the world cities.

As manufacture and trade have come to cater for a wider market so has another of the staple businesses of the world cities – the provision of entertainment. The traditional opera houses and theatres and concert halls and luxurious restaurants, once the preserve of the aristocracy and the great merchant, are now open to a wider audience, who increasingly can pay their price. They have been joined by new and more popular forms of entertainment – the variety theatre and revue, the cinema, the night club, and a whole gamut of eating and drinking places.

The staple trades of the world cities go from strength to strength. Here and there, a trade may wither and decay: thus shoemaking in nineteenth-century London, diamond-cutting in twentieth-century Amsterdam, shirt-making in twentieth-century New York. In the long historical view, even the world cities may themselves decline. Where now is Bruges – a world city of late medieval Europe? But such cases are conspicuous by their rarity. Nothing is more notable about the world cities than their continued economic strength. Not for them the fate of depressed regions which see their staple products decline: regions like the coalfields of Northumberland–Durham in Britain and Pennsylvania–West Virginia in the United States, or the agricultural and light industrial areas of the Massif Central of France and the Rhine Uplands of Germany. For as the economies of the advanced nations become more sophisticated, so does the emphasis shift to those industries and trades most aptly carried on in the metropolis: industries and trades dependent on skill, on design, on fashion, on contact with the specialised needs of the buyer. Associated with these trends, white-collar jobs grow faster than factory jobs: for every producer of goods, more and more people are needed at office desks to achieve good design, to finance and plan production, to sell the goods, to promote efficient nation-wide and world-wide distribution.

All these trends help to swell the populations of the world cities. Table 1 shows that around 1970 there were twenty-four metropolitan centres in the world each with a population of over four million; eighteen with over five million; five with over ten million. Not all these are world cities: even among the real giants, urban complexes like Osaka-Kobe, Chicago or Los Angeles have a regional, not a national or international significance. And conversely, some of the complexes near the foot of the table – like the Dutch Randstad – play a world role as centres of trade, of finance, of culture, which is far greater than the mere total of population might indicate. This book therefore will study seven centres among the twenty-four. Six of them are the greatest urban agglomerations of the world. First we look at two west European capital cities – London and Paris – which have tended progressively to grow at the expense of the provincial areas of their two countries, giving rise to very similar problems of congestion at the centre, economic decline and underemployment in the provinces. Then we turn to two urban complexes – the Randstad, or Ring City, of the Netherlands, and the Rhine–Ruhr complex of Federal Germany – which are world cities of a very special form. Instead of concentrating all the metropolitan functions into a single, highly centralised giant city, these countries have managed through accidents of history to distribute them among a number of smaller, specialised, closely-related centres. This 'polycentric' type of metropolis has special interest for planners and citizens in those countries which have to grapple with the centralised city. We look at eastern Europe, where Moscow proves to be a rapidly-growing, multi-million metropolis with many of the problems of its western European counterparts. In North America the gigantic New York urban complex, biggest in the world in terms of population, presents many of the essential problems of the metropolitan city in a particularly acute form; it shows that a high degree of affluence may bring extra difficulties to the planner. Lastly Tokyo stands as the most advanced example of the fast-growing cities of eastern Asia. Its phenomenal rate of population growth – by far the most rapid of any metropolis considered here – demonstrates the potential problems in store for cities in many developing countries; and its peculiar difficulties of physical planning offer a warning for countries whose financial and technical resources are still very limited.

Forces behind metropolitan growth

Most of this book is an examination, in more detail, of the growth of these seven city-complexes; of the causes behind that growth, the problems which result, and of the attempts to solve those problems. But because the book is mainly about the particular problems of particular cities, it is important to understand from the outset the general forces, which all over the world are contributing to the continued growth of the world cities. There are three such. The first is that population is increasing, and threatens to go on increasing in almost every country in the world. True, by the late 1970s many developed countries had experienced a drastic reduction in growth from the high levels of the 1950s and 1960s, when birth rates peaked. But modest growth is still likely – and this is especially important for the developed nations, in which so many world cities are concentrated.

The second factor is the continued shift of mankind off the land, and into industry and service occupations in the cities. This is a trend which has been observable in all advanced countries since the industrial revolution, and which has now spread in some measure to almost every country in the world. Progressively, more and more of the world's population is becoming urbanised.

The third factor is that a large part of the total urban growth is being concentrated in the great metropolitan areas. It is difficult to generalise about this: though nearly all world cities seem to be attracting a progressively greater share of the populations of their

Table 1 The world's metropolitan areas *c*. 1970

(C = Census, E = Estimate)

1	Tokyo–Yokohama	1970(C)	23,873,000
2	New York– Northeastern New Jersey	1970(C)	16,179,000
3	Osaka–Kobe–Kyoto	1968(E)	12,300,000
4	London	1971(C)	12,037,000
5	Rhine–Ruhr	1970(C)	10,924,000
6	Moscow	1970(C)	10,718,000
7	Los Angeles–Anaheim– San Bernadino	1970(C)	9,593,000
8	Paris	1968(E)	8,850,000
9	Buenos Aires	1968(E)	8,600,000
10	Calcutta	1968(E)	7,900,000
11	Shanghai	1968(E)	7,800,000
12	Chicago– Northwestern Indiana	1970(C)	7,612,000
13	Mexico City	1970(C)	7,314,000
14	São Paulo	1968(E)	6,600,000
15	Rio de Janeiro	1968(E)	6,100,000
16	Cairo	1968(E)	5,900,000
17	Bombay	1968(E)	5,650,000
18	Philadelphia–Trenton– Wilmington	1970(C)	5,621,000
19	Peking	1968(E)	4,750,000
20	Detroit–Windsor	1970(C)	4,423,000
21	Leningrad	1968(E)	4,350,000
22	Seoul	1968(E)	4,175,000
23	San Francisco–Oakland– San José	1970(C)	4,175,000
24	Randstad Holland	1970(E)	4,100,000

Source: Richard L. Forstall and Victor Jones in Simon Miles, *Metropolitan Problems* (1970), updated in part from 1970/71 Census.

countries, some – London, Randstad, New York – are relatively losing ground. Whatever the relative rates of growth, however, in absolute terms most of the world cities are still increasing; and this alone creates enormous problems of land-use competition, transportation, urban renewal and local government.

In the rest of this chapter we will look at these forces in statistical terms. First, because it is fundamental, is the general growth of population.

Population growth:
the mid-twentieth century revolution

The great world cities are still disproportionately concentrated in the most advanced industrial countries of Europe and North America. So it is important to understand a most potent factor in modern metropolitan growth: the profound change, amounting to a double revolution, in the pattern of population growth of these advanced countries.

Table 2 Total increase of population in advanced industrial countries

	1935–9 average	Postwar 'hump'	per cent per year 1950	1960	1970	1974
Canada	0·98	2·11	1·97	2·13	1·51	1·58
USA	0·75	1·95	1·67	1·60	1·08	0·72
Belgium	0·30	0·34	0·29	0·54	0·31	0·41
Denmark	0·74	1·18	0·97	0·75	0·61	0·60
France	−0·75	0·90	0·81	0·99	0·89	0·73
Western Germany	0·89	1·94	1·61	1·11	1·43	0·11
Italy	0·87	0·68	0·64	0·63	0·94	0·84
Netherlands	1·06	1·74	1·59	1·18	1·16	0·74
Norway	0·58	1·16	0·96	0·84	0·78	0·76
Sweden	0·37	–	0·83	0·35	1·00	0·25
Switzerland	0·34	–	1·19	2·12	0·96	0·78
United Kingdom	0·58	0·64	0·58	0·73	0·32	0·09
Japan	3·30	2·59	1·37	0·83	1·19	1·22

In the 1930s the population texts, like Sir Alexander Carr-Saunders' *World Population*, gave no hint of what was to come. Then, it appeared that population in every country followed a fairly simple pattern. In primitive countries, and in all the world until about 1750, a high 'natural' birth rate was offset by high infantile mortality, arising from malnutrition and lack of medical knowledge, and a high adult death rate caused by wars, epidemics and famines. Later, rapid medical advance and better diets caused a big reduction in the death rate, while the birth rate remained high, resulting in a rapid natural increase of the population; this condition prevailed in western Europe and North America between 1750 and 1900. Later still, the spread of contraceptive knowledge caused a fall in the birth rate in advanced countries of western Europe and North America; but the death rate had already been cut so low that it could not fall as fast as the birth rate, so that the rate of population increase in such countries declined, and by the 1930s in some cases was approaching zero. The

Natural increase of population in advanced industrial countries

	1935–9 average	Postwar 'hump'	per cent per year 1950	1960	1970	1974
Canada	1·05	1·93	1·80	1·91	1·00	0·81*
USA	0·61	1·57	1·39	1·41	0·88	0·59
Belgium	0·20	0·47	0·44	0·40	0·23	0·07
Denmark	0·72	1·30	0·94	0·70	0·46	0·40
France	−0·05	1·06	0·78	0·66	0·61	0·48
Western Germany	2·69	0·66	0·44	0·63	0·17	−0·16
Italy	0·93	1·09	0·98	0·88	0·71	0·61
Netherlands	1·16	2·17	1·52	1·36	1·00	0·58
Norway	0·48	1·32	1·00	0·82	0·64	0·50
Sweden	0·28	–	0·64	0·37	0·37	0·28
Switzerland	0·38	–	0·80	0·70	0·69	0·44
United Kingdom	0·31	0·83	0·44	0·60	0·44	0·11
Japan	1·18	2·17	1·73	0·96	1·20	1·28*

* 1973.

population experts in most advanced countries were therefore convinced that at some date – perhaps 1940, perhaps 1960, perhaps 1980 – the population curve would turn down, as had already occurred in France. Dr Enid Charles forecast in 1935 that on the basis of the then-current trends the population of England and Wales would fall from 40·5 million to 4·4 million in 2035. Professor Alfred Sauvy in France projected that there would be a decline from 41·9 million to between 30 and 39 million in 1975. German experts postulated a decline; so, assuming no immigration, did United States demographers. Carr-Saunders in Britain thought that the trend would spread eventually through all Europe. Economists were everywhere considering the consequences of a declining population.

Table 2 shows the changed situation since those years. It is clear first that the *total* increase of population is tied very closely to the *natural* increase. True, immigration has been important in the late 1930s into the United Kingdom, from 1945 into Federal Germany and from 1950 into Sweden, Switzerland and Canada until the recession of the 1970s; emigration reached very high levels in the late 1930s out of Nazi Germany and was quite important in the 1950s out of Italy. But these exceptions apart, for the explanation of recent changes in population growth we need to look at natural forces, and in particular – since death rates are low and almost static in advanced countries – at births.

Natural increase, or in other words the birth rate, was low in the 1930s in all advanced countries save Canada, the Netherlands, Italy (all with big Catholic populations) and Germany (where Nazi propaganda encouraged births). Japan was then at an earlier stage of demographic evolution. The birth rate stayed low almost to the end of the Second World War, though in Denmark it humped sharply up as early as 1945 – a foretaste of what was to come in every country of the group, save the two neutrals, between then and 1949. (Federal Germany, the defeated member, was interestingly the last over the hump, in 1949.) The hump represented the postwar 'baby boom', which demographers confidently explained as births delayed by the war. And indeed by 1950 birth rates, and therefore natural increase, had fallen sharply in all these countries.

But the new 'low' birth rates were in nearly every case much higher than the low ones of the 1930s. (The exception was Germany, where the rate in the 1930s was artificially high.) And in the 1950s they did not decline in any consistent pattern. It is true that they did fall somewhat in some countries, but nowhere radically save in Japan (which was entering a new stage of demographic development) and Sweden; and they remained much higher than before the war.

Then – from the late 1950s in the United States, from the mid-1960s in much of western Europe – birth rates turned down again; and in the 1970s in many countries they plummetted. By 1974 Germany had a natural decrease; Britain's natural increase was near-zero. National differences, political factors and, above all, age structures are still important: there is all the difference between Belgium with its relatively old population and its rate of increase of only 0·07 per cent (in 1974), and Canada with its exceptionally young population and its increase of 0·8 per cent (in 1973).

Thus the demographic problem has changed rapidly. In the mid-1960s all these countries were showing sustained population growth through natural increase, and the immediate problem was to accommodate the extra people. But by the late 1970s there was the prospect of a near-static population. This can be seen by comparing the official population forecasts. In 1955, when the 'baby boom' seemed to have spent itself in Britain, the Registrar General calculated that the United Kingdom population would rise from 51·2 million (then) to 52·8 million in 1995. But just at this time the birth rate began to bound up – and this meant a big increase in fertility, for it was not accompanied by an expansion in the child-bearing female population. By 1960 the forecast was 62·1 million for 1995 and 63·8 million for 2000; by 1965 it was up again, to 74·6 million for 2000. Then the birth rate turned down again; by 1970 the projection for 2000 was down to 66·0 million. By 1975, with birth-rate at its lowest-ever level of 12 per thousand, the prospect was of an almost static population of some 55 million down to the century's end. In the United States, the Census Bureau's 1955 forecast was between 206·9 million and 228·5 million in 1975, depending on different assumptions. In 1958 the population was running so far ahead of the forecasts that the figures had to be revised upwards to a range of 215·8 to 243·9 million in 1975. By 1972, with the 1970 figure running below the 1958 projections at 205 million, the President's Commission on Population Growth and the American Future was accepting a projection of between 271 and 322 million in 2000. Again, by the mid-1970s' these forecasts had been drastically cut back. In both Britain and the United States, therefore, fertility – and, belatedly following, official population projections – went up and then went down again;

the turning point in the United States came in the late 1950s, in the United Kingdom in the middle 1960s.

In all advanced countries today the big population riddle therefore concerns the pattern of fertility. Even highly sophisticated forecasts – such as that of the French expert, Jean Bourgeois-Pichat, for the countries of western Europe in 1953 – have gone wrong because they assumed that sooner or later fertility would return to a 'normal' pattern. It now seems clear that after World War Two fertility went up in a number of advanced western countries. In the United States the average number of children per woman, implied by the birth rate, rose from a low point of just over 2·0 in the 1930s to a peak of about 3·7 in the mid-1950s; but it then sank nearly to 1930s levels by the early 1970s. In Britain, it appears that women who started childbearing in the 1930s were producing on average about 2·0 children each – a bare replacement rate; those who began in the 1950s seemed likely to produce 2·4 or more children each, but with a probable fall in the number for the mothers of the late 1950s onwards.

In the late 1970s, therefore, demographic prospects were mixed. For most advanced countries, the forecasts gave low or nil growth; for the developing world, the certainty was continued buoyant increase – albeit at a declining rate. But in advanced countries, a near-static population was dividing itself into more and more, smaller and smaller households – a result of rising numbers of older people and of social changes which caused younger people to desert the parental home, plus rising divorce rates. Thus a static population could still produce a rising demand for homes. The question was where those homes would be; and thus the second factor – the pattern of urbanisation and of urban growth – becomes an acute problem.

The world pattern of urban growth

In 1899 Adna Ferrin Weber, a young graduate of Cornell University in New York, published a thesis on *The Growth of Cities in the Nineteenth Century*. He manipulated with great skill a mass of statistics from different countries to show that urbanisation had been one of the most distinctive, and most universal, features of the nineteenth century. Thus in England, the percentage of the total population that was urban had risen from 16·9 in 1801 to 53·7 in 1891; in the United States from 3·8 in 1800 to 27·6 in 1890; in France from 24·4 in 1846 to 37·4 in 1891; in Prussia from 25·5 in 1816 to 40·7 in 1895.

Since Weber wrote, the process has continued unabated. It is now recorded by the United Nations Statistical Office in their *Demographic Yearbook*, on which table 3 has been based. This diagram makes it clear that with variations, the most highly developed

Table 3 Percentages of population in urban areas

CANADA
1921, 49·5
1931, 53·7
1941, 54·3
1951, 62·9
1956, 66·6
1961, 69·6
1966, 73·6

USA
1920, 51·2
1930, 56·2
1940, 56·5
1950, 64·0
1960, 69·9
1970, 73·5

BELGIUM
1920, 57·3
1930, 60·5
1947, 62·7
1961, 66·4
1968, 86·8

FRANCE
1921, 46·4
1931, 51·2
1946, 53·0
1954, 55·9
1962, 63·4
1968, 70·0

SWEDEN
1920, 29·5
1930, 32·5
1940, 44·4
1950, 47·5
1960, 72·8
1965, 77·4
1970, 81·4

SWITZERLAND
1920, 27·6
1930, 30·4
1941, 32·9
1950, 36·5
1960, 51·3
1970, 54·6

ENGLAND AND WALES
1921, 79·3
1931, 80·0
1951, 80·8
1961, 80·0
1971, 78·3

USSR
1926, 17·9
1939, 31·7
1959, 47·9
1970, 56·3

WEST GERMANY
1939, 70·5
1946, 68·6
1950, 71·1
1961, 76·8

NETHERLANDS
1920, 45·6
1930, 48·7
1947, 54·6
1960, 80·0
1969, 78·0

NORWAY
1920, 29·6
1930, 28·4
1946, 28·0
1950, 32·2
1961, 32·1
1970, 42·5

JAPAN
1920, 18·1
1930, 24·1
1940, 37·9
1950, 37·5
1955, 56·3
1960, 63·5
1965, 68·1
1970, 72·2

AUSTRALIA
1933, 64·0
1947, 68·9
1954, 78·9
1961, 81·9
1971, 85·5

industrial nations are the most intensively urbanised. (And conversely: at the 1970 count 3·5 per cent of the population of Rwanda is recorded as 'urban', in New Guinea 4·7 per cent, in Malawi 5·0 per cent.) It is notable too that the countries which undergo the most rapid economic development also record a rapid increase in urbanisation – as Japan in table 3, which went from 18 per cent urban to 72 per cent in the half-century from 1920 to 1970. Indeed there is a close relationship between the figures of table 3 and the figures of the industrial structure of the labour force, which Colin Clark published for various dates in his book *The Conditions of Economic Progress.* England and Wales stands at one extreme, with 40 per cent of its labour force in manufacturing and 80 per cent of its population urbanised. Experience in Norway, Sweden and Switzerland shows that industrialisation *can* take place on a largely-rural basis, especially with the aid of hydro-electric power; but these countries prove exceptions to a very general rule. The indication is that most countries will continue to shift part of their workforce off the land, so that the urban percentage of the population will grow; that there will however be a limit to this, as the example of Britain shows; but that even when the urban population does not grow proportionately it may still grow absolutely, as long as high birth rates in the advanced countries continue.

In such international comparisons there is one great snag, which Weber first faced. One country's definition of an urban place, or of urban population, differs from another's: in Denmark a place with 250 people is urban, in Korea a place with less than 40,000 is not. In 1956 an American research team, International Urban Research, sought to correct this. They took as basis the Standard Metropolitan Areas of the United States Census, and sought equivalents in other countries, so as to provide a world-wide list of urban areas based on a common, standardised, functional definition. The definition they employed was *an urban unit containing a population of at least 100,000 people, being an area embracing a central city or cities, plus adjacent areas with an economic relationship with that city and with 65 per cent or more of their economically-active populations engaged in non-agricultural activities.*

This scheme has two advantages. It permits precise international comparisons of the degree of urbanisation, and of the growth of urban populations over time. And it provides a ready, functional definition of the metropolitan region of each country – the area around the metropolitan or capital city, be it commercial, administrative, financial or industrial.

The time-comparison has been made by the director of International Urban Research, Kingsley Davis, and his team, using a modified version of the urban definition just quoted; they show that while in 1950 about 28 per cent of the population of the world was urbanised, by 1970 the proportion had risen to 38 per cent. As table 4 shows, the rate of increase of the urban population was fastest in the developing parts of the world, where generally the proportion of urban to total population was lower in 1950. The explanation seems to be a fairly simple mechanical one: as urban areas account for progressively greater proportions of the total populations of their countries, they have progressively less chance of maintaining their rate of growth, because the pool of non-urban population which supplies them becomes relatively smaller. Even developed countries, though, probably have some scope for further urbanisation. The most metropolitan continent in 1970 was Australasia (because it was dominated by Australia and New Zealand), with 84 per cent of its population in metropolitan areas, but North America, northern and western Europe were close behind with 73–76 per cent urban populations.

World city-regions and their growth

What matters here, though, is not merely the general growth of population, not even the general growth of the urban population, but a third factor: the growth of the world cities, *vis-à-vis* the other urban populations and the populations as a whole. And this leads to major problems of definition.

For every major country of the world it should be possible, with the aid of the original metropolitan area definitions from International Urban Research, to distinguish a distinct metropolitan region: a single dominant metropolitan area, surrounding and growing out from a world city. Sometimes, indeed, in some highly centralised states of western Europe, this is perfectly simple. There can be no doubt that the United Kingdom's metropolitan region is the London metropolitan area, to which should be added nineteen smaller contiguous areas giving a total population at the 1971 Census of 12,036,900 or 21·8 per cent of the total United Kingdom at that time. Similarly with Paris, where a single metropolitan area contained 8,850,000 people or 17·8 per cent of the French population in 1968; or

Table 4 Per cent of population in urban areas, in continents and their subdivisions, 1950–70

| | Urban population as per cent of total population | | Rates of population growth | | | |
	1950	1970	1950–60 total	1950–60 urban	1960–70 total	1960–70 urban
Africa North	24·6	34·6	2·4	4·3	2·6	4·2
West	10·6	19·7	3·4	6·9	3·1	6·2
East	5·6	9·9	2·5	5·5	2·5	5·3
Middle/South	6·6	15·4	1·8	7·7	2·0	4·9
South	39·1	50·4	2·5	3·9	2·3	3·5
America North	63·8	75·1	1·8	2·7	1·4	2·2
Middle	39·2	53·0	3·1	4·8	3·7	5·1
Caribbean	35·2	42·5	2·2	3·1	2·4	3·5
Tropical South	35·8	53·1	3·1	5·4	2·8	4·6
Temperate South	59·1	70·2	1·9	2·8	1·9	2·7
Asia East	12·1	25·3	1·8	6·0	1·3	4·8
Japan	37·4	83·2	1·1	6·6	1·0	3·7
South East	13·6	20·1	2·5	4·6	2·7	4·7
South West	24·2	35·5	2·7	4·7	2·5	4·4
South Central	15·2	17·8	1·9	2·7	2·3	3·1
Europe North	69·5	74·9	0·4	0·8	0·7	1·0
West	63·2	73·0	0·9	1·6	1·1	1·8
East	42·4	54·6	0·9	2·2	0·7	1·9
South	40·5	50·7	0·8	2·0	0·9	2·0
Australia–New Zealand	70·0	84·3	2·3	3·4	1·8	2·6
Oceania	4·9	7·8	2·7	4·8	2·5	5·1
USSR	42·5	62·3	1·8	3·5	1·3	3·5

Source: Kingsley Davis (1969).

Brussels (2,070,000 people in 1968, 21·5 per cent of the nation); or Copenhagen (1,385,000 or 28·4 per cent in 1968); or Stockholm (1,275,000 or 16·1 per cent in 1968). In Japan the twin-headed metropolitan area of Tokyo–Yokohama (23,873,000 people in 1970, 23·0 per cent of the Japanese population) is clearly the 'metropolitan region'. But difficulties emerge when the administrative capital is separated from the commercial and financial capital, as in the United States where the true metropolitan region is not Washington (2,861,000 people in 1970) but New York–Northeastern New Jersey with 16,179,000 people or 8·0 per cent of the total United States population in 1970. They become more acute still when the administrative capital is a relatively small place and a number of large metropolitan areas exist some distance away: as in Australia, where the largest metropolitan area is Sydney with 2,600,000 people in 1968, 21·6 per cent of the population of the Australian Commonwealth. They tend to be equally complex when there is a very widely spread 'metropolitan region' containing several contiguous (or nearly contiguous) metropolitan areas. This pattern occurs in two west European countries: Germany, where an extended Rhine–Ruhr metropolitan region embraces seven metropolitan areas with a total population in 1970 of 10,924,000 – 18·4 per cent of the population of the Federal Republic; and the Netherlands, where the extended Randstad, or Ring City, takes in seven areas with a combined population in 1970 of 4,100,000 – 31·5 per cent of the Netherlands' population. Finally, in one European case the problems are so difficult as to be almost incapable of resolution. This is Italy, where political power was concentrated in Rome when unified nationhood was achieved in the 1860s, while commercial and industrial power remained in the rival metropolitan centre of Lombardy, with its great twin cities of Turin and Milan. In 1968, the Rome metropolitan area had a population of 2,810,000 – 5·3 per cent of the total Italian population; but Milan had 3,365,000 (6·4 per cent) and Turin another 1,480,000 (2·8 per cent).

In so far as they can be defined, the metropolitan regions have seen continuing and even accelerated growth since the revolutions in transport and industry of the first half of the nineteenth century. That is well illustrated by the cities which are described and illustrated in this book, as table 5 shows. In many of them, as we shall see, the central core city is now in decline; but, as population and its jobs move out, the entire retains its dynamism.

The metropolis in recent history

One critical factor in this extraordinary growth was suggested as
early as 1915 by a visionary pioneer of town-planning theory, the
Scotsman Patrick Geddes, in his book *Cities in Evolution*. The first
industrial revolution, Geddes pointed out, was based on inventions
like Darby's coke-smelting process for iron (1709), Crompton's mule
(1779) and Cartwright's power loom (1785); these inventions
harnessed coal and they produced the age of coal and iron, of heavy
industry dependent on coal and rooted to the coalfields, of black-
country landscapes like those of the Birmingham district in England,
Lille in France, the Ruhr in Germany, Pittsburgh in the United
States. But after 1850, a whole series of further inventions created a
new technology, which passed into general industrial use after 1900
and ushered in a new era: the 'neotechnic era'. They included the
electric circuit (Siemens, 1850), the telephone (Bell, 1876), the power
station (Edison, 1882), the oil well (Drake, 1859), the petrol motor
(Daimler, 1883), the radio (Marconi, 1896) and many others. The
new technology, and the industry it created, were almost the
obverse of those of the first industrial age: instead of heavy crude
products, light and increasingly complex ones; instead of coal,
electricity; instead of the universal railway, increasing dependence on
the motor vehicle; instead of concentration in congested centres,
freedom of location through improved communications.

Industry, it could now be argued, was free to locate almost
anywhere, provided that blind inertia did not multiply new industrial
plants in old industrial regions: the logical pattern of neotechnic
industry was almost complete decentralisation. This was Geddes'
thesis, and it was the thesis of writers who followed and developed his
ideas: Lewis Mumford in the United States, after the First World
War, and Jean-François Gravier, in France, after the Second.
Unfortunately, as was all too clear to Mumford and to Gravier as
they wrote, something very different was occurring: instead of
decentralisation, the neotechnic era was resulting in new concentrations of industry and services and population away from the
coalfields, in the great metropolitan regions. Both writers tried to
explain this by artificial reasons of policy: in Mumford's view the
modern megalopolis was the product of finance capitalism and of
imperial bureaucracies bent on war; in Gravier's analysis the growth
of Paris was a simple consequence of the policy of ruthless
centralisation pursued by every French government from the

Table 5 Growth of the world cities

Area*	Population, c. 1800		per cent of national total
London	(1801)	850,000	8·1
Paris	(1801)	547,000	2·0
Randstad	(1975)	400,000	21·3
Rhine–Ruhr	(1816)	280,000	2·2
Moscow	(1860)	360,000	0·5
New York	(1800)	600,000	1·1
Tokyo–Yokohama	(1785)	1,400,000	4·7

Area*	Population, c. 1950		per cent of national total
London	(1951)	11,374,000	23·2
Paris	(1954)	6,737,000	15·7
Randstad	(1947)	3,297,000	32·9
Rhine–Ruhr	(1950)	8,139,000	17·1
Moscow	(1939)	5,600,000	3·3
New York	(1950)	12,912,000	8·5
Tokyo–Yokohama	(1950)	9,049,000	10·9

Area*	Population, c. 1970		per cent of national total
London	(1971)	12,037,000	21·8
Paris	(1968)	8,850,000	16·8
Randstad	(1970)	4,100,000	31·5
Rhine–Ruhr	(1970)	10,924,000	18·4
Moscow	(1970)	10,718,000	4·4
New York	(1970)	16,179,000	8·0
Tokyo–Yokohama	(1970)	23,873,000	23·0

* Total 'metropolitan area.

Revolution of 1789 onwards. Now it is fairly evident that deliberate policies have affected the *rate* of metropolitan growth in certain countries and at certain times. But it is equally clear that the *phenomenon* of growth is universal. It has occurred alike in centralised and decentralised countries, and also both in capitalist and communist states. A more general, and perhaps a more complex cause must be sought.

Even before the general application of neotechnic technology a very significant revolution occurred, during the 1860s and 1870s, in the organisation of industrial and commercial enterprises. Up till 1850 and even later, almost all enterprises – alike in industry, trade, mining, shipping, finance – had been one-man or family firms or partnerships, financing themselves out of profits or the savings of their owners, or at most borrowing on a modest scale from local banks. But it then became evident that this form of small-scale organisation was quite unsuited to new and expanding types of activity like mining, railways or gas supply. The result was the joint-stock company with limited liability: between 1855 and 1870 England, France and Germany all made it relatively easy to form this sort of company. From then on, a critical split developed: the actual productivity process was still in the hands of the industrialist, but the more important decisions – what to produce, how much, for what markets – were henceforth in the hands of individuals remote from the factories, who held controlling interest in the new companies. In that era, these men were characteristically financiers, who at that time were uniquely fitted to decide whether a new company was worth floating, an idea worth supporting, an existing firm worthy of short-term credit.

Thorstein Veblen in 1904 pointed out a most important consequence of the change: costs were cut, not so much in manufacturing as in manufacture and selling. For the change was associated with a revolution in marketing. The popular consumption market was expanding rapidly, with rising living standards. More and more purchases were being made by corporate institutions, and (because of the increasingly complex nature of industry) by industrialists. The processes of consumption were speeded up, obsolescence became more rapid, style achieved popular significance for the first time in history. And the financiers could take advantage of these trends as the old-style manufacturing capitalist could not. The period after 1870 is one of rapid developments in marketing: of speculative production in advance of demand; of advertising to create new wants and shift existing ones; of the conscious manipulation by industry of style and fashion.

Contemporary observers of these changes – Marx and later Hobson in England, Sombart in Germany, Veblen in the United States – rightly described them as a shift in *capitalist* organisation, from early capitalism to high or finance capitalism. But that was because the characteristic and universal mode of production was the capitalist one; we cannot say how any other system of industrial organisation might have changed as it matured. The real change was deeper, deeper perhaps than the change in the identity of the people who wielded the power, took the decisions and drew the lion's share of the proceeds. It was a shift of interest away from the physical process of production, and towards questions of financing, decisions to produce, and marketing: in other words, from the factory to the office. In these years, an extraordinarily concentrated set of inventions created the modern office, which might indeed be called the first characteristic product of neotechnic technology: commercial shorthand (Pitman's, 1837), electric telegraphy (also 1837), cheap universal postage (1840), the lift or elevator (1857), the typewriter (1867), the skyscraper (c. 1875), the telephone (1876), the adding machine (developed commercially 1872–88), the electric light (1880), the steel-frame skyscraper (1883), the mimeograph and the dictating machine (1887), carbon paper (applied to typewriting c. 1890). And between 1849 and 1893, another whole series of developments in printing and photo-reproduction made modern advertising possible. It was logical, then, that these years also saw the very beginning of the dramatic shift towards white-collar employment associated with the rapid entry of women into the labour force, which has been especially characteristic of the twentieth century. In the United States, total white-collar employment rose from 5·1 million in 1900 to 21·6 million in 1950, or from 17 to 37 per cent of the total United States labour force, and women white-collar workers alone increased from less than one million to 8·6 million.

These changes had a critical effect on urban development. For while neotechnic industry might be decentralised, the neotechnic office was not. Under finance capitalism, the new types of office – the headquarters of railways, of public utilities, of industries, of foreign investment trusts – developed next to the financial institutions in the traditional banking centres. Soon, ancillary offices sprang up to provide specialised services for the new headquarters offices: accounting, law, advertising, management consultancy. Around the turn of the century, the increasing role of government in economic and social life manifested itself in a big increase in office employment in the political capital of each country – which, in many cases, was the commercial metropolis also. Increasingly, formal organisations grew up to represent economic or professional interests: trades unions, employers' federations, professional institutes. These needed to have the ear of government and of government officials, and so they naturally gravitated to the administrative capital or the administrative quarter of the metropolitan city. (A little later, in communist countries, headquarters offices of productive and transport organisations were grouped near the government offices, from which overall economic plans came.) The new communications industries, which combined factory and office functions – newspapers, magazines, radio, television – naturally located in the centres of affairs. For all these activities, the transmission of news was all-important; and it could most readily and economically be obtained in the metropolitan centre. The twentieth century saw a great expansion of higher education, especially in scientific and social-scientific research; this too tended to develop in the metropolitan centres, which were the traditional seats of education in most countries and which were close to important sources of research funds. And developments in transportation technology – the electric tram or streetcar, the electric train, the underground train, the motor bus – allowed increasing numbers of workers to be concentrated close together right in the centres of the great metropolitan cities.

The growth of white-collar occupations of all kinds, then, is without doubt the most important single explanation for the growth of the world cities in the period since 1850. But there are many other contributory causes. Retail trade grew in most metropolitan cities faster than did the demand of the immediate population; for these centres provided a shop window for national and even international markets. Certain types of manufacturing industry – women's fashions, men's bespoke tailoring, jewellery and precious metals, high-class furniture – had always been distinctively metropolitan trades. In the twentieth century they were joined by a host of new industries, which were the creations of neotechnic technology, and which for one reason or another needed to be close to the centre of affairs. Most characteristic of all is the manufacture of expensive, complex, custom-built electronic apparatus for scientific purposes, much of which goes into metropolitan business houses or laboratories or hospitals, or is ordered by the metropolitan offices of government departments. Such goods, like the bespoke suits and dresses of an older industrial age, have to be made in close and immediate contact with the final purchaser and specifier.

In the light of these features of modern technology and economic organisation, the rise of the giant city appears natural, even inevitable. In the words of the American economist, R. M. Haig, who studied the forces behind the growth of cities in 1926:

> Instead of explaining why so large a portion of the population is found in the urban areas, one must give reasons why that portion is not even greater. The question is changed from 'Why live in the city?' to 'Why not live in the city?'

In 1926, Haig could find few possible technological trends which would substantially diminish the role of the metropolis in the future. And since he wrote, most metropolitan cities have been growing noticeably faster in population than the countries of which they form a part. Table 5 shows that during the 1950s and 1960s three of the metropolitan cities described in this book – London, the Randstadt and New York – were growing less rapidly than the total population of the countries to which they belonged. The others were all gaining population, relatively, from their provincial areas. In another decade the details might have been different: in the 1930s, for instance, it was Paris which for a time was losing population to the rest of France, while since 1945 it has experienced unparalleled immigration from the French provinces.

But considered within a wider spatial framework, few metropolitan cities experience any permanent setback. In London, the Randstad and New York, even the metropolitan area definition is no longer quite wide enough; growth is dispersing outward in ever-increasing circles, to a ring of smaller metropolitan areas beyond the central one. The movement into this wider metropolitan complex is not a trend that will easily be reversed, whatever the official policy and however strong the official powers.

The Problems

Yet such growth brings problems, which are familiar to people in the world cities of every land. The extra thousands of households, created each year by natural increase, in-migration or household fission, must be housed. If new housing is not provided, the result is extra overcrowding and the creation of new slums in the already congested inner districts of the city. If housing is provided without care, the result is endless suburban sprawl which eats far into the surrounding countryside. The migrants generally find jobs – the range and variety of employment is after all one of the major attractions of the world cities – but the job may be far from the place where a home is found, and the result is extra strain on the city's transport system. In the cities of the west, this problem has acquired an extra dimension: high average living standards bring widespread ownership of private cars, and the temptation to use the car on already congested city streets. The climate of economic growth naturally creates pressures, in capitalist free-enterprise economies, for renewal of central areas so as to accommodate more intensive commercial uses of the land. But the outworn residential areas, which invariably exist around the central core of the city, are left untouched unless the community moves in to redevelop – and that brings problems of land acquisition and finance. The spread of the city rapidly outruns the existing means of city government, which is apt to reflect conditions of the era before last; yet natural inertia, and powerful built-in political pressures, may defeat any attempt at reform. As population and jobs migrate outwards from the congested and obsolescent core to the suburbs, the central urban government may face demographic and economic decline, and thus an increasing economic and fiscal crisis.

The rest of this book is an examination, in detail, of the growth of some of the greatest of the world cities; of the problems this growth brings in train, and the attempts being made to solve those problems.

2 London

Even Londoners find it difficult enough to know what they mean by London. Because there has hardly been a decade of recorded history when London was not growing physically, it has never been easy to determine with any finality where London ended and the rest of Britain began. Paradoxically, in the 1970s it has become both easier and more difficult than ever before. Easier, because since 1945 the outward growth of London has been limited by one of the most powerful systems of land-use planning ever introduced in any country. More difficult, because though the intention was to stop the growth of London altogether, in fact the metropolis has gone on growing – but in subtler and more complex forms than ever before (see map 2.1).

By 1938, aided by the development of suburban electric railways in the two decades since 1918, the suburbs of London had sprawled out to a temporary limit roughly 12 to 15 miles from the centre. In that year, the temporary limit became permanent: an Act of the British Parliament, the Green Belt Act, created the means to fix a girdle of permanent open countryside round the existing sprawl, thus preventing further erosion of the countryside. And in 1947, when the Town and Country Planning Act introduced at last a complex system of local machinery to control the land use of every acre of Britain, the preservation and even extension of the Metropolitan Green Belt became a major policy objective. It happened that the built-up area of 1938 coincided fairly neatly with a definition of London commonly used for statistical purposes: Greater London, now known in British official statistics as the *Greater London Conurbation*. And since 1 April 1965, following major reform of London's government, this unit has become the territory of London's new administrative units: the Greater London Council, which administers the broader

functions appropriate to the conurbation as a whole, and the thirty-
two London boroughs which together with the ancient City of
London administer the more local functions. The Greater London
Council is responsible for an area of 610 square miles (or 1,580 square
kilometres) which in 1971 had a population of 7,452,346. So, from
1965, in London a situation obtains which is rare in any world city:
physical reality, statistical reality and administrative reality are all
approximately the same.

The difficulty is that there is another, deeper, sort of reality: the
economic and social reality of people's jobs and homes, and the way
they travel between them. Even at the point when it came into being,
Greater London was becoming less great: between 1961 and 1971 it
lost 540,000 people, 7 per cent of its 1961 population; between 1971
and 1975 it lost another 330,000 people, and its population –
7,110,000 – was some one and a half million less than in 1939. Yet in
one sense this is an illusion. In fact, since 1945 London has continued
to grow, and grow rapidly: but because the planners would not let it
sprawl, because it has been hemmed in by the Green Belt, it has grown
in new ways. In the zone beyond the original 5-mile-wide Green Belt,
that is between 20 and 40 miles from central London, the existing
towns have swelled; and new towns have grown out of villages, or on
virgin fields, into major centres. Altogether, this 'Outer Ring' added
nearly one million to its population in the decade 1951–61,
representing two-fifths of the net growth of the British population;
from 1961 to 1971 the growth was much slower, only a little more
than a quarter of a million. Of course, not all these people look to the
Greater London Conurbation for a living; but many – some 539,000
– travel across the Green Belt into London's centre or its suburbs,
each workday morning, to earn their daily bread. So, in an important
sense, towns 20 to 30 miles out, like Guildford, Reading, Chelmsford
and Maidstone have become parts of London too. Yet since 1945
they have grown in the way they always grew, not a part of a single
sprawling urban mass, but as separate entities each with its own
individuality: planning has seen to that.

In consequence a new sort of London has been appearing since
1945, a London so complex in form and function that it is difficult to
describe or delimit it. The most useful working definition is the
London Region (or Metropolitan Area) defined in British official
statistics: it embraces an area of 4,412 square miles (11,427 square
kilometres) bounded by a roughly circular line with a radius 40 miles

(70 kilometres) from Charing Cross (map 2.1) and it contained a population of 12,684,760 at the 1971 Census.

British research, following earlier work by International Population and Urban Research, gives a slightly smaller London but it also makes London the second biggest metropolitan area in Europe (after Paris) and the world's eighth biggest in 1971. Its London Standard Metropolitan Labour Area contained 1,498 square miles (3,880 square kilometres) and a Census population of 8,634,200 in 1971. But in fact this area was surrounded by an almost continuous ring of nineteen smaller Metropolitan Areas, which together with London recorded a combined population of 12,036,900 at the 1971 Census.

Greater London plus Outer Ring, therefore, equal London Region. These are the important definitions. But even within Greater London there are important social and economic distinctions between one ring and another. It is necessary to look now at the problems of the different parts of London in more detail: and the most logical place to start at is the centre.

Congestion at the centre

Most of the least tractable of London's problems stem from the centre, even if they do not manifest themselves there. It is not merely a question of the increasing volumes of traffic on an inadequate street system, or of the increasing congestion of people in streets, cafés, restaurants, pubs; for the problem of the centre expresses itself also in the ever increasing crush on the suburban trains from Maidstone or Reading, the traffic congestion in the morning rush hours in Lewisham or Croydon or Leytonstone, and the problem of the isolated suburban wife in the 'commuter country' of Camberley or Three Bridges or Chelmsford, outside the Greater London Conurbation and 30 miles or more from London.

As defined for the 1971 Census, London's 'conurbation centre' is rather bigger than that of most other world cities. It covers just under $10\frac{1}{2}$ square miles (26·9 square kilometres), mainly on the north bank of the Thames where it is bounded by the main terminal railway stations, but stretching about a mile south of the river as far as the traffic junction of the Elephant and Castle where government and other new office blocks began to go up in the early 1960s. With a resident population in 1971 of 230,010, the central core had a daily workforce of some 1,241,000 – just over one-fifth of the 6,029,000

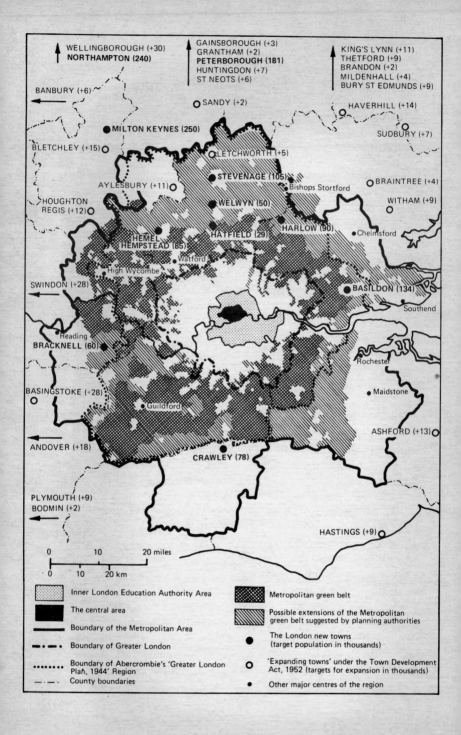

WELLINGBOROUGH (+30)
NORTHAMPTON (240)

GAINSBOROUGH (+3)
GRANTHAM (+2)
PETERBOROUGH (181)
HUNTINGDON (+7)
ST NEOTS (+6)

KING'S LYNN (+11)
THETFORD (+9)
BRANDON (+2)
MILDENHALL (+4)
BURY ST EDMUNDS (+9)

BANBURY (+6)

SANDY (+2)

HAVERHILL (+14)

SUDBURY (+7)

MILTON KEYNES (250)

BLETCHLEY (+15)

LETCHWORTH (+5)

STEVENAGE (105)

BRAINTREE (+4)

AYLESBURY (+11)

Bishops Stortford

WELWYN (50)

WITHAM (+9)

HOUGHTON
REGIS (+12)

HATFIELD (29)

HARLOW (90)

HEMEL
HEMPSTEAD (85)

Chelmsford

Watford

SWINDON (+28)

High Wycombe

BASILDON (134)

Southend

Reading

BRACKNELL (60)

Rochester

BASINGSTOKE (+28)

Maidstone

Guildford

ANDOVER (+18)

ASHFORD (+13)

CRAWLEY (78)

PLYMOUTH (+9)
BODMIN (+2)

HASTINGS (+9)

0   10   20 miles

0   10   20 km

	Inner London Education Authority Area		Metropolitan green belt
	The central area		Possible extensions of the Metropolitan green belt suggested by planning authorities
	Boundary of the Metropolitan Area	•	The London new towns (target population in thousands)
—·—	Boundary of Greater London	○	'Expanding towns' under the Town Development Act, 1952 (targets for expansion in thousands)
··········	Boundary of Abercrombie's 'Greater London Plan, 1944' Region	•	Other major centres of the region
—·—	County boundaries		

workers in the London region. However, from 1961 to 1971 the central area recorded a loss of over 173,000 workers – a sharp contrast to the gain of 80–100,000 recorded during 1951–61. And independent counts of peak hour commuters into the central area show a steady decline after 1964 – with an overall drop of 175,000 commuters between the 1962 peak figure and 1973.

Over 80 per cent of these central area workers were in the tertiary sector, and about 60 per cent were in office occupations. This in turn reflects the concentration of office floorspace there, which rose from 146,640,000 square feet in 1957 to 168,100,000 square feet in 1961 and 179,594,000 square feet in 1966 – this last figure representing some 60 per cent of all office floorspace in Greater London. This situation changed little thereafter, despite central government controls after 1964: central London had 29 per cent of the country's commercial office floorspace in 1967 and almost 25 per cent in 1974.

The overall decline in central area employment in the 1960s was dominated by falls in manufacturing jobs – including associated offices. There were also declines in routine clerical jobs. But there was a pronounced increase in high-grade office and other work in specialised financial and professional services. Central London, in other words, is becoming economically more specialised.

The new offices have powerfully changed the London skyline since 1950. The planners have eased the old rigid regulations which for centuries limited the height of London buildings, and the traditional landmarks of London are becoming lost among the new office towers. Yet London's skyscrapers represent only a physically different expression of a very old phenomenon. Office employment in Britain has been traditionally concentrated in London ever since the first offices were built by the government and the banks in the eighteenth century. But until the last decades of the nineteenth century, office employment was limited in scope. It was mainly restricted to the government offices at Westminster and the traditional commercial and financial functions of the City. Then, as the economy became

2.1 *The London region.* For local government, London means Greater London, an area roughly within 12–15 miles of the centre, which is similar to the 'conurbation' used for statistical purposes. Outside this is the Green Belt, and then the new towns created after 1945. The London region recognised for planning purposes stretches up to 40 miles from the centre; while some towns receiving London's overspill population are still farther out.

more sophisticated, all sorts of new office functions multiplied: head offices of manufacturing organisations, concerned with sales; ancillary services like advertising, consultancy and operations research; non-profit organisations like trades unions, higher education research and professional organisations; journalism and broadcasting. The new functions colonised new areas; especially parts of the West End, which changed within a few decades from the home of the rich to office quarters, as deserted at night as the City. This was a change paralleled in other cities, for in the same decades offices took over from residences in the *Grands Boulevards* of Paris and in the Midtown district of New York.

The growth of offices has brought problems, of which the most obvious is traffic congestion. But here caution is necessary. Londoners are fond of saying that London's traffic is grinding to a halt: they have been saying it for at least a century, and probably since the Middle Ages. Though traffic volumes in central London have increased, according to police censuses, three to ten times between 1904 and 1973, the evidence is that improvements in traffic control, and in the speed and flexibility of vehicles, have just kept pace. No major street works were undertaken in central London between the creation of Kingsway in 1900 to 1910 and that of the Hyde Park Boulevard in 1962; but the capacity of the existing streets was expanded enormously by increasingly complex systems of traffic-light control, waiting restrictions, parking meters – which already by 1965 extended almost right across the central area – one way street systems, and then after 1973 computer-controlled traffic lights. Nor is it necessarily true that conditions for pedestrians or the ordinary worker and traveller have deteriorated. Few now remember the horrors of noise and smell which were the inevitable accompaniment of horse-drawn traffic on cobbles or wooden paving. Nevertheless, in 1963 an officially-sponsored report appeared with the revolutionary suggestion that in terms of civilised urban life, to keep pace was not enough. *Traffic in Towns*, the report of a working party under Professor Colin Buchanan, was published by the Ministry of Transport with government blessing in autumn 1963. The report's central argument was that it was possible to define an environmental standard for any street or street network – a standard in terms of noise, fumes, danger and inconvenience – and that this standard would then automatically determine the amount of traffic which could be allowed to pass through the system. Once given the standard and the existing system, the amount of traffic could be increased only by comprehensive reconstruction.

For central London, the implication of this approach would be a very costly reconstruction. Here, it is clear that congestion and regulations have long kept traffic flows well below potential maximum. Annual traffic counts over the period 1961–73 have shown that during the morning peak period (0700–1000 hours), only 11–13 per cent of passengers entering the central area were using private transport. Almost 75 per cent, in fact, were using rail transport – either London Transport underground, or British Rail trains into the major termini, or both. The London Transporation Study shows that the majority of the vehicles on central London streets on working days are carrying people rather than goods; but they represent commercial traffic, which can be displaced only with difficulty. An economist, Christopher Foster, has calculated the total costs of the more ambitious types of alternative reconstruction in the report at £6,500 million for inner London alone. This compares with the projected primary road network for Greater London which was estimated in 1972 to cost £2,280 million.

The other critical effect of office growth is on the journey to work. Though total commuting to the centre appears to have fallen from 1962 to 1970, almost certainly this conceals a big fall in short-distance travellers and a big rise in longer-distance riders from beyond the Green Belt, that is from places more than 20 miles away. A reliable estimate was that the number of commuters to the centre from outside the conurbation, only 100,000 in 1951, had risen to over 200,000 by 1961, and then more modestly to 260,000 in 1971 – though this figure was not exactly comparable with the earlier ones. These long-distance commuters represent a new element in the social geography of London. Like their New York counterparts, they make relatively long journeys on express trains every morning, and then must transfer at the terminals to buses or tube trains which take them to their offices. Their journeys may take up to two hours each way; their fares are proportionately heavy.

And, if money has to be found to provide extra capacity – which has occurred during the 1960s and 1970s, with electrification works on the main lines out of Waterloo, Euston, Kings Cross and St Pancras, and expensive track works in south London – then, even with central government aid in the form of grants and writing off accumulated deficits, some money may have to be found from commuters themselves. Indeed, rail fares have risen sharply in this period (map 2.3).

East and West

Surrounding central London in a close-built, 5-mile-wide belt is the Inner Ring of the London Region. Together with the central area, it represents the physical growth of London before 1914, before electric railways allowed the suburbs to sprawl; and the two together are roughly coincident with an important administrative unit, the area of the Inner London Education Authority. The ILEA area of 117 square miles contained 2,772,131 people at the Census of 1971: 23,693 on average to the square mile, compared with only 9,304 to the square mile in the interwar suburbs just outside. But Inner London is still built up to an extraordinarily low density by international urban standards. Its 23,693 to the square mile compares with 44,530 for Manhattan and Brooklyn (a bigger unit of 4,141,245 in inner New York) in 1970, or 56,500 in the *Ville de Paris* (population 2,291,000) in 1975. The difference stems from London's unique development since medieval times. As Steen Eiler Rasmussen points out in his book *London the Unique City*, London grew rapidly outside its medieval city walls, establishing a tradition of low-density suburbs for almost everyone, which has persisted ever since. London did not build apartment houses to accommodate its enormous nineteenth-century influx of population, as almost every other city of the world did; up to 1914 and in large areas up to the present day, the commercial core of London gives way immediately to separate houses with gardens, or at least small yards. Alike in the tiny, two-storey labourers' cottages of the East End, in the solid bourgeois houses occupied by city clerks and professional men in the streets and squares of Islington, and in the great stuccoed terraces of the rich in Kensington, this pattern persisted. It makes London, to this day, the airiest and least oppressive, and in summer the greenest, great city of the world.

Within Inner London, for centuries the classic distinction has been between east and west. In 1662 William Petty wrote that London was growing westwards to escape 'the fumes, steams and stinks of the whole easterly pyle'. The east, lying alongside the busy river port downstream from the city, was then already the home of London's poor, while the suburbs of the rich spread westwards and north-westwards from the court in Westminster. In the nineteenth century, the East End took in many of the poorest of the new arrivals in London, as an industrial revolution occurred in industries like clothing and furniture and as hundreds of thousands of Jewish immigrants fled here from persecutions and privations in eastern Europe between 1880 and 1910. In the late 1880s and early 1890s Charles Booth conducted the first large-scale modern social survey here: 12·45 per cent of East Enders were found to be 'very poor', who 'live in a state of chronic want', and another 22·79 per cent were 'poor', 'living under a struggle to obtain the necessaries of life and make both ends meet'. In the years after Booth, conditions improved slowly. The popultion of the inner East End – the modern London borough of Tower Hamlets – fell from 597,000 in 1901 to 308,000 at the outbreak of the Second World War in 1939; then, evacuation and bomb destruction reduced the population still further to 231,000 in 1951. By 1971, the figure had fallen to 166,000 – a little more than one quarter the level of seventy years earlier.

The bombing gave a unique chance for London to rebuild the East End; and London seized the chance. In the middle of the war, in 1943, appeared London's blueprint for reconstruction: the County of London Plan, prepared by the notable town planner Sir Patrick Abercrombie, in association with the planners of the old County of London which gave way to the Greater London Council in the reform of 1965. This Plan devoted much space to the problems of rebuilding bombed and blighted areas like the East End. Its analysis concluded that if the majority of East Enders were to be given housing suitable for family life, with houses and gardens on the traditional London pattern for the bigger families, then some people would have to move out of the area. Thus two important concepts were born, which have governed London planning ever since: the *net residential density* of 136 persons on each residential acre, which was to be applied to areas like the East End (and, in the event, to most of inner London), and the associated concept of *overspill* into new and expanded communities far from the congested redevelopment areas.

Working from this plan, even before the war ended, London took powers to designate a huge area within the modern borough of Tower Hamlets as an area of comprehensive redevelopment, which meant that all reconstruction would be carried through according to a master plan prepared by the planning authority. In the 1950s and 1960s this area of nearly two square miles was still the biggest area of comprehensive development in Britain. The plan involved nothing

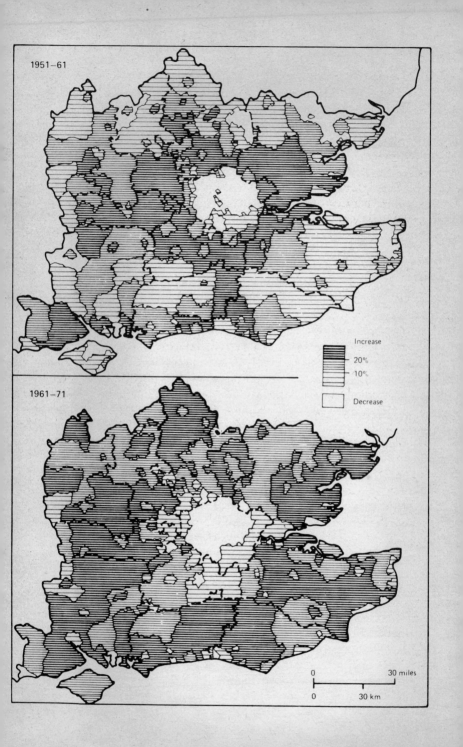

1951—61

1961—71

Increase
20%
10%
Decrease

0   30 miles
0   30 km

less than the creation of a new town within the heavily built-up area of inner London, to hold close on 100,000 people – compared with over 100,000 in 1951 and over 200,000 in 1939. It is expected to be virtually finished by the late 1970s, and it has already been joined by two other schemes on the northern flank which will increase the total area under comprehensive reconstruction by nearly one-fifth as much again. The result, in the mid-1970s, is dramatic for anyone who recalls the old East End. Huge areas are already transformed into totally new neighbourhoods, dominated by tall blocks of flats and by the lower terraces of three- and four-storey apartments, standing in spacious landscaped areas. Only a few yards away stand the reminders of the past: the long, squat rows of cottages inhabited by dock labourers or Jewish tailors. But they invariably already have the air of waiting for the demolition men.

The biggest comprehensive developments are concentrated east of the City: north of the river within the borough of Tower Hamlets, south of it in the Bermondsey area within the Borough of Southwark. These schemes were in large part conceived in the late wartime years of 1943 and 1944, to deal with the slum problems of the London of 1939. They are well on the way to completion; and, for the generation of planners of the 1970s, London's biggest housing problem lies in a different quarter. It is the west, home of London's rich; and paradoxically, the problem stems from that fact.

Though the landscape of inner London is almost everywhere still dominated by houses built for occupation by single families, these houses are very different in east and west. In the east, they are the small terraced cottages built in the 1840s and 1850s for the labourers who fled from the countryside into London's docks and industries; in Chelsea and Kensington and Paddington, they are the town houses of the rich and comfortable middle class of the mid-Victorian era, built on three or four floors above their basement kitchens. But progressively, as land values have risen, in inner London, after the First World War, and as the trek to more distant suburbs has taken place, the big houses of west London have been broken up into separate apartments or flats. Thus, in an area like North Kensington,

2.2   *The London region: population changes, 1951–61 and 1961–71.* In the 1950s Greater London had a net population loss of 165,000, while the Outer Metropolitan Area (15–40 miles from the centre) gained 960,000. During the 1960s Greater London continued to decline – by no less than 540,000; the Outer Metropolitan Area grew by 800,000.

middle-class houses have become working-class flats; they are occupied by people who drive buses or vans, or wait in restaurants and bars in central London and who have to live near their work. These people have been paying low rents for rather poorly equipped and poorly maintained property, and since rents were frozen as a result of two world wars, the maintenance has got worse and the property has deteriorated. In other areas, like Earls Court, houses have been fragmented into 'bed-sitters' for students and secretaries without families, who can pay relatively high uncontrolled rents to be near their work in central London. As the growth of the central London economy has swollen the ranks of these people, so they have displaced others unless rent control provided a barrier. Now, as a result of partial decontrol of rents in 1957 and the constant pressure of demand for owner-occupied housing, many working-class families are finding themselves displaced. In some cases their homes pass to new immigrants, from the West Indies or other parts of the Commonwealth, who are willing to pay high rents because of colour discrimination elsewhere. Others pass perhaps after a spell in the occupation of black immigrants, to professional and executive workers who are willing to pay high prices to buy and re-convert them to one-family occupation. Yet others are converted by property developers into luxury apartments. The process has made big profits for those who bought cheap and sold dear; but here, the professional speculator finds common cause with the middle-class owner-occupier, whose infiltration of working-class areas has given a new word to the English language in the early 1970s – gentrification. It is this process, above all, that has caused a catastrophic loss in the population of several inner London boroughs between 1961 and 1971; 59,358 or 25·4 per cent in Islington, 38,970 or 17·1 per cent in Camden (map 2.2).

The Milner Holland report on London housing, published in March 1965, was a milestone in the systematic statistical analysis of inner London's housing problems. It identified the worst areas of housing stress: they formed a wide arc surrounding central London on its north and west sides. And it found a systematic association between overcrowding, lack of basic facilities (like exclusive household access to kitchen and bathroom), multi-occupation of housing, and rented housing – especially in the furnished lettings. Nor has this situation altered subsequently. The 1971 Census showed that though 75 per cent of all households in Greater London had exclusive access to hot water, fixed bath and inside w.c., for furnished tenants this proportion fell to 35 per cent. And though only 3 per cent of all households lived at more than $1\frac{1}{2}$ persons per room, for furnished tenants it was 13 per cent.

But there is no simple answer to the problem of 'multi-occupation' of former one-family houses in areas like west London. The local authorities have already been given considerable powers, under the Housing Acts, to prevent mismanagement of rented housing. But a problem is bound to remain as long as population in London grows by natural increase and by rapid immigration; as long as coloured immigrants suffer prejudice and are so driven to offer high rents for cramped, insanitary accommodation; as long as London continues to attract disproportionate numbers of well-paid professional and executive workers who can afford high prices to buy houses near the centre. To build outwards is no necessary answer, for the pressure of people on space near the centre will remain; and no government could seriously contemplate the abandonment of the Green Belt policy. Yet to build higher and more densely in inner London is no necessary answer either: it will make at best a partial contribution because much of inner London does not need replacement; it will probably be more expensive, in real terms, than the present density standards for rebuilding; and as the housing authorities have stressed, it will almost certainly be less satisfactory for children. At bottom, the problem is not capable of solution; it may be relieved by giving people the maximum possible opportunity, incentive and help to move out of inner London, and even out of the crowded south east of England altogether.

The problem is complicated by the fact that by the middle and late 1970s inner London was in demographic and industrial decline. Total employment began to fall from the early 1960s: between then and the mid-1970s the entire Greater London area lost about half a million jobs, mostly from the inner boroughs. Most of this was in manufacturing, where between 1966 and 1974 alone there was a decline of some 27 per cent; by the mid-1970s, 70 per cent of London's jobs were in services. The reasons for the decline of inner city manufacturing are complex: economic recession, rationalisation associated with takeovers, redevelopment and clearance of the areas that included many small factories and workshops, labour supply problems. Certainly, since the loss of factory jobs in London was four times as rapid as in the country as a whole, a 'London factor' was

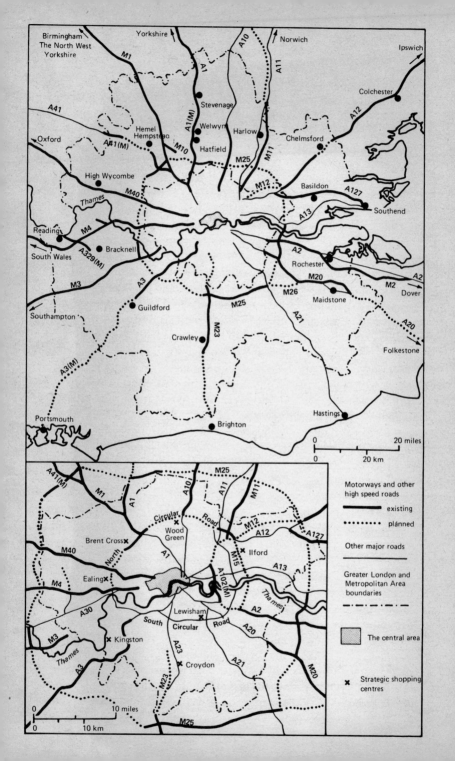

Motorways and other high speed roads

existing

plánned

Other major roads

Greater London and Metropolitan Area boundaries

The central area

× Strategic shopping centres

at work: the metropolis is now an unfavourable location for manufacturing. But the resident labour force has fallen even faster, with a net outflow of 100,000 people a year – mainly from the inner boroughs.

The experts are not in entire agreement as to whether this decline really represents a major problem. On one hand, the Greater London Council and the inner boroughs argue that it is producing an ill-balanced population, with many rich and many poor and too few middle-income workers, and that it is putting an increased strain on local authority finance as the rateable value (local tax) base is eroded. On the other, some experts think that London and Londoners can only benefit from the thinning-out process. The official inner area study of Lambeth in south London, commissioned by the Department of the Environment from consultants and published in 1977, suggests that many Londoners would like to leave the city but are prevented by housing problems. It argues that efforts to provide more jobs in Lambeth should be matched by training schemes to upgrade the skills of the local labour force and – more controversially – by measures to help those who wish to leave to do so. Certainly the right answer to inner city decline – in London, Birmingham, Liverpool and other large British cities – was not clearly in sight when the inner area studies appeared.

The interwar suburbs

About five to seven miles from the centre of London, the outward-bound traveller passes, quite abruptly, from the more densely built inner ring to the suburbs built between 1918 and 1939. During the period 1921–39 the population of Greater London grew by about 1·2 million or 16·6 per cent; but the built-up area grew over three times. By 1939, the zone between about 5 and 12–15 miles from the centre was almost uniformly built up with housing at an average density of 12–14 to the acre. The new houses were not only more widely spaced than ever before; they were also built in much freer patterns, for it was everyone's ambition to own a house slightly different, in design or position, from his neighbour. The frequent corner shops of the old

2.3 *The London region: transport improvements.* The map shows the end-1976 position. Since the Greater London Council abandoned its ambitious urban motorway plans, the conurbation lacks circumferential access except for the North Circular Road, which is being upgraded. Further out the M25 Orbital Motorway, through the green belt, is the first priority for completion in the mid-1980s.

London were replaced by shopping parades, often built around the electric railway stations which took commuters into central London.

The interwar suburbs, in fact, were built on good communications – better than London had known before. Ironically, in the middle 1970s perhaps the chief problem they present is the problem of getting about. Between 1918 and 1939, the underground railways took their lines far into what was then open countryside, opening up the suburban ring to the commuter in areas like Hendon, Edgware, Wembley, Harrow or Ruislip; south of the river, the Southern Railway electrified its suburban lines and built some new ones, with the same result. Underground or Southern suburban lines stretch, on average, some 15 miles from central London. They have frequent stops so that journeys – especially on the underground – are relatively slow. Because of considerable overloading on the inner stretches, again especially on the underground, they are also often rather uncomfortable. Those suburbanites who earn their living outside the centre – the majority, in most suburban areas – may travel by car, and many suburbanites travel exclusively by car in the evenings and at weekends; the 1971 Census shows that in the average London outer borough, 45–65 per cent of households owned cars. But here too, their journeys are far from smooth. The arterial roads which sweep through the suburbs are now thirty-five to forty years old, and are congealed with a volume of traffic for which they were never conceived. They are bad traffic carriers, with frequent side-road access and frontage developments, including some major shopping centres. Already, in the middle 1960s, some are being relieved by new motorways (freeways), while others are being reconstructed as motorways. But it looks as if extensive improvements and new roads may be called for, on a much bigger scale, to deal with the traffic volumes expected in the 1970s (map 2.3).

Despite these disadvantages, it does not yet appear that the interwar developments are losing favour with commuters in competition with the newer suburbs farther from the centre, as may be happening in New York. Like the Bronx, many interwar suburbs of London are now experiencing slow population decline as their original inhabitants grow old and their children move away. The suburban zone as a whole has lost population since 1951 (map 2.2); most of the individual boroughs were losing population in the decade 1961–71. Many of the houses are already being bought by a second generation of occupants. These young people do not appear to find the houses of the suburbs obsolescent by the standards of the 1970s, possibly because fewer own cars than their New York counterparts, and even fewer own two cars. And to London suburbanites, the more distant suburbs appear less attractive because the Green Belt puts them so far away. So without any firm evidence, it would be wrong to suppose that the interwar suburbs will suffer rapid obsolescence. Pockets of older, smaller suburban housing, near to factory areas, may pass into the hands of coloured immigrants escaping from the overcrowded multi-occupied housing of the inner rings: a process observable in the immigration of factory workers from the Indian sub-continent into Southall. By 1971 indeed two outer London boroughs, Brent and Haringey, had the highest proportions in all London of immigrants from the so-called New Commonwealth countries: 14·0 and 14·4 per cent of their total populations, respectively. But this will make relatively little impression on the suburbs as a whole. Overall, change is likely to be very gradual.

Green Belt and New Towns

London is the city of a thousand suburbs, but that perhaps is no longer the most remarkable fact about it. The unique thing is that the suburbs suddenly stop, to be replaced by open countryside. London's physical growth, some local rounding and infilling apart, has been stopped by the planners' edict at the point it happened to reach in the summer of 1939. The Green Belt has even grown. There is now the agreed Belt, about 5 miles wide, which still closely corresponds to the Belt shown in Abercrombie's Greater London Plan of 1944; around it there is a much wider penumbra, proposed by local authorities for inclusion in the Belt, but still to be approved by the central government (map 2.1). Some of this land was approved in 1972, so that by 1974 the firm Green Belt included almost 900 square miles.

In the period of rapid building in south east England since the mid-1950s, the Green Belt has been subject to intense commercial pressures; for the planner's decision to re-zone an area, from agriculture to housing, can put astronomical fortunes into private pockets. In the face of these pressures, successive governments have reiterated that the Belt is to be rigidly preserved. But in successive policy statements, from 1963 to 1973, governments have admitted the principle that areas of doubtful agricultural or landscape value might be re-examined, to see if their inclusion in the Green Belt served any useful purpose. A frequently quoted example is the area of abandoned glasshouses in the horticultural district of the upper Lea Valley north east of London. The strong argument is that if land must be found for housing, it is preferable to take this sort of land than better land farther out.

This, though, is unlikely to make more than a marginal difference to the size and form of the Belt. The *South East Study* published by the government in 1964, and the later *Strategic Plan for the South East*, published in 1970, specifically reject more radical solutions such as the replacement of the present belt by a series of green wedges running in less developed land between the main transport lines. Though this form is almost certainly preferable for a rapidly growing metropolis like London, these studies point out that London has been planned on the basis of a Green Belt for nearly twenty years and that the Green Belt is now an accepted part of the structure of the London region. But this does not at all weaken the force of the criticism that the function of the Belt needs re-thinking. The Scott Report on Rural Land Use in 1942, and the Abercrombie Greater London Plan of 1944, could not have anticipated the postwar explosion of population in Britain, and especially in the south east – or the threat of universal motorcar ownership by 1980. In wartime, and against the background of agricultural depression in the 1930s, it was natural that planners of 1942–4 should have been influenced by the need to preserve farming above all. But in the Britain of the 1970s, it is arguable that the needs of the city dweller should take first place, and his rights of access to the countryside should be greatly strengthened. It seems anomalous, to say the least, to find from David Thomas's careful study that in 1960 only 5·4 per cent of the Green Belt was used for recreation – and only 3·4 per cent was open to the public for their enjoyment. Country Parks, opened by local authorities and private bodies with government grant following the Countryside Act of 1968, may remedy this to a limited extent; a bigger hope is to incorporate them in larger regional parks, such as the Lea Valley Park in east London – well advanced in the mid-1970s – and the proposed Colne Valley Park west of London.

Strategically sited, at the outer edge of the original Abercrombie Green Belt or a few miles beyond, are the eight London New Towns (map 2.1), a complementary part of Abercrombie's grand strategy for London. Abercrombie proposed, and government and local planners accepted, that London should be developed at relatively low densities of population – 136 to the residential acre over much of inner

London, rising to 200 in a very small area at the centre but falling to 100 or less at the periphery of the Inner Ring. The inevitable consequence was a huge overspill population – 1,033,000, in the calculation of the Greater London Plan – who must be re-housed elsewhere by public action, with perhaps another 250,000 moving privately of their own accord. A central feature of Abercrombie's plan was that these people should not be housed in outgrowths of the existing suburban sprawl; the Green Belt was to stop that. But as a complement to this restrictive policy, there was to be a positive programme of new, fully planned communities to receive the overspill beyond the Green Belt: the New Towns in the 20–35-mile ring, the expansions of existing small towns in the same ring and farther afield. Here people and jobs would move together, so that there would be no additional commuting problem.

The New Towns represent a uniquely British solution to a universal problem of metropolitan growth. They are communities of a finite size – generally 60,000 or less in the first conception, since increased to up to 100,000 – built according to the English tradition at fairly low densities of fourteen to sixteen houses to the acre, with relatively few people housed in multi-storey blocks of flats. By the end of 1975 they had reached a combined population of 505,000, almost exactly four-fifths of the way to their final target population of over 640,000 – a figure which itself is appreciably higher than the original combined target of 1946–50.

The New Towns have on every criterion been a triumphant success. They have proved phenomenally attractive magnets to industry, so that out-commuting has been kept to a minimum; their shopping centres, better adapted to the motor age than those of the older towns, have attracted shoppers from far afield; as examples of comprehensive and humanist planning they have attracted admiring visitors from all over the world. Their most serious limitation perhaps is that, dominated as they are by skilled and semi-skilled factory jobs, they have failed to attract substantial proportions of the lower income groups who remain trapped in poor housing within Inner London.

Yet curiously, their very success reflects a deeper failure of the Abercrombie policy. In his concept, they were instruments of a once-for-all planning operation – the removal of hundreds of thousands of Londoners from congested surroundings to new communities set among open countryside – within a London region which was no

longer attracting jobs and people from outside. These postulates have
not been fulfilled. Industry has grown rapidly in the New Towns
partly as a reflection of the rapid growth in the south east as a whole;
people, especially skilled workers, have come to the New Towns not
only from London but from the rest of Britain; the rise in the birth
rate is causing unexpected growth both in the New Towns and in
London where it creates a new and a continuing overspill problem.
Thus the problem of the growth of London, which the overspill policy
was designed to solve once for all, has been exported to the New
Towns and the ring of countryside within which they lie.

   This belt – the Outer Ring of the London Region, between twenty
and forty miles from Piccadilly Circus – has, however, witnessed even
more radical and disquieting departures from the orderly planned
development which Abercrombie foresaw. The ultimate effect of the
Abercrombie Plan would have been to give this Ring a population of
4,224,000 – 1,166,000 above the level of 1938. Of this increase, all but
about 250,000 would have been accommodated in fully planned
communities. The postwar reality has been very different. By 1975,
the original New Towns programme was largely completed and the
programme for planned town expansions – the other important
instrument of Abercrombie policy for the Outer Ring – was about
half-way advanced to its target figures with a combined overspill
population of about 170,000 already housed in towns up to 100 and
more miles from London. Yet the population had by then reached
5,280,000 or more than 1 million above the 'ultimate' Abercrombie
level; and the increase of population in the period 1961–75 had been
896,000, some 30 per cent of the net increase of the whole British
population. The explanation lies of course in continued growth of
population in the London region through natural increase, and in
'spontaneous' migration into privately built houses, on a scale that
Abercrombie never contemplated. Every one of the major towns in
this ring – Reading, High Wycombe, Luton, Bishops Stortford,
Chelmsford, the Medway towns, Maidstone, Guildford – has been
ringed by a maze of new speculatively built estates in the 1960s.
Further, the ring of strongest population growth has moved steadily
farther out from London: whereas in the 1951–61 decade it was on
average 15–35 miles from London, by 1961–71 it was 30–60 miles
away (map 2.2). This is London's new 'commuter country', inhabited
by people who make long journeys of thirty, forty or fifty miles to the
London termini each morning. One point though needs stressing:

these long distance commuters, in most cases, form only a small minority of the total working population of the Outer Metropolitan Area. Though their total numbers are rising, the areas where they live – the areas round such towns as Reading, Guildford, Maidstone or Chelmsford – are quite self-sufficient labour markets in themselves. Thus the London region is becoming a more polycentric city region; though, it must be said, the new towns are considerably more self-contained than other towns at similar distances from London.

There is an important difference between these new suburbanites and their New York counterparts. London's new commuters live in separate self-contained communities separated from each other by open land, because the Green Belt policy is being applied in practice around most of these towns. They also live at higher densities than the one-house one-acre American commuter, densities on average about the same as those of the interwar suburbs of London, but which the government planners are trying to raise still further in the future. London and New York commuters, however, suffer the same problems of the rising cost, discomfort and uncertain future of their commuter rail services; their children face the prospect that when their turn comes, the house they buy may be ten or twenty miles down the line.

So finally, this tour of the London region brings us round in full circle. The problem of the new commuter estates is also the problem of the centre. In London since 1945, the central set of problems has been the same as that of the decades before 1939: the continued growth of London, the dynamism of its economy, and in particular the attraction of the small area at the very centre for new jobs, especially the white-collar jobs which form an increasingly important part of the British economy.

But the very success of the new suburbs, ironically, was attracting unfavourable attention by the late 1970s – for the simple reason that the suburbs were continuing to drain the inner city of people and jobs. One possible government answer, announced in the spring of 1977, was to scale down the future growth of the new towns programme – which meant particularly the three latter-day new towns started long after the rest, in the mid-1960s: Milton Keynes, Northampton and Peterborough. Yet in fact the new towns were together a small and insignificant part of the whole decentralization process – most of which was as fully spontaneous as its North American counterpart.

People and jobs in London:
past, present and future

The Abercrombie Plan of 1944 started from the simple and comfortable assumption that there would in future be no extra jobs and no extra people within the London region. This belief, incredible in the 1970s, was not then entirely unreasonable. For one thing, the official forecast was that the population of Britain, 46·6 million in 1940, would be only 47·2 million by 1960; so plans could be made on the assumption of virtually no natural increase of population. (The actual 1971 population was 53·8 million.) For another thing, migration into London could also be discounted, because the Barlow Commission on the Distribution of the Industrial Population in 1940 had concluded that steps could, and should, be taken to control the establishment or extension of factory industry in the London area, thus stemming the inter-regional drift of population at source.

But after 1945 the planners were overtaken by two events. The population increased in every region because of a high (and, from 1955 to 1964, an increasing) birthrate. Between the 1951 and 1971 Censuses the population of the London Region rose by over 1 million but all of this represented natural increase – the excess of births over deaths. In fact, after 1961 the London Region was losing population by migration to the rest of the country. Secondly, employment increased also. It was true that, as the Barlow Commission had recommended, an elaborate apparatus of control was established after 1945 to limit the growth of factory jobs in the London area. But this apparatus did not concern itself with shop and office jobs, which were the hard core of the London problem. Within the London Region, a high proportion of the new jobs were in service industries, the location of which was subject to no central control until the Office Development Permit procedures were introduced in 1964–5. And even in factory industry, small-scale extensions fell outside the control net. Office jobs have in fact moved out of London at an estimated rate of 10,000 a year between 1963 and 1975, aided by the propaganda efforts of the Location of Offices Bureau and the ODP controls. But most do not move more than 40–50 miles away.

The continued strength of the London regional economy reflects structural trends in the British economy as a whole. Certain types of job – the services mentioned above, and manufacturing industries like electrical goods and vehicles – are increasing very rapidly. They have always been strongly concentrated in London and the South

East, and it is very hard to break an established pattern of industrial location, because the existence of an industry in an area automatically tends to foster its further growth there. In addition, certain of these trades, especially the services, are extremely sensitive to the so-called 'external economies' which stem from the close concentration of many firms in the same area. These external economies now seem to work over a larger area than before, so that not only factory and routine jobs but even headquarters' offices are now able to move 40 to 50 miles from London, to centres like Southend, Reading and Basingstoke.

The future pattern of jobs and homes:
Strategic Plan and GLDP

Thus it is not likely that the future growth of the London region, either of people or jobs, will be easily stemmed. In 1964 the official government *South East Study* caused controversy by recommending acceptance of a population increase of $3\frac{1}{2}$ million over the period 1964–81 in South East England (including East Anglia) with a second generation of new towns and cities, at greater distances from London than the first round, to house the growth (map 2.4). Such a scale of population growth had come to seem inevitable by the early 1970s – if only because it represents the natural increase of the region's own population. The much debated 'drift south' became a myth in the early 1960s: in fact the entire South East Region records a modest net loss of population by migration each year. So the expected scale of population growth – in 1970 estimated at over $4\frac{1}{2}$ million for the South East during the period 1966–2001, but later scaled down drastically – does not necessarily rob the development areas of northern England, South Wales or central Scotland of their populations. What it may do is compete for scarce footloose industry – which is a more serious matter.

This is the background to two definitive plans for the future of London and its region: one, a statutory development plan for London produced by the Greater London Council, on which a panel of inquiry gave critical views to the central government in 1973; the other, a strategic plan for the whole South East, produced by a joint team of central and local government planners, published in 1970 and accepted by the government a year later as the future framework for planning the growth of the whole region down to the century's end. The relationship between these two plans – one covering an area of

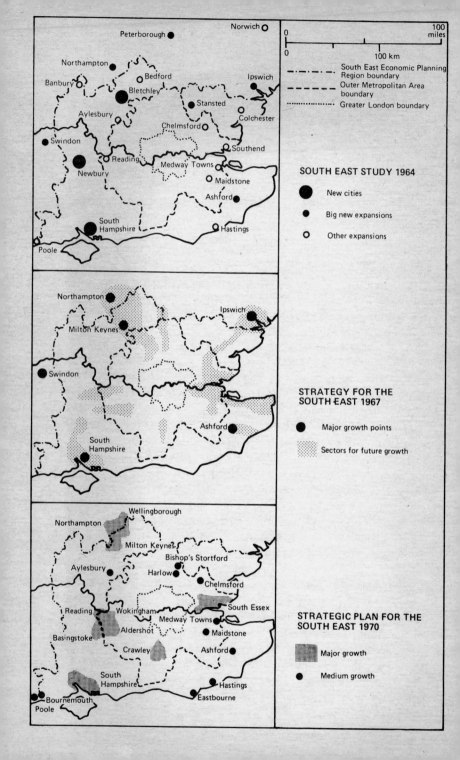

South East Economic Planning Region boundary
— · — · —
Outer Metropolitan Area boundary
— — — —
Greater London boundary
· · · · · · · ·

0   100
|——|
miles
0   100 km

SOUTH EAST STUDY 1964

● New cities

● Big new expansions

○ Other expansions

STRATEGY FOR THE SOUTH EAST 1967

● Major growth points

▓ Sectors for future growth

STRATEGIC PLAN FOR THE SOUTH EAST 1970

▓ Major growth

● Medium growth

Map 1 — South East Study 1964

Peterborough
Norwich
Northampton
Banbury
Bedford
Bletchley
Ipswich
Aylesbury
Stansted
Chelmsford
Colchester
Swindon
Reading
Southend
Newbury
Medway Towns
Maidstone
Ashford
South Hampshire
Hastings
Poole

Map 2 — Strategy for the South East 1967

Northampton
Ipswich
Milton Keynes
Swindon
Ashford
South Hampshire

Map 3 — Strategic Plan for the South East 1970

Wellingborough
Northampton
Milton Keynes
Bishop's Stortford
Aylesbury
Harlow
Chelmsford
Reading
Wokingham
South Essex
Basingstoke
Aldershot
Medway Towns
Maidstone
Crawley
Ashford
South Hampshire
Hastings
Bournemouth
Eastbourne
Poole

620 square miles and a population of 7·4 million, the other extending outwards to take in over 10,000 square miles and 17 million people – is critical for the future of both areas. And, in vital respects, the two plans are in conflict.

The *Greater London Development Plan* (or GLDP) is a general plan setting the broad guidelines for London's development; within these, local plans will be made by the ancient City of London and the 32 London boroughs. During the prolonged 237-day inquiry, the great bulk of the 28,000 objections were into one aspect only: the controversial plan for a £2,000 million motorway network for London (map 2.3), which was accepted in part by the inquiry panel and then by the government but was then rejected by the GLC itself in 1973 after a change of administration at County Hall. But more basic than this, and more important, is the controversy that has taken place only among the professional planners and their critics: on the interlinked questions of London's future size and patterns of economic activity.

At the time of Abercrombie's 1944 Plan, and for long after, planners at both national and local level agreed on the need to limit London's growth: hence the green belt and the planned overspill programme into the new and expanded towns. But as we have seen in this chapter, since 1945 London has lost people at accelerating speed; while since 1960 it has also lost employment. From $8\frac{1}{2}$ million at its peak in the late 1930s, Greater London's population was down to just over 7·1 million by 1975; this last figure is actually below the GLC's original 7·3 million target for 1981, now been scaled down to 6·8 million. Jobs, too, have fallen catastrophically – by more than three-quarters of a million between 1966 and 1975 alone, with especially big declines in manufacturing, in dock employment (due to the shift of the Port of London downstream towards Tilbury) and in routine office jobs. (It should be noticed that this was a time of declining employment nationally and in the South East.) Further, it was mainly the middle income jobs – the skilled and semi-skilled factory jobs, the

2.4 *Regional Strategies for South-East England.* The *1964 Study*, based on a projected population increase of 3·5 million to 1981, provided for three new cities at more than 50 miles from London. The *1967 Strategy* developed 'growth points', linked back to London via partially-urbanized sectors along major transportation corridors. The *1970 Strategic Plan*, accepted by the government, provides for five major growth centres plus a larger number of medium growth centres; this was reduced in 1976 to adjust to falling population projections, but the main strategic features survived.

routine office jobs – which moved out; increasingly, the jobs that
remained were either high-paying (senior management or professional jobs) or low-paying (service jobs in transportation, hotels
and bars, associated particularly with the tourist explosion). Thus the
outward movement was associated with a danger of social
polarisation, with London divided increasingly into rich and poor.
And the loss of both people and jobs contributed to a progressive
erosion of the Greater London Council's tax base; in the words of the
GLC's former chief strategic planner, David Eversley, it led to rising
costs and static incomes. As yet this has not led to a crisis like that in
New York and other American cities; the welfare burden for the low
income groups is less onerous in London, and both it and other costs
are cushioned by central government subsidies in a way that has not
so far applied to the United States. Nevertheless the danger is present
– particularly since the GLC, like other British local authorities, is
almost completely dependent upon the local real estate tax, or rates,
for its own income.

Table 6 Projected Employment in the South East, 1966–81
(from the Strategic Plan 1970)

	1966*	Change 1966–81	
Greater London	4,450,000	− 367,000	(−8·2%)
Outer Metropolitan Area	2,060,000	+ 422,000	(+20·5%)
London Region	6,510,000	+ 55,000	(+0·8%)
Outer South East Region	1,709,000	+ 320,000	(+18·7%)
South East Region	8,219,000	+ 375,000	(+4·6%)

* Corrected Census figures

Table 7 Planned Population in the South East
(from the Strategic Plan 1970)

	1966	1981	1991	2001
		(millions)		
Greater London	7·8	7·3	7·0	7·0
Outer Metropolitan Area	5·1	6·4	7·4	8·2
London Region	12·9	13·7	14·4	15·2
Outer South East	4·0	4·9	5·7	6·4
South East Region	17·0	18·7	20·1	21·6

Table 8 Major Growth Centres in the South East
(from the Strategic Plan 1970)

	Distance from London, miles	Population, millions		Population, growth, millions 1966–2001
		1966	2001	
Reading–Wokingham– Aldershot–Basingstoke	35–50	0·5	1·2	0·7
South Hampshire	70–90	0·8	1·4	0·6
Milton Keynes– Northampton	90–120	0·3	0·8	0·5
South Essex	50–60	0·6	1·0	0·4
Crawley–Gatwick	40–60	0·2	0·5	0·3
5 major growth areas	–	2·4	4·9	2·5
South East Region	–	17·0	21·6	4·6

The *Greater London Development Plan* therefore argued for an attempt to stabilise both population and employment – particularly through the retention of factory jobs by a system of floor-space targets. But the inquiry panel rejected the GLC's arguments, both because they doubted the desirability of keeping jobs, and because they thought the GLC lacked the powers to achieve it. One hope might be if land could be found for extensive public housing schemes to provide for factory workers, especially in east London which has recorded big losses of manual jobs. But, apart from a windfall gain of land in east London's abandoned docklands – the subject of a special study in 1976, which suggested major redevelopment and economic regeneration at a cost to the public purse of over £1,100 million – the problem is that escalating land prices may price local authorities out of the market. And the outer, lower-density boroughs of Greater London do not want extensive public housing projects to house inner London overspill, for both social and political reasons.

This is why the Strategic Plan for the South East is particularly relevant. Though the Plan accepted the then GLC population target of 7·1 million for London in 1981 – a target the GLC themselves later had to scale down to 6·8 million, and which the GLDP inquiry panel believed should be replaced by a projection of only 6·4–6·5 million – its underlying philosophy is one of dispersal. The central feature of the Strategic Plan, in fact, is the rapid development of a number of major growth centres near London – five of them, some as near as 40 miles from the centre, some up to 80 miles distant. These centres, and the smaller centres of growth which would be based on a number of towns, incorporate some of the ideas for new towns and new cities in the 1964 South East Study; they also bear a relationship to the notion of growth sectors radiating from London, suggested in a 1967 report from the South East Regional Economic Planning Council (map 4.5). The major centres in the Plan would be built up to sizes between half a million and one and a half million – equivalent to major English urban agglomerations like Sheffield or Tyneside – and would thus become real counter-magnets to London, both as employment and service centres. They would take the lion's share of the total expected growth of the region's population in the last thirty-five years of the century: 2·5 out of 4·6 millions (map 2.4).

All this would happen while Greater London's population and employment both declined. Thus there would be a continued overspill of people and jobs from the capital to the rings of growth around it. Many of the jobs that would move out, research reports for the plan make clear, will not be able to move far – especially the office jobs, which are expected to move out at the rate of 15–20,000 a year. This is a critical constraint on the location of the growth centres, and it will mean an open-minded application of central government controls on new office and factory floorspace, so as to encourage selective migration of employment into the Outer Metropolitan Area. But this is unlikely to find much favour either from advocates of vigorous development in areas like northern England, Wales or Scotland, or from the Greater London Council which may want to continue to argue for retaining as many jobs as possible within its own boundaries.

In its own terms, the Strategic Plan offers a contemporary version of the same policies that animated the Abercrombie Plan of 1944. Whereas Abercrombie saw the solution to London's problems in the form of new or expanded towns for around 60,000 people each, the 1970 plan sees it in terms of planned urban agglomerations for a million and more each. These would themselves contain a whole variety of settlements, ranging from large cities through small towns to villages, all set against a background of open space, and interlinked internally by good communications. This vision may appear very modern; but it merely represents a rediscovery of the almost forgotten last chapter of Ebenezer Howard's famous 1898 tract *Garden Cities of Tomorrow*, where he advocated building new towns as part of just such a poly-nuclear Social City. Thus the Plan will transform the South East radically, from a region dominated by a single agglomeration at the centre, to one with a number of strong concentrations of people, jobs and services. Whereas London in 1970 still had almost half the population of the South East, by 2001 it will have less than one third. But in this process, there will be a profound resorting of both people and economic activities. In particular, London seems destined to continue losing factory jobs and more routine white-collar jobs, while adding massively to those activities which it is uniquely qualified to perform: the higher decision-making professional and managerial jobs, as well as continued growth of tourism and international business. This should guarantee continued prosperity for the London of 2000, despite a smaller population.

The drastic fall in birth rate, coupled with the unexpectedly high loss of people and jobs from Greater London, and the rapid growth of new households, already caused the government to update the Strategic Plan only six years after its first publication. The *1976 Strategy Review* assumes that the 1991 population of the entire South East region – including the GLC area, the Outer Metropolitan Area and a wide zone beyond – will be 17·1 million: a sharp fall from the 19·8 million assumed in the 1970 version; the assumed population growth between 1975 and 1991 is only 174,000, against nearly 2·8 million six years earlier. But, since London's forecast population would be only 5·7 million – against 7·0 million in the earlier plan – the forecast reduction for the rest of the region would be more modest: 11·4 million against 12·8 million. In the Outer Metropolitan Area the reduction is only 700,000 – from 6·7 million to just under 6·0 million. Thus, all the five major growth zones of the 1970 plan are still assumed to be necessary – albeit on a somewhat reduced scale. The advantages of concentrating people, jobs and services in a few quite large growth centres, the 1976 authors say, are still telling – though they stress that these centres would not be unbroken masses of building, but rather clusters of settlements separated by intervening open land.

In all this, the 1976 plan is adamant that there is little that either central or local government can do to reverse the outward flow from London itself. It will not be feasible to slow down the exodus, the authors say, until London can supply a quality of life that persuades

Londoners to stay. And that, of course, may be some way off. This answer will be unlikely to satisfy the London authorities – and it may be that central government politicians, faced with their demands, may launch a major diversion of resources in order to reverse the flow. Whether they can succeed is another matter. For, as shown in remaining chapters of this book, urban decentralisation is now a world-wide force in all highly industrialised countries.

But two associated problems, stressed by the GLC planners, will remain. They are the growing burden of an under-privileged, under-skilled, underpaid minority; and the possible gap between the GLC's spending burdens and the revenue needed to meet them. No single neat solution will meet these: a bundle of policies may be needed, including more determined dispersal of low income groups to the new towns (as Peterborough new town, for instance, has attempted), new sources of revenue for the GLC such as a sales tax or tourist tax or lottery; and, most controversial of all, a possible extension of the GLC's boundaries to take in the ring of growth all around. But, with English local government outside London reorganised in a new mould from 1974, this last intriguing possibility seems rather distant.

3 Paris

Most non-Frenchmen like to think they can claim an easy knowledge of Paris: they can pick their way from the Louvre to the Musée de l'Art Moderne, or from the night spots of the Place Pigalle to a hotel on the Left Bank; in between, if they are motorists they may even be able to navigate the one-way street system without too much trepidation. But they seldom think of the Paris they may glimpse beyond: the streets and houses and factories which make it the fourth urban agglomeration of Europe (outside the USSR) and the eighth in the world. And it is doubtful whether most of them spare more than a thought for the problems of one of the fastest-growing urban complexes in the developed western world.

The Parisian planners, who have to grapple with these problems every day, think of a very different Paris from that of the tourist. Their *Région Parisienne* extends to between 60 and 90 kilometres (40 to 60 miles) from Notre Dame (map 3.1). It stretches halfway to Rouen in the west – and two-fifths of the way to the Belgian frontier in the north. Since the administrative reform of 1964, it embraces the *Départements* of Paris (i.e. the city of Paris), Hauts-de-Seine, Seine-St-Denis, Val-de-Marne, Val d'Oise, Yvelines and Essonne – all of which are new creations – plus the old *Département* of Seine-et-Marne. The *Région Parisienne* thus extends over 4,600 square miles – 2·2 per cent of the land area of France. It contained, at the Census of 1975, 9·88 million people – 18·8 per cent of the national total. (The 'metropolitan area' defined by International Urban Research is smaller, with an estimated 8·8 million in 1968.) But in the eight years from 1954 to 1962 the Paris region augmented its population by 1·1 million; 32 per cent of the national increase. From 1962 to 1968 it added 780,000 more, 24 per cent of the total French growth; from 1968 to 1975, another 630,000, 22 per cent of the total. The rate of growth during the whole 1954–75 period ran at between 90,000 and 135,000 a year: 1·0 to 1·8 per cent annually, well above the national average rate of growth.

Some of this phenomenal increase arose from 'natural' causes – the excess of births over deaths, which since the end of the Second World War has been exceptionally high in France. Coming after a long period of stagnation, the rise in the birth rate to one of the highest in western Europe has been hailed in France, with some reason, as a demographic miracle. The rate of natural increase in Paris has actually been a little higher than in France as a whole – partly because Paris contains a high proportion of young adults of childbearing age. But natural increase accounted for just over half of the 130,000

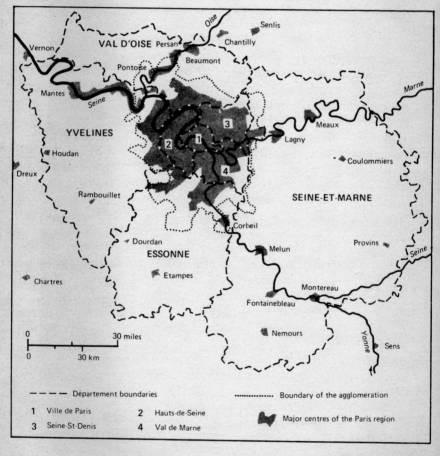

annual average increase during the 1960s. The other half have arrived in Paris by migration – drawn there by the magnetism of the capital. Yet it is important to note that the provincial cities of France have been exerting an even greater magnetism; as compared with a 1·5 per cent annual increase in Paris during 1962–8, Grenoble recorded 4·4, Lyon 2·5 and Marseilles 2·4 per cent. The fact is that France is witnessing a very rapid structural change in the economy, associated with a very high rate of natural population increase: agriculture is contracting, relative to total employment, while the labour force in industry and services expands. This in itself is a matter for national self-congratulation; but the effect on an urban agglomeration already as large as Paris is to create some very large planning problems. These problems have been examined very expertly – and imaginative and far-reaching solutions have been posed to them – in two official documents: the great *Plan d'Aménagement et d'Organisation Générale de la Région Parisienne* (or PADOG) of 1960, and the *Schema Directeur d'aménagement et d'urbanisme de la région de Paris*, a revised plan of 1965 by Monsieur Delouvrier, the Prime Minister's special delegate for the Paris region and latterly the supreme *Préfet* for the whole region. What is particularly interesting is that the second plan starts from quite different premises as compared with the first, and so reaches quite different conclusions. These differences must be examined in detail in the later pages of this chapter.

The structure of Paris: the inner city

How to begin to analyse this great urban complex? The 4,600 square miles of the planners 'Parisian region' contain many strangely assorted landscapes – some of them curiously un-Parisian. They range all the way from the intense bustle of the Grands Boulevards or the insanitary, close-packed tenements of the East End of Paris to the open-field landscapes of the plateaux of Brie and Beauce and the Île de France, or the great forests of Fontainebleau and Chantilly – areas where one could travel for many hours and very nearly forget the existence of a capital of nine million people (map 3.1).

3.1 *The Paris region.* As with most great metropolitan cities, there are several possible definitions of Paris. The planners' *Région Parisienne* extends up to 60 miles from central Paris and embraces 4,600 square miles, with a population of 9·8 million. Much smaller, but still ten times the area of the historic city of Paris, is the *agglomeration*, where over 9 million lived at the 1975 Census. The *Ville* (*city*) had a population of 2·3 million, which was in decline.

But in fact Paris means many different things to different people. We have chosen the Parisian region because it is the most liberal possible definition. But it is helpful to start by looking at other, narrower concepts of Paris.

For the real purist, Paris is the historic city of Paris – *la Ville de Paris*. Based on the great route crossing, where the great north–south route from Flanders to the Mediterranean makes an easy passage across the Seine, in the centre of the fertile Île de France, Paris like London was a Roman creation. Like London it remained small in the Middle Ages – the first wall, built between 1180 and 1210, enclosed 675 acres, almost exactly the same area as the medieval City of London – but unlike London it remained tightly enclosed within its walls until the seventeenth century, and as late as 1860 – the time of Napoleon III – its urban area was surrounded by a ring of fortifications. Despite desperate attempts by the French kings to limit its growth, from the sixteenth century onwards, Paris continued to swell. By the middle of the nineteenth century it had a million people, and it was then – in 1860 – that the City of Paris received its final extension. Most people are familiar with the twenty *arrondissements* into which Paris is divided: ten of these – the 11th to the 20th – were taken in by the last extension, and form the 'peripheral arrondissements'. This Paris of 1860 has remained fixed since then, its limits marked by the gates in the fortifications, long since swept away – Porte des Lilas, Porte de la Villette, Porte de Clignancourt, Porte de Versailles, Porte d'Orléans, Porte d'Italie and others. The tourist knows these names well, because most of them define the outer termini of the *Métro* or underground network, which took shape in the decade after 1900.

The dominant feature of the city of Paris, its overpowering problem, is congestion – congestion of people, of jobs, of traffic, of physical equipment. The congestion of people can be demonstrated vividly in statistics. At the 1975 Census, the city of Paris numbered 2,300,000 people packed on to 105 square kilometres (which include the great open spaces of the Bois de Boulogne in the west and the Bois de Vincennes in the east). Translating, that is 99 people per acre of ground, to say nothing for a moment of all the other things – roads and railways and offices and factories and warehouses and entertainments – that have to be fitted on to these same square kilometres. In comparison, the average for the equivalent area of London (Inner London) in 1971 was 37 per acre. The highest recorded density for a London borough – 62 per acre in Kensington and Chelsea, which probably has the worst housing conditions in London – was lower than that for any of the twenty *arrondissements* of Paris, even the exclusive 16th in the west; it compares with a density in the 11th *arrondissement* of 175 to the acre (in 1975). Of course, high density need not mean poor housing; partly it reflects a

3.2 *The Paris region: population changes, 1962–68.* The region's growth – 780,000, or 24 per cent of national growth – was very unevenly distributed: the historic city was in decline, and the ring of maximum growth was 20–30 miles from the centre. During 1968–75 the decentralization trend continued strongly.

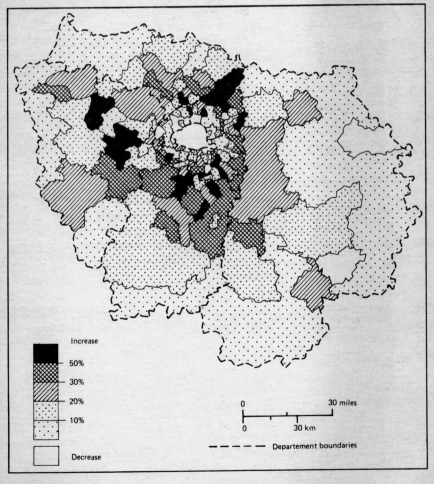

different tradition of close, in-city living in France. But as we shall see, in much of inner Paris these high densities reflect a housing problem of gargantuan proportions.

The congestion of jobs is most vividly illustrated by the central core of Paris. The Parisians have not been able to agree on what precisely constitutes the centre of their city, any more than any other city dwellers have; in Paris the problem is exceptionally difficult, because jobs and residential areas are so closely intermingled right through the inner city area, in the peripheral *arrondissements* as in the central ones. But a convenient definition is the ten 'central' *arrondissements* – the 1st to the 10th, representing roughly the built-up Paris of 1840. These form an oval area conveniently bounded by the big terminal railway stations – St Lazare in the north west, Nord and Est in the north east, Lyon and Austerlitz on opposite banks of the Seine in the south east, Montparnasse in the south west. Within this area, at the Census of 1968, 965,000 found employment; that is approaching one quarter of the total labour force of the Paris region, crowded on to less than 9 square miles – one five-hundredth part of the total area of the region. This central concentration extends marginally into the 16th *arrondissement*, to the west, and the 17th, to the east.

Although many of the peripheral *arrondissements* also have a high density of working population, the employment pattern in the central area is distinguished by one feature, which makes for an extra planning problem: employment at the centre creates longer journeys to work than employment elsewhere. In 1968 1,100,000 people both lived and worked within the City of Paris. But every morning they were joined by another 935,000 commuters from beyond the historic gates of the city. Thus, of a total workforce of 2,035,000, some 46 per cent were in-commuters. (The flow in the opposite direction, by comparison, was negligible.) This throws an exceptional strain on the transport system of the whole urban complex – and as we shall see, the system is ill-adapted to the job.

This pattern of journey to work arises from the character of the jobs at the centre, and from the social composition of the people who work at them. Central Paris is the hub of *les affaires*. It contains the financial centre, around the Bourse, in the 1st, 8th and 9th *arrondissements*; the area of luxury shopping to the west of this, but partly overlapping it, in the 1st and particularly the 8th *arrondissement* (Champs Élysées, Rue Royale, Place Vendôme, Rue du Faubourg St Honoré); the centre of administration, especially around the Invalides in the 7th *arrondissement*, south of the river; and the university and its associated institutions (libraries, institutes and bookshops) south of the river in the 5th and 6th *arrondissements*. The jobs of the central area are overwhelmingly professional, managerial and clerical; the people engaged in them are those who have progressively deserted the city of Paris for homes in more or less distant suburbs. Within this area, increasingly the centre of gravity of employment has shifted westwards, towards the Grands Boulevards and the former exclusively residential area of the 16th *arrondissement* – strictly a peripheral *arrondissement* but now, due to the postwar development of international agencies such as UNESCO, functionally a part of the central area. These have helped Paris retain its role as world city, though in many respects – finance, tourism, international company headquarters, air travel – it stands second to London.

In the peripheral *arrondissements* the employment pattern throws up different problems. Particularly in the East End of the 11th, 12th, 19th and 20th *arrondissements* – the traditional home of the Paris poor – we find the home of densely-packed small industrial and commercial undertakings, packed cheek-by-jowl with the homes of the people who work in them, to the mutual discomfort of both. The figures show that here the amount of travel to work, across the boundaries of the *arrondissements*, is much less. The problem here is rather how to refurbish and replan the pattern of housing and industry. It will certainly involve the large-scale transfer of many people, and many industrial undertakings, out of the city of Paris altogether – a phenomenon already occurring on a large scale by the 1970s.

Paris, in fact, is a typical western European inner city: an area in decline. Between the 1968 and 1975 Censuses it lost 300,000 people – a decline of 11·6 per cent. In most inner *arrondissements* the figure was over 15 per cent.

Seine-Banlieue and the outer suburbs

Beyond the gates of the city, we enter a world which the foreign tourist to Paris hardly glimpses, except on his journey by rail or from the airport, or on his ritual trip to the Flea Market just beyond the Porte de Clignancourt. In every sense this is a strange twilight world. It is administratively ambiguous, being in Paris but not of it: this is the area the French call *Seine-Banlieue*, that is the part of the former

Département of the Seine beyond the Paris city limits. (The *départements*, originally created by the revolutionaries in 1790 for the better management of French provincial government, now number ninety-five since the administrative reform of 1964–7; the Seine *département* has been split into four, one of which is the City of Paris, the others – Hauts-de-Seine, Seine-St-Denis and Val-de-Marne – constituting the *Banlieue*.) The Administration here, then, is in large measure severed from that of Paris and is conducted separately by a multiplicity of separate communes.

Seine-Banlieue corresponds pretty closely to the 'suburban ring' of the London region (the area outside Inner London, but within the conurbation). Like London's suburbs, it has been developed almost continuously between the late nineteenth century and the mid-twentieth. After about 1880 the French bourgeoisie progressively deserted the densely built-up housing of the centre; between 1881 and 1911 the *banlieue* added more people than the city, and after 1911 the population of the city at last began to turn down. (The corresponding date for Inner London was 1901.) We saw that after 1951 the population of the London suburban ring reached stability, and even began to turn down. But the Paris *banlieue* has gone on growing: between 1962 and 1968 alone it added nearly 400,000 people, between 1968 and 1975 another 144,000 (map 3.2). It can do this, despite a much smaller area than its London counterpart, by carrying a relatively high density of population. In 1971 the 500 square miles of the London suburbs held 4,680,215 people – 15 per acre. In 1975 the Paris suburbs – 249 square miles in extent – contained 3,977,000 people, at a density of 25 per acre. The density of these inner Paris suburbs, then, is intermediate between the Inner London area (37 per acre) and the London suburbs. This reflects again, a real difference in social preferences as between the French and the Anglo-Saxon peoples. One-family dwellings are mixed with 'high-rise' structures to an extent unimaginable in England, Germany or the American suburbs. As most of the *banlieue* was developed between the wars in conditions of rampant speculation, the only object was to find plots which would command a ready sale, so that large tracts of less attractive land were left – . generally those with less adequate communications. In recent years many of these have been developed by the public housing organisations known as HLM (*Habitations à loyer modéré* – Dwellings at regulated rents) with large blocks of flats. Many are concentrated in the large estates, called *Grands Ensembles*, where one Parisian in fourteen now lives; the biggest, Sarcelles, is designed for 80,000 people. The resulting landscape is often so ragged and anarchic as to be bizarre; high blocks stand next to still-undeveloped, weed-covered plots. It stands in sharp contrast to the well-kept monotony of British, American or German suburbs.

The housing pattern is heavily interspersed with industry of the newer, space-using sort, which has, however, particularly concentrated in the north-west sector, along both banks of the Seine: between the two great industrial nodes of Boulogne–Billancourt, west-south-west of Paris (the home of the giant Renault works), and the plain of St-Denis in the north. Engineering in various forms, particularly the electrical and vehicle-building branches, is the dominant industry here, as in the corresponding zone of London. This zone principally accounts for the fact that two-thirds of the region's industrial jobs are outside the city: 21 per cent in the Hauts-de-Seine, another 13 per cent in the Seine-St Denis. This type of industry has developed in the course of the present century, and stands in sharp contrast to the congested small workshop industry – light engineering, clothing, furniture, fur – of the East End of Paris.

The industrial areas are big labour magnets, drawing workers from outside. But much of the travel is relatively short-distance in character: of that part of the total workforce of the Paris region that works outside the city (2,321,000 out of 4,254,000 in 1968, or just over half), the great majority – 1,817,000 – do not commute across the boundaries of their own *départements*, but find work fairly close nearby. Many of these short-distance commuters are manual workers: in 1968 in Seine-Banlieue, manual workers travelled on average only 3·2 kilometres, while white-collar workers – mainly bound for jobs in Paris – averaged 4·1 kilometres. (For example: Boulogne-Billancourt draws heavily on the residential areas immediately to the south and south-west, within a radius of 6–10 miles.) Further, while 78 per cent of commuters from the suburbs to Paris use public transport, 53 per cent of commuters within the suburbs use private cars. And at least this movement does not throw such intolerable strains on the transport system as do the radial flows towards the centre. The real problem of the suburbs does not lie here, but rather in the poverty of the physical equipment. Haste and lack of plan were the distinguishing features of development in the suburban zone. Villages like Pantin, Aubervilliers, Boulogne, even towns like St-Denis, were swallowed up in the urban flood. They became nodes of building simply because they lay on the main roads from Paris. In consequence they frequently remained ill-adapted to their new function. Too often, today, the old villages fail to provide proper urban shopping, entertainment and social centres; the road system is basically the rural road system, engulfed by the town; the whole landscape resembles nothing so much as a vast, ill-conceived, hastily constructed emergency camp to house the labour force of Paris. As in Paris itself, so in the suburbs, a clear distinction exists between east and west: the western suburbs – Meudon, Sèvres, Chaville – were early settled and have better housing and a more coherent urban structure; but the inner suburbs of the north and east, from St-Denis through Aubervilliers and les Lilas south almost to the Bois de Vincennes, presents almost the limit of urban degeneration.

After 1918 the expansion of Paris could no longer be limited even by the bounds of the former Seine *département*. It spread in long tentacles along the main lines of communication, into what are now the neighbouring *départements* of Seine-et-Marne to the east and (especially) Val d'Oise to the north, Yvelines to the west and Essonne to the south. Together these three peripheral *départements* and the three closer-in ones form the Parisian *banlieue* or suburbs. In consequence French statisticians and planners have been driven to find a working definition of the urban area of Paris, which can be revised from time to time to keep pace with reality. This unit is the Parisian *agglomeration*: in 1975 it was comparable in size with the Greater London Conurbation, and had a population of over 9 million. The outermost fringe of the *agglomeration* – the area within the three peripheral *départements* – was the fastest-growing area of the Paris region between 1962 and 1968, as map 3.2 shows. But here there is a distinct falling away in the degree of urbanisation. The density of population in the entire area of the four outermost *départements* of the Paris region, in 1975, was only 10·3 per acre, considerably less than that of the entire 'suburban ring' of Greater London. As one travels out from the centre, the areas of housing, often built in rigidly formal patterns around the stations, are separated by increasingly wide tracts of rural land. The uniform suburban sea of housing progressively gives way to a more distinct urban structure, with towns that were already important when they were swallowed up by Paris – l'Isle Adam, Villeneuve-St Georges, Poissy, Pontoise. Here the great problem of the planners is to control and limit growth: to guide it so that the land is used as economically as may be, with a proper balance between development and open space. This indeed has been one of the most important objects of recent planning in the Paris region.

The central problems of the Paris region

In this rapid journey across the vast *Région Parisienne*, we have touched upon the central planning problems of Paris, as they superficially appear. It is now time to sum them up, and to probe them more deeply. The problems that make the most obvious impression in Paris are:

Traffic. The Parisian transport system – or, as the French delight in calling it, the transport infrastructure – is increasingly incapable of performing adequately the functions it is called upon to perform. For this it is possible to blame a number of past mistakes.

The history of planning in Paris is bound up, more than that of any other city of the world, with the name of one man: Baron Haussmann, Prefect of the *département* of the Seine during the reign of the Emperor Napoleon III, from 1853 to 1870. Haussmann transformed inner Paris, tearing away the narrow lanes and alleys and replacing them by the great boulevards which today are the envy and admiration of all visitors. But in some ways Haussmann's legacy to Paris is an unfortunate one. His boulevards give a deceptive impression that Paris is a city capable of ready adaptation to the age of the universal motor-car. But that is by no means so: for their great size, the boulevards are strangely inefficient carriers of great traffic volumes, because so many of them converge so often on *ronds-points* which are quite incapable of handling the resulting flows. In one respect only was Haussmann perceptive, and that by accident: he refused to widen existing streets, but built his new boulevards parallel to them (as his great north–south artery, the Boulevard de Sébastopol, next to the Rue St Martin). As a result, since 1949 the Parisian traffic planners have been able to adapt his boulevards to the most extensive one-way street system in Europe: a system which has compensated for some of the worst errors of Haussmann's road planning. The other great criticism of Haussmann's planning was that he created plenty of space for traffic to move, but none for it to park, except on the roadway itself. As, in addition, he made sure that his new boulevards were lined by lucrative commercial properties, there was every incentive for kerbside parking. In 1860, with traffic flows only one-tenth of the volume of a century later, that was perhaps an adequate solution. Today, with one of the highest car ownership rates in Europe – 2·9 million vehicles in the Paris region at the start of 1972, one for every 3·9 people – it is reponsible for acrimonious wrangles between the Paris police, who are trying to banish the stationary vehicle from the main arteries of their central 'blue zone', and the shopkeepers who depend on the kerbside to unload their goods and receive their customers.

One other great error was made in the planning of the pattern of Parisian circulation, and that concerns the urban railway network. It was only logical, in Paris as in other European cities, to forbid the main-line railway system to enter the central heart of the city. But if this system was to prove adequate to demands, two things were necessary; and neither happened. One was effective liaison between the terminal stations and the centre of the city. Here Haussmann failed in an essential task, because the stations are frequently sited on inadequate offshoots from the main boulevard system, and are in consequence the scenes of some of the worst traffic congestion in Paris. This particularly applies to the Gare St Lazare, which is by far the most important commuters' station, bringing in well over a quarter of a million commuters every working day in the 1960s. The other was that the main-line railways be relieved of pressure in the inner suburban area, by a separate network of short-distance stopping trains, such as is provided by the London underground system. This too failed to happen, because with a few exceptions the *Métro* system was not extended beyond the gates of the municipal area. In addition, it was built on a restricted loading gauge, and could not be connected with the main system. As a result travellers bound for the Seine-Banlieue area have to transfer to the bus system at the *Métro* termini, which throws an increasing strain on the street system at these points at the morning and evening rush hour, and needlessly congests the main radial highways out from the city in the zone between three and five miles from the centre.

Housing. Curiously, the second problem of Paris may also be laid, in some measure, at Haussmann's door. Haussmann destroyed quickly, without thinking too closely or too clearly where the poor of the Paris slums would go. In fact, they were merely displaced outwards; because rents were too high on the new apartment blocks that rose on the cleared sites, they went to badly built new housing in the peripheral *arrondissements* – where, today, some of the worst housing problems are concentrated. At a time of such very rapid reconstruction, the essential minimum was an adequate sanitary law; but that did not come until 1902.

Partly as a result of this failure, the city of Paris today suffers from a gargantuan problem of obsolescent and substandard housing. It would be wrong to pretend that this is solely the problem of Paris; it is the problem of France, one that the 'economic miracle' under the four-year plans, since 1946, has begun to touch only on any scale during the 1960s.

Statistics tell the tale. At the 1962 Census, in the entire Paris region, the average dwelling had only 2·6 rooms against a national average of 3·1 rooms; in the city of Paris the average dwelling was even smaller, 2·25 rooms. (By 1968 the figures were 2·8 for the region, 3·3 for France and 2·3 for Paris.) 54 per cent of all dwellings in the region, and two thirds in the city, had one or two rooms only in 1962; by 1968 the regional figure had fallen to 47 per cent but the figure for the city was still 65 per cent. (It should be noticed, though, that households, too, were smaller in the city than elsewhere.) On average in the Paris region there were nearly 1·1 people to a room in 1962, just under 1 in 1968; in 1962, according to official definitions, 12 per cent were acutely overcrowded and 21 per cent moderately so. (The corresponding 1968 figures were 10 and 30; but the basis of the calculation was quite different.) The average Parisian, then, lacks space.

Furthermore, the space he has is often old and poorly equipped. In 1962, 54 per cent of all dwellings in the Paris region dated from before World War One; 19 per cent from before the Franco–Prussian War of 1871. At that date 65 per cent of all dwellings still lacked a bath or shower; 44 per cent an internal w.c.; 13 per cent even lacked running water. (The 1968 Census recorded quite a big improvement, with 45 per cent lacking bath or shower, 36 per cent a w.c. and only 4 per cent running water.) It is small wonder that in a survey in 1963 30 per cent of households thought themselves badly housed and that 37 per cent desired to change their home.

Basing their calculations on these figures and on future population projections, the planners of the Paris region estimated in 1966 that some 170,000 dwellings were needed to meet current shortages; that 580,000 dwellings, or 20 per cent of the 1962 stock, should be condemned by 1975; and that the overall need was for an approximately 50 per cent increase in the rate of new residential building above the 1962–5 average, coupled with an increase in the average size of new dwellings from 3·3 to 3·6 or even 3·8. This is the scale of the programme needed to cope with the chronic failure to provide new homes in the period of stagnation between the two World Wars, coupled with the explosive population growth of the region since 1945.

The shortage of social capital. Paralleling the lack of adequate housing has been an inadequacy in the capital equipment which must be provided, as a social obligation, by public authorities. The effects were scathingly described by M. Delouvrier in the *Livre Blanc* – a 1963 survey of the needs of the region:

The home that you only reach late in the evening because of the lack of convenient transport, the sanitary installations paralysed in summer for lack of water, the career missed or abandoned for lack of a place in a technical institute, the leisure hours wasted because of physical obstacles ...

Some of this deficiency is general, arising from the failure of the public authorities to provide in time for the explosion of population within the Region: thus the water supply, which nearly failed completely in the hot summer of 1959, or the disposal of sewage – at least *half* of which was put straight into the Seine without treatment down to the mid-1960s. Another type of shortage – that of open space – is peculiarly the problem of inner Paris: the presence of the Bois de Boulogne and Bois de Vincennes hardly compensates for the chronic lack of parks within the city. But the most chronic deficiency of social capital, by the early 1960s, was experienced in the suburbs. While the suburban zone expanded mushroom-fashion, after about 1880, a strange paralysis attacked the organs of local government in the region. Some of the resulting incongruities were bizarre: thus the town hall of Argenteuil, occupying a private house bought about 1890 when the population of the commune was 10,000, then serving 90,000 people; or areas like Nanterre (90,000), Vitry-sur-Seine (78,000) or Maisons-Alfort (53,000) which completely lack even a police station. There was a serious lack of places in secondary education in the suburbs, especially in technical branches; there was not a single university establishment in the suburbs, with the exception of the decentralised faculty of science of the Sorbonne at Orsay. Apart from a very small number built between the two wars, the suburban zone was entirely lacking in hospitals; all cases were removed to the city hospitals, which mainly date from the nineteenth century and which were chronically overloaded. On average in the early 1960s there was only one swimming bath, in the whole Paris region, for 200,000 people (though plans provided for five times the number by 1970). The superb cultural facilities, which the visitor enjoyed, were all concentrated in the Paris he knew: beyond the tourists' regular haunts, they simply stopped. The whole of Paris outside the centre, a region housing six million Parisians, was virtually devoid of theatres, museums, cultural centres and libraries. Thus was the state of the suburbs in the early 1960s – a time when Parisian planning was transformed, with dramatic results.

Redevelopment versus conservation. In the 1960s, under de Gaulle, Paris continued to demolish and redevelop on a vast scale – even after other European cities had come to stress conservation. The result is a new Paris, very different in scale and atmosphere from the old. The Boulevard Périphérique, a completely new motorway, was driven along the line of the old fortifications which mark the edge of the historic city of Paris; completed in the early 1970s, it actually involved tunneling under the famous lakes in the Bois de Boulogne. A new one-way expressway was driven along the historic *quais* on the right bank of the Seine, and another was projected for the left bank. In the Fronts de Seine development in the 15th *arrondisement*, 2,500 new flats were provided in high tower blocks on an old factory site. In the vast Maine–Montparnasse scheme on the site of the Montparnasse station, 20,000 office jobs and 1,000 flats were provided together with shops, hotels, a congress hall and parking. A complete redevelopment was proposed for the old market site at Les Halles in the heart of the city. All these went ahead except for the Left Bank Expressway, which was abandoned after fierce protests. But the Montparnasse scheme and above all the redevelopment of Les Halles proved bitterly controversial, and by the mid 1970s it seemed unlikely that such large-scale redevelopment would ever be repeated in the historic city. In other areas, such as the historic Marais not far from Les Halles, the state was encouraging and subsidising a generous programme of conservation.

Physical growth. The four problems so far described all basically arise from the mistakes of the past. But they are all greatly aggravated by the continued growth of Paris and its population, which throws an

increasing strain on the urban transport system and the central
streets; which creates a persistent demand for new housing
construction, thus competing with the vital job of renewal of the
outworn structures in the centre; and which further exposes the
paucity of communal equipment in the suburbs. The question is not
merely one of a once-for-all onslaught on these deficiencies of social
capital; it is how far we need to go on providing more such capital –
and planning its provision a good deal more effectively than in the
past – for a growing population. Shall Paris grow? That is the
fundamental question, which has given rise to intense debate in
France ever since the fact of rapid population increase became
manifest.

Paris et le désert français

In 1947, a 32-year-old geographer, employed in economic planning
for the Ministry of Reconstruction, published the work which was to
set this debate in motion. *Paris et le désert francais*, by Jean-François
Gravier, illustrated the extraordinary imbalance in the structure of
the French population, which hardly has a parallel elsewhere in the
world. He showed, with a wealth of telling illustration, the
extraordinary concentration of French life in Paris, which had
resulted from the long tradition of administrative centralisation – a
tradition that had passed through from the *ancien régime* through all
the revolutions since 1789. He illustrated the effects on the
administration itself, where affairs, which would be treated locally in
any other country, are transacted through Paris; on the universities,
where the Sorbonne dominates French university and cultural life to
an extent almost unimaginable elsewhere; and in finance, where a
strong tradition of provincial banking had collapsed in the nineteenth
century. Gravier showed how the process of centralisation had fed
itself: how the railways, planned deliberately to focus on Paris in the
mid-nineteenth century, tended to ignore communication between
the provincial centres, and so encouraged the further concentration
of commerce and industry in the one centre. Gravier demanded that
this vicious circle be broken – by means of a positive policy of
decentralisation and a fundamental reorientation of French life, to
give more effective power to the provincial centres.

The decentralisation policy

Gravier's book created intense public interest in France in the techniques of positive regional planning, and since 1949 the French Government has pursued an active policy of industrial decentralisation. Up to 1955 policy was limited to positive inducements to industry to set up in decentralisation areas, by means of grants from special funds; from 1955 this policy has been made more effective by the development of new types of grant – e.g. special equipment premiums – and the establishment of more effective regional development societies, charged with co-ordinating efforts over wide areas. But perhaps even more important, since 1955 such measures have been supplemented by negative restrictions on industry – and, latterly, on commerce – in Paris itself. In 1955 new industrial construction in the Paris region was limited; from 1959 the establishment of offices of over 500 square metres (5,382 square feet) were also made subject to official agreement; in 1961 a system of charges began to operate for building new offices or factories, and with it a parallel system of grants for the reconversion of industrial or commercial premises into houses or schools. During the 1960s the permit system was applied with increasing rigour so that the proportion of permits to build or extend factories in the Paris region dropped from 26 per cent (in 1954) to 8 per cent (in 1969): in 1967 even more stringent controls, including tax penalties, were introduced for all new building in the Paris region above a certain size limit.

There is no denying that these measures have had an effect – but it is a curiously limited one. Perhaps 500,000 new jobs have been created outside Paris. But the majority of the factories have not gone any very great distance out of Paris. A ring of *départements* immediately around the Paris region, and forming in effect an extension of it at distances up to 200 miles from Paris itself, with some big cities (Rouen, Le Havre, Amiens, Reims, Troyes, Orléans) and many small country towns, took 75 per cent of all the moves and 60–65 per cent of the decentralised jobs. Significantly, many of these were small branch operations for main plants that remained in Paris; nearly half of them, representing nearly three-quarters of the new jobs, were in mechanical or electrical engineering. And, of course, manufacturing industry only represents a minority of all jobs in the Paris region – some 37 per cent in 1968. In the tertiary sector, over one quarter of the national total of employment is in the Paris region, and there is no reason to expect any early substantial change in this situation. It is too early yet to draw conclusions on the restrictions on office development. But it is perhaps significant that between 1962 and 1970, new office floorspace in the Paris region totalled some 30 million square feet, or 4 million square feet a year – with a particularly large share in the western suburbs just outside the historic city limits. And during 1971–75, the projected total gain was 10 million square feet a year – mostly in the city or the adjacent western suburbs where more than 90 per cent of the office space is concentrated. Interestingly, this average gain was close to the average loss of manufacturing floor space in the city during the 1960s. With more than 60 per cent of all employment in the region in the tertiary sector, Paris like London and New York is fast becoming a non-manufacturing city.

The future growth of Paris

We have in fact already seen that during the period of operation of this policy, Paris added 1·9 million to its population – 1·1 million from 1954 to 1962, 0·8 million from 1962 to 1968 – and was increasing at double the national rate. However, it is very important to realise that in terms of population, it is now unrealistic to talk of *et le désert français*. Provincial France may be a desert culturally, intellectually, in social provision; but not in population. When Gravier was writing, the experience of the previous century (1851–1946) showed that the Parisian agglomeration had in effect accounted for the entire net increase of the population of France. But in contrast, between 1954 and 1962 – as we have seen – the Paris Region accounted for only 32 per cent of the increase; the proportion declined to 24 per cent in 1962–8 and to 22 per cent in 1968–75. True, there is still a considerable number of 'under-endowed' regions of France where population is stagnant or even decreasing – Brittany, the Massif Central. But the great provincial urban agglomerations of the provinces are proving viable enough: their average rate of increase was slightly greater than Paris in 1954–62, and considerably greater in 1962–75. Furthermore, the decision in the Fifth Plan to designate eight of the most important (Marseilles, Lyons, Toulouse, Bordeaux, Nantes, Nancy, Strasbourg and Lille-Roubaix-Tourcoing) as 'equilibrium metropolises', or counter-magnets to Paris, will surely strengthen their growth rates in the 1970s. The question now is not whether Paris will suck the life blood from France; but rather the precise rate at which Paris is to grow, relative to the provincial cities, given that both of them seem destined to grow very fast.

Forecasting the future population of a major metropolis like Paris is a hazardous business. There is room for doubt about the course of future national population and about the proportion that will go into the cities as a whole; but above all there is room for debate about the proportion of the urban population that will go, or should go, to Paris. The PADOG plan in 1960 worked on the basis that migration into Paris could be reduced from over 100,000 a year (the average for the late 1950s) to only 50,000 a year, to give a total increase of about 100,000 a year. Because it accepted that migration could be limited, PADOG was led to propose that a limit be put on the physical growth of the agglomeration, as Abercrombie had proposed for London in 1944. Further, this limitation was not to be balanced, as in the London plan, by large schemes for new towns or town expansions within the wider urban region. PADOG firmly rejected new towns, on the grounds that they would attract more people into the region. At most it countenanced a limited expansion of towns like Meaux, Melun, Creil, Mantes and Étampes, from 20–30,000 people to double that size, plus some smaller increases elsewhere. Really big increases could be allowed only in towns well outside the Paris sphere of influence, 60 miles and more away: Rouen, Amiens, Reims, Troyes, Orléans, Le Mans. The growth of Paris itself must be accommodated within the boundaries of the agglomeration (map 3.3).

These assumptions, and the resulting policies, did not go unchallenged. M. Delouvrier, in his *Livre Blanc* of 1963, took as example a minimum hypothesis which was lower still than that of PADOG: that migration could be cut to 25,000 a year. Even this, he showed, would give Paris a population of 12 million by the year 2000 – an increase of nearly 50 per cent on the 1962 figure. And it would demand that the other urban agglomerations must more than double their populations by 2000: Lyon must reach more than 2 million, Marseilles, Lille and Nancy–Metz between 1·5 and 2 million, Bordeaux 1 million. M. Delouvrier, however, also gave a 'maximum' forecast, based on a high national rate of increase, a high rate of urbanisation and a Paris which was growing as fast as the total urban population. That would give a total increase of nearly 200,000 a year – double the PADOG estimate – and a population of 16 million by 2000, double the 1962 total. The *Livre Blanc* argued that the growth of Paris is merely a matter of time: be it in 2050, or 2100, the 16-million mark will be reached, and at that time the built-up area will have extended to encompass the whole Paris region. M. Delouvrier's view

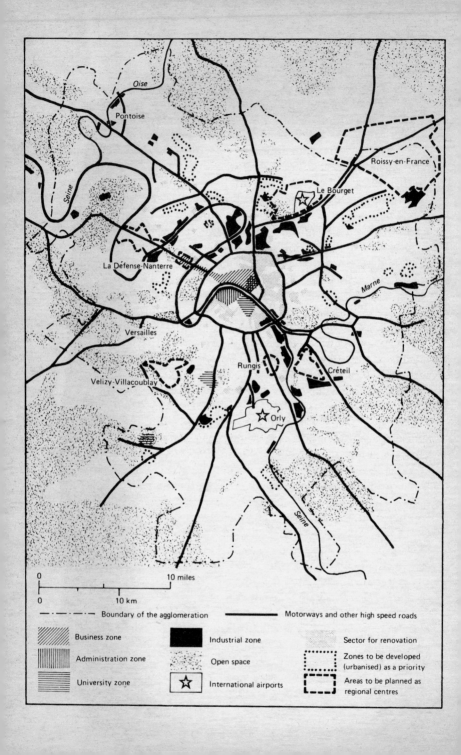

0		10 miles
0		10 km

— · — · — Boundary of the agglomeration ———— Motorways and other high speed roads

Business zone

Administration zone

University zone

Industrial zone

Open space

☆ International airports

Sector for renovation

Zones to be developed (urbanised) as a priority

Areas to be planned as regional centres

Oise
Pontoise
Seine
Roissy-en-France
Le Bourget
La Défense-Nanterre
Marne
Versailles
Rungis
Créteil
Velizy-Villacoublay
☆ Orly
Seine

was reinforced by trends between 1962 and 1964: the Paris population grew by an average of 165,000 a year – three times the PADOG assumption – of which 65,000 represented natural increase, 50,000 internal migration and 50,000 repatriation from Algeria. In February 1964 M.Delouvrier calculated that on a 'reasonable' hypothesis, the population of the Paris region would top the 12-million mark by 1985. To justify his forecast, between 1960 and 1965 the authorities granted special limits to build 25,000 houses outside the limits of the agglomeration set by the PADOG plan, and the total population of the region topped the 9 million mark by the mid-1960s.

Against such a statistical background, the attempt of PADOG to limit the physical growth of Paris began to appear misconceived. In 1961 M.Georges Pilliet, in a powerful criticism (*L'Avenir de Paris*) claimed that the effect of PADOG policy would be to cripple the most active wealth-creating enterprises in Paris and to deny France the opportunity of becoming the capital of Europe. 'The Parisian agglomeration', he concluded, 'is thus neither too big nor is it overpopulated, it is badly-built, badly-serviced and badly-equipped'; and he argued for a plan to develop the whole of the Paris region. This theme was taken up by M.Delouvrier, who in the *Livre Blanc* said flatly that whatever artificial factors are blamed for the shortage of land in the Paris region – the slowness of the planning machine, the excessive areas reserved by public authorities for future use – the fundamental trouble was that not enough land is allocated for development. 'The truth,' he writes, 'is that once again the barriers of Paris are bursting.' To make land available for development is not to return to the speculative anarchy of the 1920s; it is to plan effectively and to provide necessary public services in good time. That cannot be done while holding the existing limits of the agglomeration: PADOG worked on this basis, but according to the *Livre Blanc* the attempt was doomed to failure.

3.3 *The Paris region: PADOG plan 1960: regional objectives.* The essential philosophy of the PADOG plan is to limit further physical growth of the Parisian agglomeration. The plan firmly rejects new towns because they might add to the attraction of the Paris region. At most a limited expansion of peripheral towns can be allowed. But most of the planned population growth must be accommodated within the existing bounds of the agglomeration by developing new regional nodes: La Défense-Nanterre to the west, Velizy-Villacoublay to the south-west and Le Bourget to the north.

A new plan for Paris: The 1965 Schéma Directeur

This is the background to the 1965 Plan: the *Schéma Directeur d'Amenagement et d'Urbanisme de la Région de Paris* (map 3.4). Prepared by the staff of M. Delouvrier, it starts from the frank recognition that Paris will expand: according to the assumptions set out at the beginning of the plan, from 9 million in 1965 to 14 million by 2000, representing a middle position between the extremes forecast by M. Delouvrier in the *Livre Blanc*. This growth is likely to be accompanied by 2 million extra jobs – three-quarters in the tertiary sector; a quintupling of purchasing power; a doubling or trebling of the car fleet; and a twofold increase in dwellings. All in all, according

3.4   *The Paris region: Schéma Directeur 1965.* Rejecting the policy of restraining the region's growth, the Plan provides for Paris to grow from 9 to 14 million people via giant new cities, each with up to half-a-million, aligned along two preferential axes north and south of the Seine.

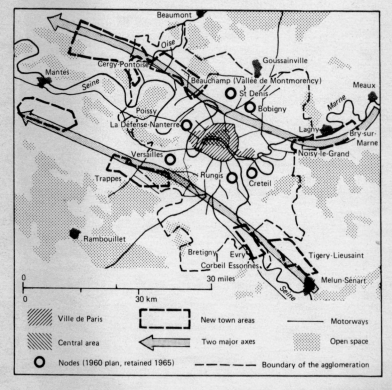

to the calculations of the authors, these changes imply nearly a doubling of the developed area: from 460 to 850 square miles (1,200–2,300 square kilometres). This is the essential basis of the radical physical provisions of the 1965 plan – a basis quite contrary to the assumptions of PADOG in 1960.

The starting point is the location of employment. This, at present in the Paris region, is dominated by the contrast between the over-concentration at the centre and the underdevelopment in the suburbs. Paris contains no intermediate level of service centre between the centre of the world city, serving the agglomeration and even beyond, and the purely local suburban service centre serving at most 30,000; there is no centre of the level of major provincial cities, such as Toulouse or Strasbourg. One aim should be to create centres of this size to contain the fast-growing service sector of employment; they would include higher education, cultural facilities, sports facilities, department stores, luxury restaurants, major hotels, and the centre of the prefecture. Such centres would serve populations of between 300,000 and 1 million, depending on the location and the level of services provided.

The next element in the 1965 plan is the distribution of new residential areas. This will be conditioned by the need to remedy the glaring lack of living space in the region now. In 1962 there were 6 million rooms in the region; to reach London or New York standards at that time, there should have been 9 million. The number of dwellings is expected nearly to double (3·2–6 million) by 2000, the number of rooms to treble. The surface area needed for housing may well quadruple, because the evidence is that most people prefer a one-family house. At present the effective choice is between a small and under-equipped apartment, nearer the place of work, and a bigger and better-equipped house, far from work and with poor travelling conditions. To remedy this, there will need to be a bigger range of work near the home, and faster, better travel.

Open space in the region at present is lacking. As we have seen, the inner area at present is developed to a very high density with a corresponding lack of open space; the growth of the suburbs in a series of annular rings, with no proper planning, has left an insufficiency there too. The plan will remedy this by reserving the Seine valley, between major urban developments on the higher ground on both sides, as a recreational zone wherever land is not used for industry. The forest of Versailles will also be extended westwards;

to the east of Paris, the fine forested land between the Seine and the Marne valleys will be left open.

The transportation element in the plan is based on the necessity to reduce travel time and fatigue. To supplement the existing structure of transportation lines in the region, which radiate from the centre like spokes of a wheel (but with a certain concentration in the Seine valley both above and below Paris), new transportation lines will be developed in accordance with the preferential east–west axis of development. These will be based on the principle that the inner agglomeration must still depend principally on public transport, especially for work but that in the new extensions dependence on the car will be almost complete. There will be a new 260-kilometre system of express Métro lines running both east–west and north–south (but these last will fan out to serve some of the new extensions both to west and east); and a 900-kilometre network of radial and concentric motorways which serve more local networks of secondary and tertiary routes, connecting with the new centres. These in fact are inherited from the 1960 plan, and by the early 1970s several of the motorways radiating from the new circumferential Boulevard Peripherique which encircles the city of Paris (north to Brussels, south to Marseilles, west to Rouen and south-west to Chartres) were open; so were two sections of the new express Métro, with the connecting middle section under construction for a scheduled opening in 1978 (maps 3.5, 3.6).

These different elements of the plan powerfully condition the urban structure, which is reached through the elimination of alternatives. As starting point it is recognised that development must take the form of major sub-regional service and employment centres, catering for between 300,000 and 1 million people. The plan rejects the concept of grouping these into a 'second Paris', on the ground that such a centre could not hope to compete for many years with the existing national centre. It rejects also the idea of a ring of new towns with an intervening green belt, on the English model, chiefly on the grounds that it would hinder the development programme in more distant towns 60 miles (100 kilometres) or more from Paris, such as Orléans, Chartres, Rouen and Reims (a programme retained from PADOG); additionally, it is argued that the intervening green belt would tend to fill up along the radial lines of transportation into Paris, however draconian the planning powers. The central concept of PADOG – the development of suburban nodes – is retained as part of the new plan; but it is recognised that this development is physically more difficult, and its scale more limited, than the development of new city units on land outside the existing agglomeration.

From this analysis springs the concept, common also to plans for other European capital cities such as Stockholm and Copenhagen, of

3.5   *The Paris region: Highway Proposals.* The 1965 plan contains an investment programme of new and improved highways, partially completed by the late 1970s. In this the *Boulevard Peripherique*, encircling the historic *Ville de Paris*, connects the main national radial motorways.

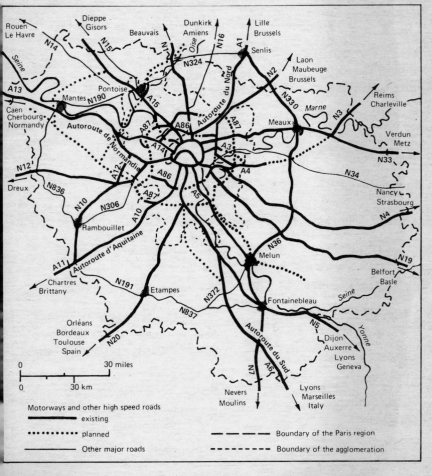

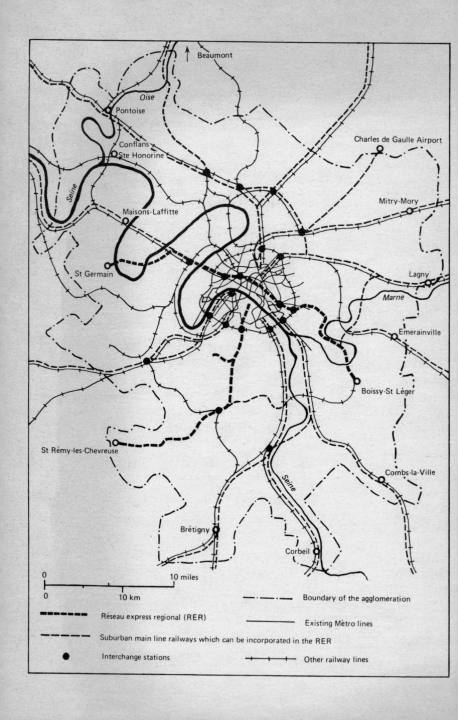

Beaumont

Oise

Pontoise

Conflans
Ste Honorine

Charles de Gaulle Airport

Seine

Mitry-Mory

Maisons-Laffitte

St Germain

Lagny

Marne

Emerainville

Boissy-St Léger

St Rémy-les-Chevreuse

Combs-la-Ville

Seine

Brétigny

Corbeil

0		10 miles
0	10 km	

Boundary of the agglomeration

▄▄▄▄ Réseau express regional (RER)

Existing Mètro lines

▄ ▄ ▄ Suburban main line railways which can be incorporated in the RER

● Interchange stations

╁╁╁ Other railway lines

grouping the new units along preferential axes representing main lines of transport. Throughout the history of Paris, the authors of the plan point out, the form of the major transportation axes has literally controlled the form of growth of the agglomeration; in the past this occurred spontaneously, for the future it can be planned. Up to now, the radial-concentric system of transportation lines produced the agglomeration of today; in future, different directions are possible. The preferred solution of the 1965 Plan is to develop along a very few preferential axes. This solution, the plan argues, will alone guarantee access to open space and open air recreation to the great majority of the people of the agglomeration; it alone will exploit at minimum cost the new and planned investments in rail routes and motorways. It is also the only way the planners can see of readily decentralising industry and other economic activities into new towns, since it exploits the observable tendency, on the part of both people and economic activities, to move outwards along roughly radial lines.

The critical question is the choice of axes. In the view of the planners, more than one axis is necessary to exploit the natural tendencies towards outward radial movement. But too many axes will sacrifice the critical advantages of access to countryside and low investment costs; further, they will lead to the familiar historical process, whereby the gaps between the 'fingers of the glove' fill up with development. It is mainly for this reason that the plan finally emerges with the concept of a principal axis which is double, taking the form of two parallel lines: one 40 miles (75 km) long, north of the Seine from Eaux to west of Pontoise, the other 55 miles (90 km) long, south of the Seine from Melun to Mantes. To this are attached a number of short secondary axes, designed to give some room for the natural development of the agglomeration. The major new towns are strung out along the two new axes – on the northern line at Cergy-Pontoise, Beaumont (Vallée de Montmorency), and Vallée de la Marne (Bry-sur-Marne/Noisy-le-Grand), on the southern axis near Mantes, at Trappes (later renamed St Quentin-des-Yvelines), at Evry-Corbeil, and at Tigery Lieusaint (later renamed Melun-Sénart). The two axes, in their central sections, are tangential to the

3.6   *The Paris region: Mass Transit Proposals.* A new Regional Express Métro (RER) will run under the historic E-W axis of Paris, connecting centres like La Défense with the historic urban core. Another N-S axis will connect the centre with several of the new cities of the 1965 Plan.

edge of the existing agglomeration and thus can incorporate many of the ideas for new nodes in the existing Parisian banlieue – a central concept of the 1960 Paris plan, here retained.

Polycentric Paris

This in fact was the most revolutionary notion of the 1960 Plan: to revertebrate the suburbs (the word was Gravier's) by establishing gigantic new nodes of employment, social equipment and housing at a few selected points in the suburban zone. To choose such areas was a delicate task, because they needed considerable land and also good transport facilities. This was a little easier in Paris than (say) in London, because of the characteristic we described earlier – the chaotic pattern of Parisian suburban development, which has left many open or half-developed spaces.

PADOG finally lighted on a number of major nodes, and the 1965 Plan retained them. The first and most dramatic is the zone known as La Défense – a 1,700-acre site, then largely undeveloped, lying only 2·5 miles west of the Arc de Triomphe, and immediately west of the exclusive inner suburb of Neuilly, on the direct continuation of the line of the Champs Elysées. For decades the central heart of Paris has been drifting westwards – a trend partly associated with the rise of new types of 'central area function', such as headquarters offices, advertising and public relations, business consultancies and institutes. (The trend is parallel to the one which has changed the West End of London, during this century, from a residential into an office zone.) The 1960 Plan recognised this trend, but sought to guide it. Already a pioneer undertaking – the *Centre National des Industries et des Techniques* – had settled at La Défense. Around it the plan grouped offices, shops, showrooms, and public buildings, together with the homes of 800,000 people. To provide for the increased traffic flows, the area would be served by the new west–east express *Métro* and by an ambitious system of new roads, culminating in a complex multi-level system of junctions at the heart of the development. Largely complete, but still a bewildering mass of construction works in the mid 1970s, La Défense promises to be one of the most exciting pieces of twentieth-century central area development of any city of the world – though in the early 1970s it was already being criticised by a younger generation of architects and planners for monolithic soullessness. The general development extends westwards to take in the vast 'Paris No. 10' University at Nanterre – scene of some of the main events in the May 1968 revolutionary disturbances.

The second great node lies west of Paris – and south of La Défense. Immediately east of Versailles lies the plateau zone of Velizy-Villacoublay, then occupied by a military aerodrome. This was badly sited, especially in relation to Orly; its removal released a considerable space for housing and for new central area activities.

The third node is in some ways the most important for the suburban zone itself. It represents a gigantic effort to renew the most impoverished and desolate sector of the whole inner suburban zone – the industrialised sector of St Denis, Aubervilliers and Bobigny. On the outer edge of this zone lies the former second airport of Paris – Le Bourget – which has become inadequate with the arrival of bigger planes. In 1973 it was replaced by a new airport further north, at Roissy-en-France, which will become the first Paris airport. This is a position peripheral to the main agglomeration – a position which will hopefully permit supersonic operation without intolerable discomfort to the neighbouring population. The existing airport will be redeveloped during the 1970s as a service and residential node, a node exceptionally well-served by rail facilities and by the *Autoroute du Nord*. This central focus will be ringed by major new housing developments in the northern suburbs.

Lastly, in the south-east the 1965 Plan borrows from PADOG the idea of a major zone of redevelopment of growth based on Rungis – the new location for the famous wholesale food markets of Les Halles, moved here in 1969 – and the adjacent centre of Créteil. Together with Versailles-Velizy-Villacoublay, this node relates closely to the southern development axis of the 1965 Plan – just as St. Denis-Bobigny-Le Bourget are incorporated into the northern axis.

Implementing the Plan

Combining as it did many of the more ambitious elements of the 1960 Plan – the new suburban nodes, the radial and circumferential motorways and the regional express *Métro* – together with the eight completely new towns, the 1965 Plan amounts to a formidable programme of investment, one of the most heroic of any major urban area in the world. Only in a country like France, with one of the highest rates of growth of GNP of any advanced industrial country during the 1960s and 1970s, would it be possible to contemplate such a scale of investment at the same time as a vigorous programme of development was being carried through in the other regions of France

– particularly in and around the eight *métropoles d'équilibre*.

In fact, as early as 1969 broad structural plans had already been prepared for the development of all eight of the new towns and for no less than eleven major redevelopments in the suburban nodes. And, by 1971, five of the new towns – Cergy-Pontoise, Evry, St. Quentin-des-Yvelines, Vallée de la Marne, and Melun-Sénart – were in process of detailed planning by official study groups. At Cergy-Pontoise, 20 miles north west of Paris on the future *Autoroute* to the Channel tunnel, the plan proposes a target of 400,000 people by the end of the century. One of the first of the new towns to start construction, Cergy-Pontoise, already had over 2,000 new homes complete by 1971; its first commercial centre, with a hypermarket and specialised shops, was opened in stages during 1972 and 1973. It will be the location of a new university and is the administrative centre (prefecture) for the new *département* of Val d'Oise. The other new town to start construction in the late 1960s, Evry, occupies a similar position on the opposite south east side of Paris; it, too, is the seat of administration for a new *département*, Essonne. The area of the new town already had a population of 150,000 at the end of the 1960s, and was being planned for an eventual total of half a million.

Perhaps the most ambitious new town plan of all, that for the Valley of the Marne east of Paris, was unveiled in 1970. It will be an elongated linear city, 13 miles long and only 1–2 miles wide, with a population of 600,000 living in a series of urban villages close to unrivalled outdoor recreation facilities. Served by the future *Autoroute de l'Est*, which will be a vital artery of the Common Market linking Paris with central Germany, and also by a branch of the regional express *Métro*, the new city will have a major commercial and cultural centre at its end nearest Paris, at the small town of Noisy-le-Grand. The new city of Vallée de la Marne is intended to serve as a major residential area for the workers at the new Paris Nord airport at Roissy-en-France to the north, since it is one of the nearest available areas outside the zone of serious aircraft noise. But more than that, the Parisian regional planners see it as a counter-magnet, reversing the long continued trend of business and other service industries to move westwards from the centre of Paris.

At the same time, the suburban nodes are not being ignored. La Défense, the biggest central area redevelopment in Europe and probably in the world, was well on the way to completion by the mid 1970s; to the south of Paris, and close to the decentralised Les Halles at Rungis, Créteil was being developed as a regional centre for 100,000 people, complete with university, teaching hospital and office centre. All this, furthermore, was being accomplished within the framework of a fairly cumbrous administrative and financial structure. The French have not developed a specific machinery to build new towns, like the development corporations in Britain; they must rely on a cooperative structure incorporating central and local government interests, which has somehow to ensure the necessary coordination of finance from a number of different central government Ministries.

One feature of the French operations, however, might well be envied by planners in other countries – including Britain. Land values are frozen in areas scheduled for major development, and the profits from assembly and resale of the land are retained by the public bodies responsible for the planning operation. Though private enterprise is represented on these bodies in a minority role, it is expected to win its profits from development contracts – not from financial speculation in land. Thus, with the aid of financial guarantees from the state, the French system ensures that land values created by community action revert to the benefit of the community as a whole.

The 1965 Plan ten years after: the 1975 Review

A decade after the historic 1965 Plan it was already clear that some basic assumptions must be modified. The general slackening in growth, so typical of big cities in advanced countries, had occurred here too. Population growth in the Paris region from 1968 to 1975 was down to 1·4 per cent a year against 2 per cent between 1954 and 1962; net migration was now outward to provincial France, though still inward from abroad; and there was marked outward movement within the region, with a declining city and a fast-growing outer ring. Employment growth was less than had been expected, mainly due to a big fall in manufacturing; in the city this had been compensated by increases in tertiary jobs, but in the eastern inner suburbs there was an actual problem of declining job opportunities. Though there had been a prodigious effort to modernise housing, the result had been social polarisation, since little public housing had been provided in the city or inner suburbs. The new towns had taken off, with between 60,000 and 70,000 new homes in five years and one-fifth of the new factory floorspace in the region; but progress had been slower than planned, due to the scale and complexity of the whole operation.

Yet overall the 1965 Plan, truly audacious in its plan to restructure Paris within thirty-five years, was working. The need now was to readapt it to projections of slower growth: 12·5–13 million by 2000 if trends continued, or 12 million if restriction was successful, against an expected 14 million a decade earlier. But employment would grow, by between 500,000 and 800,000, needing major new construction of offices and factory floorspace.

Faced with this evidence, the authors of the 1975 *Schéma Directeur* – produced by the Prefecture for the Paris region together with the Institut d'Aménagement – reassert the fundamental principles of the 1965 Plan. Paris is to grow into a polycentric city along the two main axes; major poles of growth, both within the existing urban fabric and in the new town centres, are to be planned for maximum diversity; open space is to be defined and protected, especially by so-called *Fronts Ruraux* which will limit urban growth; the transportation system is to be planned deliberately so as to tie together the elements of the future multi-centred region.

It is in details, therefore, that changes occur. In the city of Paris, the objectives now are to maintain the residential function for all groups of the population, and to stabilize employment – especially industrial employment in the east. In the inner suburbs, the aims are to maintain and improve existing built structures, to improve local environment, and to develop the service and employment 'poles' at places like Vélizy, Rungis, Créteil, Rosny, Bobigny and la Défense. These, and the new towns farther out, will be tied together by a new orbital motorway through the suburbs, about 10 kilometres further out from the centre than the already complete *Boulevard Peripherique*; important parts of this system will be complete by 1990. The express Métro (RER) will be developed in two north–south links (one joining the existing Ligne de Sceaux to the new line from the Gare du Nord to the airport at Roissy, the other joining two existing Métro lines southwards to Velizy) and two east–west lines (one, nearing completion in the late 1970s, from Cergy to Marne la Vallée, the other from St Quentin-en-Yvelines to Juvisy). An important new notion developed in the 1975 Plan is that of a *Rocade*: a new line of route embodying a motorway and a public transport line using its own tracks. Such a notion will permit rapid access both by road and by public transport from one new town to another, generally via one or more of the restructured 'poles' of the suburbs. Some of the new orbital public transport lines can use existing pieces of infrastructure, including the rail 'Ceinture' already developed in the nineteenth century. Finally, there will be particular stress on convenient interchange between one part of the public system and another, and also with the motorway system – generally at the 'poles'.

In the late 1970s and 1980s, the priority public works should already be shaping the new structure of Paris. While the city itself will be largely maintained in a state of balance, with little new employment and an emphasis on physical conservation, the eastern and southern parts of the city will see renewal. In the inner suburbs the new poles, and the connecting *rocades*, will at last provide the structure that was always lacking. And from there growth will be channelled out along the new transportation lines towards the new towns. It will be one of the most awe-inspiring programmes of urban restructuring in the world. But, given the determination and energy of the decade 1965–75, it should be achievable.

Verdict on the Parisian experience

In many respects, Paris provides a useful comparison – and a contrast – with London. In all Europe, they are the two greatest concentrations of people around a single centre of population and employment. In important respects, they are rivals for many of the important international functions which are developing so rapidly in western Europe. They are the truest world cities of a continent which boasts many examples of the genre. Both enjoy unique advantages, and yet suffer unusual social costs, from the concentration of people and their activities. In both, continued dynamism and growth led to alarm on the part of many thoughtful people, resulting in attempts at containment and decentralisation of industry to the provinces.

Yet there the similarities end. Paris has been a much more dynamic city than London, in terms of both population growth and economic growth, since World War Two – above all in the 1960s, when London began to show signs of stagnation. After a brief attempt to restrain this growth, the planners of the Paris region have wholeheartedly accepted it, and have produced a plan for vigorous expansion. True, as we saw, the London region, too, has its plan for growth; but it is significant that it is based on the creation of counter-magnets to the capital on the traditional model of the new towns policy, while the so-called new towns of the Paris region are seen as arms of the city itself. The new motorways and the regional express *Métro*, themselves symbolic of the worship of technology in the new France, are deliberately designed to bind the new towns and the old Paris, creating of them a single agglomeration both physically and functionally.

During the 1960s, in fact, the Parisians found that they could not limit the growth of their city – perhaps because finally they lacked the will to do so. This is not necessarily to say that their planning is ineffectual. In many respects – in its capacity to carry through bold schemes at speed, and in its determination to seize community-based land values for the benefit of the public – it is more effective than the British system, and among the more successful in the world. Though Frenchmen and others may have their reservations about the architectural and human quality of some of the results, few would doubt that they are – even on a world scale of comparison – impressive.

4 Randstad Holland

From the Aéroport de Paris–Orly, 10 miles south of Notre Dame, to the Luchthaven Schiphol, in the polders ten miles south west of Amsterdam's Muntplein, it is 250 miles as the crow flies and an hour's journey by jet. As the aircraft loses height and comes through the cloud cover which so often covers this part of Europe, the traveller's first glimpse may well be of water: he sees the complex distributaries of the great Rhine and Maas rivers, and the great harbour basins, mixed with oil refineries, chemical plants and warehouses, which mark the port of Rotterdam – first port of the world in the tonnage it carries. Rotterdam's heart, devastated by German bombardment in 1940 and magnificently rebuilt after 1945, lies below. The city spreads far to the west, on the northern side of the New Waterway, Rotterdam's main outlet to the sea: it has swallowed up former towns like the fishermen's centre of Vlaardingen and Schiedam, the birthplace of Dutch gin, which now appear ringed by suburbs. And as he looks west towards the North Sea, the air traveller will realise that Rotterdam – city of 679,000 people in 1970 – is only part of a much larger whole. Along the great motorway that runs straight as a die across the polders to the north west, an infinitesimal gap appears to separate the suburbs of Rotterdam from those of the old pottery town of Delft. Farther away towards the North Sea, along the same ribbon of road, an even smaller gap separates Delft from the vast urban spread of the Hague along the coastal sand-dunes. To the north of that, just inland from the coast, appear the towns of Leiden and Haarlem; north of Haarlem, right on the coast, industrial haze marks the steel town of IJmuiden. As the plane loses height rapidly, the city of Amsterdam, with its 820,000 people (in 1970), appears behind the runways and terminal buildings of Schiphol. To the right, on the higher forested ground behind the polder edge, are the suburbs which extend outwards from Amsterdam towards the radio and television masts of Hilversum, and then again southwards along the ridge of high ground to the city of Utrecht with its quarter of a million people.

Schiphol airport, in fact, lies in the centre of one of the most extraordinary urban regions of the world. All around is the polder landscape of the provinces of North and South Holland, which has always dominated the nation of which it forms a part: so much indeed that English-speaking people habitually confuse the two, and say Holland when they mean the Netherlands. Beyond the polders, just as in a landscape by Ruysdael, are the houses and spires of the nearest town. It is only from the air, or from the map, that you can appreciate the real change that has come over Holland in the three centuries since Ruysdael – indeed in the century since 1860. The cities, which Ruysdael and Vermeer and de Hooch painted, are recognisable today. But, as in their day, the cities have prospered; and they have spread far beyond the limits which they knew. Today the cities and towns of Holland have grown so close together that they form, in an important sense, one city, though a city of a particular form. The Dutch call it Randstad Holland: the ring city. It has the shape of a great horseshoe, pointing with its open end towards the south-east: a horseshoe over thirty miles in length, some thirty miles also at its maximum width, and altogether, if some supernatural blacksmith were to straighten it out on his anvil, some 110 miles in length. It runs from Dordrecht, south east of Rotterdam, through Rotterdam and along the north side of the New Waterway to the Hook of Holland on the coast; turns there through a right angle to the Hague on the coast, taking in Delft within the angle; runs in a belt, some ten miles wide, along the coast, to incorporate the considerable towns of Leiden and Haarlem, as well as the many small seaside resorts and the steel centre of IJmuiden; turns thence, north of Haarlem, through another right angle to run inland to Amsterdam; runs from there across the high ground to Hilversum, out of the provinces of Holland to Utrecht, and even beyond there towards the river Lek (map 4.1). This complex, in 1970, had three cities – Amsterdam, Rotterdam and the Hague – of between half and one million people; one – Utrecht – of over a quarter of a million; one – Haarlem – of 173,000; and one – Leiden – just 100,000. (These are city populations; the agglomerations around them are much bigger.) Its total population, according to the definitions of urban agglomerations used by the Dutch planners, on 1

January 1970, was 4·23 million or – taking into account also the Randstad's 'green heart' – about 4·4 million: 33 per cent of the population of the Netherlands, living on 5 per cent of its land area. (The complex agglomeration defined by International Urban Research's 'metropolitan areas' is smaller, with an estimated 4·1 million people in 1970.) After London, Paris, and the cities of the German Rhine–Ruhr region, it is unquestionably the greatest metropolitan centre of western Europe.

But this is clearly a metropolitan centre of a different order from London or Paris. The Dutch are prone to emphasise the essential difference – which, they claim, gives them a real advantage in planning for continued growth. It is that the traditional economic functions of the metropolitan centre, which we examined in the beginning of this book – the government, trading and financial functions, as well as the cultural, educational, manufacturing and retail developments that follow from them – are not concentrated in one centre but are spread out in several, which remain physically separate despite their closeness. In particular the government function is firmly fixed in the Hague; the port and wholesaling function, as well as the heavy industry that accompanies it, in Rotterdam; and the financial functions, many of the cultural and retail functions, and a wide range of port industries and of light manufacturing in Amsterdam, which is the capital city though it is not the seat of government. Partly as a result of this basic division, the enormous expansion of the lighter manufacturing industries which has been characteristic of all the world cities in this century has not taken place in an amorphous ring round one city, but has gone to a great extent into towns quite separate from the three big cities though within easy reach of them. Prominent among these are Leiden, Haarlem and the area known as Het Gooi around Hilversum. Thus the cities still remain physically distinct – and distinct, too, in important elements of economic structure. Each remains separated from the next by a buffer zone of open land. And, in the centre of the horseshoe, there is still a vast tract of open rural land – a feature that led the British planner Gerald Burke to christen the Randstad 'Greenheart Metropolis'.

The Randstad in history

The cities of the Randstad are nearly all medieval foundations; the Hague is the great exception, for it was only a castle up to the

sixteenth century. And in 1584, when the Netherlands won its
independence from Spain, it was the most heavily urbanised country
in Europe, with half the population living in cities. Yet even in the
seventeenth century – the 'Golden Century' when the Dutch
conquered the seas, dominated the trade of Europe and contributed
powerfully to the development of western art and science – the cities

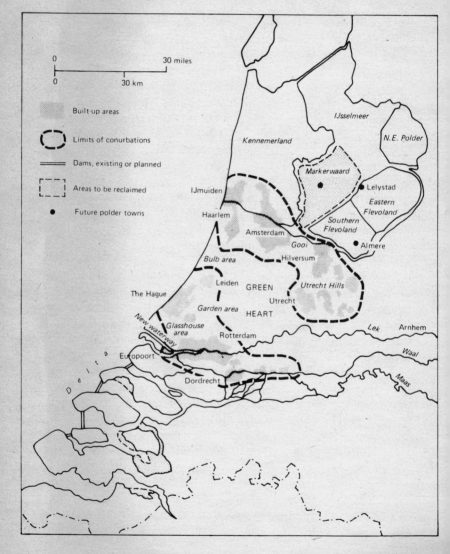

remained small.' As late as 1795, only Amsterdam had more than 200,000 people; no other city had even 60,000. And it was only at this time that the Hague – third town in size, and the centre of the government – attained city status; for two centuries the jealousy of the provinces had kept it 'the biggest village in Europe'.

The figures show, in fact, that the real rise of the Dutch cities dates from the revolution in trade and industry of the nineteenth century. In 1825 came the first Dutch steamship; in 1839, between Amsterdam and Haarlem, the first Dutch railway line. But the most significant changes of those years occurred outside the Netherlands: through the medium of the customs union or *Zollverein*, German unity was being effectively achieved. Finally, in 1871, the German empire became a reality and the Ruhr began its mushroom growth into the greatest industrial area of Europe; with it, the Rhine became western Europe's major commercial artery. But the mouth of the Rhine was the Netherlands' prize; as Germany rose to industrial might, the Netherlands rose with it to commercial power. Rotterdam benefited the most: aided by the construction of the sea canal known as the New Waterway in 1872 and its improvement in 1885, the city's population rose more than fourfold between 1850 and 1913. Amsterdam profited less: despite the North Sea Canal, a ship canal cut through to IJmuiden on the coast in 1876, it lost its position as first port of the Netherlands to Rotterdam about 1900 and its population rose only about two and a half times between the mid-nineteenth century and the outbreak of the First World War. The Hague benefited from an unprecedented growth of the functions of the central government, and its population multiplied over four times between 1850 and 1914.

This growth continued between the wars; but since 1945 it has accelerated, aided by the highest natural rate of increase of any western European population, and by the marked increase of trade within western Europe and between western Europe and the rest of the world. The progress of the cities is plotted in table 8. But the whole period since 1918 has seen the rapid acceleration of a process which

4.1   *Randstad Holland.* The complex urban agglomeration of the Randstad (Ring City) takes the form of a horseshoe open to the south-east. It contains three major conurbations, grouped round the cities of Rotterdam, The Hague, Amsterdam and Utrecht. The planners aim to preserve the agricultural heart of the Randstad and the gaps between its cities. It will grow outwards into regions like the polders, Northern Kennemerland and the Delta region.

Table 9 The growth of the Randstad cities

populations in thousands

	c.1650	1796	1850	1913	1938	1970
Amsterdam	100	217	224	588	788	820
Rotterdam	32	53	90	448	606	679
The Hague	—	41	72	295	490	538
Leiden	70	31	36	59	76	100
Haarlem	40	21	26	70	135	173
Utrecht	—	32	48	123	163	278

was already starting, in the region south east of Amsterdam known as
Het Gooi, in the 1870s: the spread of the suburbs. Though they built
their seventeenth-century houses fairly closely, the Dutch have
always had a very English (or un-French) preference for the single-
family house with its own garden. With rising living standards and
the improvement of urban transport after about 1900, the result was
rapid growth of low-density suburban housing around all the
Randstad cities, involving many annexations of surrounding

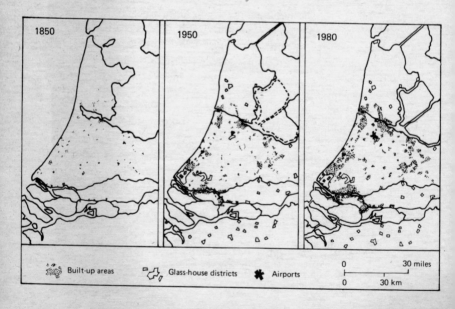

territory by the municipalities. Rotterdam extended itself on no less than eleven occasions in the century between 1860 and 1960, the Hague on five occasions. The suburbs grew especially rapidly in the attractive sandy areas outside the low-lying polders, like Het Gooi, in the wooded hills north and south of Utrecht, and in the sand-dune country along the coast. Haarlem, one of the most attractive examples of large-scale seventeenth-century town building, grew partly as a dormitory suburb for Amsterdam 12 miles away, though it also developed some light industries of its own.

The physical expression of this growth can be seen in map 4.2. In 1850 the towns of the Randstad, though close together by the standards of many areas of Europe, were still separate entities. By 1950 they had spread towards each other, to form the almost continuous urban ring of the Randstad; and the problem of future growth had become acute.

Factors in future growth

Certain forces have been at work in the growth of the Randstad since 1870, and especially since 1945. They are not likely to diminish in the remaining decades of the twentieth century; indeed, if anything they are likely to strengthen.

The first is the population growth in the Netherlands as a whole. Dutch planners have to reckon with the highest rate of natural increase in western Europe: 1·2 per cent per year on average during the middle and late 1960s, a rate only equalled in western Europe by Switzerland and much higher than that of Belgium, France or the United Kingdom. But, here as elsewhere in western Europe, birth rates were falling from 1965 onwards – very rapidly between 1970 (18·3 per thousand) and 1974 (13·8 per thousand). In consequence, like the experts of most other west European countries, the Dutch demographers have had to revise downwards their official projections of the future national population after raising them a few years earlier. The actual population at the beginning of 1975 was 13,600,000. The central Statistical Bureau, making some allowance

4.2   *Growth of the Randstad.* In 1850 the cities of the western Netherlands gave little sign of forming an incipient urban agglomeration. But beginning about 1870 in the Gooi region near Hilversum (see map 4.1) rapid suburbanization set in. Today urban activities compete for land with traditional intensive agriculture which is expanding in acreage. The dilemma can only be resolved by diverting the growth of the Randstad into new channels.

for possible net migration into the country, projected in 1976 that the total might only rise to 15·6 million by the year 2000 – compared to the 19–21 million forecast in 1965.

The second and critical question is how this increase will be distributed region by region. Until very recently the three urbanised western provinces of the Netherlands – North Holland, South Holland, and Utrecht – have been gaining population rapidly, due both to natural increase and to migration from the rest of the country. It has been the planners' aim to balance in- and out-migration, in other words to reduce net migration to zero. In fact by the 1960s the current had been reversed: the west was actually losing population, by migration, to the rest of the Netherlands. A 1965 forecast was that if the prevailing trends continued, population in the west might rise from 5·7 million in 1965 to 8·5 million in 2000, or by 2·8 million over 35 years; but a policy of increased dispersal could reduce this somewhat. In either event, the west would have a declining share of the population of the country. In the event, this proved only too true: by the 1970s the Randstad was losing population to the south of the country through migration, and this was expected to continue. So the radically revised 1975 forecast gave the west only 6·34 million by the year 2000 – a mere 200,000 increase over 1975.

Table 10 Distribution of Population in the Netherlands, 1965–2000
(populations in millions)

	1965 actual	1965 forecast c.2000 with continuation of 1960s trend	1965 forecast c.2000 with increased dispersal	1975 actual	1975 forecast c.2000
North	1·30	2·25	3·00	1·49	1·77
East	2·20	4·00	4·25	2·60	3·31
West	5·70	8·50 ⎫	12·00	6·17 ⎰	6·34
South	2·60	4·75 ⎭		0·33 ⎱	0·37
South-West	0·30	0·50	0·75	2·99	3·81
The Netherlands	12·10	20·00	20·00	13·60	15·61

Yet the result, because of a fall in household size and increased demands for space per person in and around the house, could still mean a large increase in the total urban area – and this at a time when the Dutch government are concerned to save space and reduce demands for mobility. It is altogether too much to hope for a greater degree of decentralisation, because of continuing trends in the economy of the Netherlands and of Europe. In the first place, like other EEC countries, the Netherlands is experiencing a pronounced shift of labour out of agriculture and into manufacturing and services. In 1950, 14 per cent of the working population were in agriculture; by 1964 this was reduced to 8 per cent and by 1980 it is expected to be as low as 5 per cent. Secondly, and associated with the first tendency, the Netherlands are showing a rate of industrial growth that is rapid even by contemporary western European standards. Thirdly, an important part of the fastest-growing industry is tied physically to the Randstad because it depends on the processing of imported bulky low-value goods, and so must be located on deep navigable water. The leading examples of such industry are oil-refining and the associated petrochemical industry, which is particularly concentrated on the New Waterway below Rotterdam, and the iron and steel industry, which is located in the great integrated plant at the entry of the North Sea Canal into the sea at IJmuiden. These industries will almost certainly continue to grow in the remaining decades of the twentieth century. Oil is progressively replacing coal as an energy source and as a raw material for chemicals. And where coal continues to be used, as in iron and steel manufacture, it is found cheaper to import it from low-cost producers in North America than to use European coal; while of course the ore has long been imported from Sweden or Spain. So the tendency in iron and steel manufacture has been to favour the coastal sites, as on the south Wales coast in Britain, at Bremen in Federal Germany and here at IJmuiden. Of course all the deep-water industries are capital-intensive in character: they use a relatively small labour force to produce a large volume of output. But they create a great deal of employment in ancillary and service trades, a large part of which must be close to the areas where the basic industries are located. The main growth zone for the tidewater industries will continue to be the New Waterway below Rotterdam, which will receive a powerful impetus from the completion of the great Europoort complex opposite the Hook of Holland; but Amsterdam and the North Sea Canal are improving their capacity for bulk handling of goods so as to take a share.

Other industries, it is true, are not tied to the west, and the statistical trends of the 1950s and 1960s show that they are decentralising out of the western part of the country. These are the labour-intensive manufacturing industries with a relatively high proportion of value added in manufacture; they can bear high transport costs for materials and products, but because labour costs are a large part of total costs they are particularly sensitive to wage competition from the capital-intensive industries in the west. These industries have been particularly attracted, since 1945, to the province of North Brabant in the south east Netherlands, where a strong Catholic majority produces a high natural increase of population. Between 1953 and 1960 North Brabant increased its labour force by 50,000 or 25 per cent, the highest absolute and percentage increase in the country; and by 1960 it was threatening to overtake South Holland, traditional industrial province of the Netherlands, in numbers of workers. Eindhoven, symbol of this development, has grown with the Philips electrical complex from a mere village in 1890 to a city of over 187,000 people in 1970. Elsewhere, in Limburg in the south and in Groningen to the north, chemical industries have developed, and the discovery of natural gas off the coast in Groningen province is undoubtedly giving another powerful impetus to development in the north: development even, perhaps, of capital-intensive tidewater industry. But meanwhile much of the lighter industry still remains in the west, where it is apt to decentralise into unsuitable locations: as for instance the electronics industry around Hilversum, which has led to large-scale building since 1930 in the agricultural and recreational zone of Het Gooi.

Perhaps the critical question concerns the service industries. Clearly many of them perform a purely local function for a population working in factory industry. But some are much more than local in character. Outstanding among these is government service, which is important not only for its direct effect on employment but also for the fact that the presence of government is apt to attract other, semi-official public organisations. Of the 218,000 government servants in the Netherlands (including the postal service and the coal-mining industry) no less than 42,000 were found in the Hague in 1960. In another 'industry', which is expanding rapidly in every advanced country – higher education – the concentration in the west is as marked: for out of six universities in the Netherlands only two were outside the west in 1960, and those were in peripheral locations. The area of the Netherlands outside the western provinces had in 1960 52 per cent of the population, but only 40 per cent of the student population and only 21 per cent of the resident student population. Clearly direct government action could help to alleviate this state of affairs; and in 1960 the important report on physical planning in the Netherlands recommended that a policy of government and university decentralisation should be actively pursued.

Problems of the Randstad

Regionally, then, the Netherlands is faced with a dilemma of long standing, which some other European countries have only begun to experience more recently. Whatever is done to promote decentralisation out of the west, there is bound to be a rapid growth of population in the western provinces themselves, if only because of the natural increase of an already numerous population. But this growth raises acute problems of competition for scarce land. It is a commonplace that the Netherlands is the most densely populated country in western Europe: with over 1,000 people per square mile in 1970 it stands slightly ahead of England and Wales. By 2000, if the population reaches 15·6 million, the figure could be over 1,200 to the square mile. The concentration is even more marked in the west, where already by 1970 the density was over 2,200 to the square mile.

And in the west, in the coming decades, there are four dominant types of land use, all of which will be making heavy demands for space. The first is agriculture. There is here a prosperous, intensive and efficient market-gardening industry, much of it under glass, with a very heavy capital investment on each acre. It produces 40 per cent of the Netherlands' total crop of garden products. And the market gardeners are not likely to need less land in the period up to 1980; indeed during the 1950s they took over 1,740 extra acres in the west for glasshouse cultivation. The second competitor is heavy industry and port installations. In 1958 it was estimated that in the west no less than 11,610 acres might be needed up to 1980 for heavy industry; and that the port of Rotterdam alone might increase its land needs by 14,820 acres in all between 1958 and 2000. A third and most obvious need is for housing. The average number of people per dwelling tends to fall, because of smaller families. A rise in population of 2·8 million between 1965 and 2000, as a report of 1966 suggested, might mean a need for one million or more extra dwellings, which at the prevailing urban densities in the urban areas of the western Netherlands (taking

into account all necessary services) might mean the appropriation of
140,000–190,000 extra acres from agriculture up to 1980. That is 13
or 14 per cent of the agricultural land of the west, an area greater than
the East Flevoland, which the Dutch reclaimed from the former
Zuiderzee in the late 1950s. And it does not take account of the extra

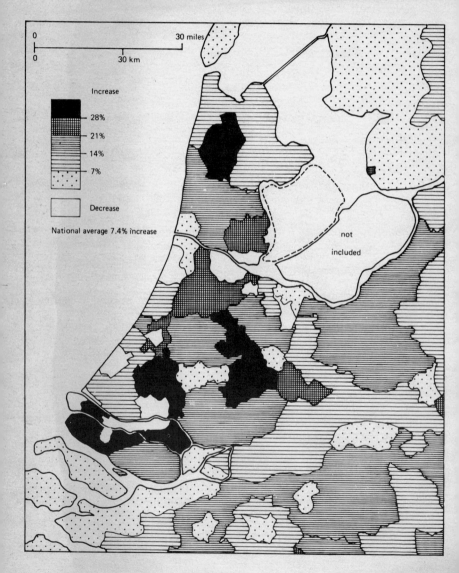

need for dwellings created by urban renewal schemes in the congested older parts of the cities, which inevitably mean displacement of some of the inhabitants. A fourth need is recreation. The west is already chronically short of adequate open space with public access, and the shortage will be aggravated by three factors: the fact that the relatively short coastline has to serve the needs not only of much of the interior of the Netherlands but also of areas as far inland as the Ruhr; the increasing population in the whole hinterland, including the areas across the German frontier; and the rapid increase in mobility, following the spread of the motor-car. Already by 1960 it was found that 25–30 per cent of the urban populations were leaving the Netherlands cities on summer Sundays, two-thirds of them for trips of 20 miles or less. If by 1970 the same proportion of the city population was seeking to find room outside the cities, this would mean about three million people. In the west alone in 1954 between one and a half and two million people visited recreation areas in the busiest week of the year, and this might rise to between two and a half and three million by 1980: yet there is capacity for only two million – one million of them along the coast.

Most serious of all is the need for housing land. Inevitably, it is being felt most acutely outside the limits of the existing cities and towns. Within the period 1950–70, the fastest-growing populations of the Netherlands, both in the west and elsewhere, were those of the suburban zones outside the municipalities. Indeed, the largest cities began to lose people by migration from the 1950s, and by the mid 1970s they were in rapid absolute decline: between 1971 and 1974 Amsterdam, Rotterdam and the Hague together lost 110,000 people. In the west these zones are concentrated in areas peripheral to the Randstad itself: they include the island of Voorne, south west of Rotterdam; the northern Kennemerland, north of the North Sea Canal between IJmuiden and Alkmaar; the polders in the agricultural centre of the Randstad, adjacent to Amsterdam; and the southern fringe of the area known as the Veluwe, east of Utrecht,

4.3   *Randstad and neighbouring areas: population changes 1965–71.* As in most other metropolitan regions of the world, the central cities of the Randstad are recording low rates of increases or even decreases (e.g. Amsterdam), while the big increases occur in the suburbs outside the cities. Especially disturbing are the rapid increases within the agricultural heart of the Randstad. These add urgency to the plans for diverting further growth outwards, as in the northern delta region adjacent to the Rhine mouth, which was already showing rapid increases in the late 1960s.

between Wageningen and Arnhem. A curious incidental result is that population in the Randstad, which is rigidly defined in terms of the highly urbanised municipalities, has been growing less fast than the areas of the western provinces outside it. During 1951–63 the population of the Randstad increased by 491,000; but this was only 13 per cent, while the agricultural area in the middle of the 'horseshoe' grew by 22·9 per cent and the areas outside the Randstad altogether – that is, the peripheral parts of the west – increased by

4.4   *Planned growth for the Randstad.* The planners' strategy is to divert growth outwards. **A** Southwards: reclamation of the delta region will allow a new town at Hellevoetsluis on the Haringvliet.
B Northwards: development can take place parallel to the coast in northern Kennemerland. **C** North-eastwards: parts of the polders will become an extension of the Amsterdam conurbation, especially around Lelystad, new 'polder capital'.

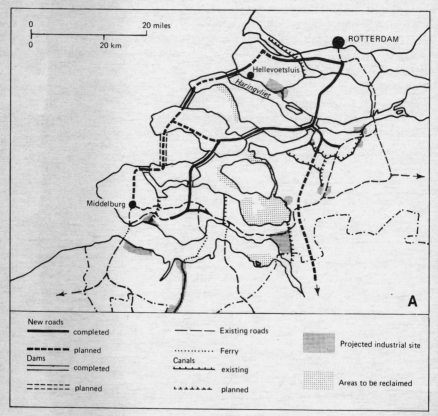

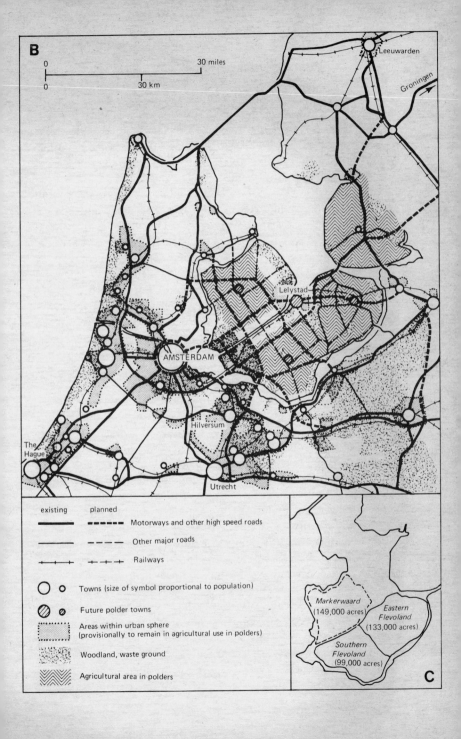

B

0 ——————————————— 30 miles
0 ——————————————— 30 km

Leeuwarden

Groningen

Lelystad

AMSTERDAM

Hilversum

The
Hague

Utrecht

existing   planned

━━━━━━   ▬ ▬ ▬ ▬   Motorways and other high speed roads

───────   ─ ─ ─ ─   Other major roads

┼┼┼┼┼┼   ┼ ┼ ┼ ┼   Railways

◯ ○   Towns (size of symbol proportional to population)

⊘ ⊘   Future polder towns

▒▒▒   Areas within urban sphere
(provisionally to remain in agricultural use in polders)

▒▒▒   Woodland, waste ground

〰〰〰   Agricultural area in polders

Markerwaard
(149,000 acres)

*Eastern
Flevoland*
(133,000 acres)

*Southern
Flevoland*
(99,000 acres)

C

21·2 per cent. By 1975 the population density in the green heart, still less than 300 per square kilometre (780 per square mile) in 1960, had risen to over 500 per square kilometre (1,300 per square mile); almost half the increase had been in-migration (map 4.3).

Here lies the real threat. It is not only that the growth of the suburbs will cause the cities of the Randstad to coalesce along the line of the 'horseshoe', so that by 1980 the Netherlands will have a continuous linear city 110 miles long; even more, it is that the agricultural heart of the 'horseshoe' will fill up, so that the Randstad will lose its unique character among the world cities and become merely another vast urban sprawl – a Dutch Los Angeles. The threat is most serious in two places: one in the north of the Randstad, where a continuous town is in process of development along the line of the North Sea Canal, connecting Amsterdam, Zaanstreek, IJmuiden and Haarlem; and in the south west, where the cities of Rotterdam, Delft, the Hague and Leiden could easily coalesce into a miniature Randstad, only about 15 miles across, the centre of which could then fill up. But there are other areas where the problem is more insidious, as in the east at Utrecht, where the city is tending to spread both north and south into attractive hilly country that is important both for agriculture and recreation (map 4.4).

Yet the concentration of population already brings social and economic disadvantages. The lack of space makes it difficult for many people to enjoy the one-family type of house which they prefer. During the 1960s, only 35–40 per cent of new dwellings completed in the towns of the Randstad (above 50,000 population) were of the single-family type. Again, costs of building of all sorts are much higher in the west – a fact attributable to a combination of competition for land and the nature of the terrain. In a large part of the west foundation costs amount to 20 per cent or more of the costs of the superstructure; this is not surprising when it is realised that in North and South Holland, 80 per cent of all houses have to be supported on concrete piles. Motorways cost nearly three times as much to construct in the west as in the east; housing two to three times as much. The cities of the west have problems, familiar the world over, of water supply, air pollution and traffic congestion. Within the west there is an acute problem of providing an adequate tax base for public works within the big cities, where the problems are most severely concentrated, because the resident population is growing in the suburban areas outside the city limits. In the Randstad these problems do not yet exist on the scale of London or Paris. But they could become serious with the growth of population in the remaining decades of this century.

Policy for the Randstad

These considerations made it apparent, from 1945 onward, that a new scale of regional planning was necessary. The Dutch have one of the oldest traditions of city planning in Europe, which arose out of physical necessity: in a difficult environment, it was early realised that all must co-operate for the common good. The idea of town planning, in some cases, goes back right to the foundation of the Dutch cities in the middle ages; and in the modern period it expressed itself as early as 1901 in a far-reaching Town Planning Act, which was responsible for many notable town-planning schemes on the edges of the fast-growing cities of the western Netherlands. But after the Second World War it was increasingly realised that municipal plans were not enough: if the Randstad was not eventually to envelop a great part of the western Netherlands, its growth must be planned as a whole, both in its relation to the development of the whole country and in its internal structure. Starting in 1949, with an official report on *The Distribution of Population in the Netherlands*, a whole series of official studies have analysed the trends of population growth, examined the problems which result, set out the planning choices and evolved a coherent set of policies for the Randstad. The most important are *The West of the Netherlands and the other Provinces* (1956), a joint study by the economic and the physical planners; *The Development of the Western Netherlands* (1958), a report by a special working party, which outlined a set of policies for the Randstad; the *First Report on Physical Planning in the Netherlands* (1960), a statement of general policies by the government Physical Planning Service, which sets out the planners' objectives for the Randstad in relation to the regional development of the rest of the Netherlands; the *Second Report on Physical Planning in the Netherlands* (1966), which updates the analysis and policy recommendations of the earlier report, and the *Third Report on Physical Planning in the Netherlands*, in two parts: the *Orientation Report* of 1974 and the *Urbanisation Report* of 1976. These documents make up a coherent whole; for in the Netherlands official policies, evolved in the course of careful analysis and exhaustive discussion, command a wide measure of agreement and are not lightly modified. Yet there has been radical modification – in the *Third Report*. And this reflects a fundamental shift in the background to the Dutch planning process between the mid-1960s and the mid-1970s.

A basic element of policy is the development of the peripheral regions of the Netherlands, outside the west. A number of cities here, and especially in the north, are to be expanded to over 100,000 and even over 200,000 people, so as to serve as adequate growth points for regional development. Cities of this size, the Dutch planners argue, are necessary for the performance of the specialised functions of business, entertainment, professional life, culture and education. The programme includes old towns and regional capitals with development potential, like Groningen, Arnhem, Nijmegen and Breda, as well as some developing industrial towns like Enschede and Tilburg.

Nevertheless, it is clear that the Randstad will remain, and that it (and even more so the areas adjacent to it) will continue to grow. So certain principles of growth must be maintained.

The first of these is to preserve the historic cities of the urban ring, as separate and distinct points of concentration. Because of the danger that some cities may soon coalesce, the 1958 report first suggested the establishment of buffer zones, at least two and a half miles wide, between all of them. This may well be difficult, as the 1960 report recognises, because often local municipal extension plans make inroads into the buffer zones, not so much for extension of the built-up area as for city-fringe land uses like parks, sewage beds and swimming pools. Amsterdam grew eastwards towards the Gooi during the early 1970s with a new town for 100,000 at Bijlermeer; while Rotterdam grew westwards towards Delft.

The second policy line consists in the preservation of the agricultural heart of the Randstad 'horseshoe'. An absolute priority will be given to agriculture in certain areas where it is of distinctive character and where it makes a particularly intensive and important contribution to national production – the glasshouse industry of South Holland, particularly south of the Hague; the bulbfields between Leiden and Haarlem and the intensive garden cultivation round the villages of Aalsmeer and Boskoop, east of Haarlem and Leiden. Any growth of population that does occur in this central area will be concentrated into a few existing historic towns, such as Gouda, Alphen and Woerden, and into the development of a new town next to the village of Zoetermeer, necessary to house the overspill from the Hague agglomeration.

The third and perhaps most revolutionary proposal, first contained in the 1958 report, concerns the growth of the Randstad. If it is not to expand laterally, by coalescence within the urban ring, or inwards, into the agricultural heartland, it can only grow outwards. Short of unplanned sprawl, two possibilities suggest themselves here. One is the establishment of a green belt, on the London model, separating the Randstad from an outer ring of towns and cities, old and new, surrounding it. The other, which the 1958 report chose in preference to the idea of the green belt, is expansion along the main transport routes – road, rail and water – in radial lines extending outwards from the Randstad. These zones of growth would themselves be separated by wedges of open land which could continue the agricultural buffer zones of the Randstad.

Four possibilities offer themselves for this sort of linear expansion: northwards, north-eastwards, eastwards and south-westwards. The first and third of these are the more conventional. To the north, development can be guided into a series of existing towns within the area known as Kennemerland, north of the North Sea Canal and the IJmuiden steel works, as far as the old cheese town of Alkmaar and a little beyond. With the completion of Bijlermeer in the mid-1970s, Amsterdam's next major development would be to the north west, in Purmerend. To the east, the Randstad must not be allowed to spill out beyond Utrecht into the fine forest and heath country of the Utrecht hills. Here, a positive policy of decentralisation must guide growth into the small towns on the far eastern side of these hills, lying in the Gelderse Valley south of Amersfoort. This valley has already demonstrated its capacity to take light industry, and it may eventually form a continuous industrial zone from Amersfoort south to Arnhem and so nearly to the German frontier (maps 4.1 and 4.5). In the early 1970s it was proposed to concentrate growth in this area around the small town of Leusden.

The revolutionary proposals are the other two; for in them the Dutch have sought to relieve the problems of the Randstad by developing outwards on to new land (map 4.4). To the north east, the drainage of the Zuiderzee polders reached a critical stage in 1968, when the dike enclosing the South Flevoland polder was completed and the polder itself began to become dry land. For this substantially changed the geography of the Netherlands: a substantial area of new land exists next to one of the most heavily populated parts of the Randstad, joining it with the mainly agricultural northern region.

Almost immediately the Dutch opened a new highway – Rijksweg (National Highway) 6 – across this polder and the adjacent East Flevoland polder, which was drained in 1955–7. By 1969, via a bridge on to the older North East Polder, it had joined the national capital, Amsterdam, direct to the major city of the northern Netherlands, Groningen, reducing journey time between the two by as much as an hour.

This new motorway will serve the new capital of the new southern polders – Lelystad, named after the engineer who conceived the whole Zuiderzee drainage scheme, which lies on the north west corner of the East Flevoland polder. Lelystad is already less than an hour's journey from Amsterdam; it stands near the mouth of a new stretch of water, the Oostvaardersdiep, which will bring 2,000-ton ships from Amsterdam and the North Sea. So Lelystad, and the land along the route to Amsterdam are uniquely fitted to relieve the population pressure in the capital and its suburbs. Though most of the new polders will be reserved for agriculture and recreation, this Amsterdam–Lelystad strip will be urbanised: the main concentrations will be at the western end of the South Flevoland polder, next to Amsterdam, and around Lelystad near the junction of the East and South Flevoland polders.

Later, in the 1970s, the last Zuiderzee polder will be drained: Markerwaard, north of South Flevoland, and separated from it by the Oostvaardersdiep. The southern strip of this polder, with direct access to Lelystad, will also be available for urban growth – though, with falling population projections, it was being suggested that more logically this would provide a site for Amsterdam's new airport.

In 1964 Lelystad was still little more than a collection of temporary buildings along a dike; by 1971 it already possessed a smart new town centre, and building was proceeding apace all around, with 4,000 people already housed and 15,000 expected by 1975. By 1980 it will be an integral part of the Randstad, and an important city in its own right, and by the century's end it is expected to have 100,000 people or more. At the south west corner of the South Flevoland polder, next to the new bridge to the mainland of the Gooi and thus nearest polder site to Amsterdam, the new town of Almere will receive its first inhabitants by 1975 and its highly flexible plan provides for an eventual population of between 125,000 and 250,000 people.

The other development – perhaps, in the long run, an even more spectacular one – concerns the isolated region of the

Rhine–Maas–Scheldt delta, on the southern border of the Randstad. In the disastrous flood early in 1953, 618 square miles of this region were inundated; a planning commission, set up immediately afterwards, produced an interim report a year later with a revolutionary proposal which was accepted. Instead of partial drainage of parts of the delta, the whole area should be diked against the sea. There were many good reasons for this: agriculture would be extended, there were important recreational opportunities, and the whole region might become an important industrial area, lying as it did between the densely populated industrial zones of the Randstad to the north and the Antwerp–Brussels region to the south. The key to the delta's historic backwardness, and to its future development, was communications. New roads and railways could connect Rotterdam direct with the Haringvliet, the stretch of water through which over half the combined waters of the Rhine and Maas reach the sea; at present almost undeveloped, this waterway could rapidly become an extension of the great port of Rotterdam. The 1958 report, taking up this idea, suggested that a major part of the overspill problem of the city of Rotterdam – estimated at a quarter of a million people by 1980 – could be met by development on the island of Voorne, between the New Waterway and the Haringvliet. This might include a new town for 200,000 people at what is now the village of Hellevoetsluis. By the early 1970s the gigantic programme of public works was already well advanced towards its scheduled completion date of 1978, with new direct communication lines from Rotterdam southwards and south westwards; the plans for urban and industrial development foresaw strong axial concentrations along the northern, eastern and southern edges, with tidewater industry along the New Waterway in the north and the Scheldt in the south, and the reservation of the islands of Voorne and Putten for residential, recreational and agricultural use.

These outward extensions of the Randstad will very neatly relieve the points of maximum pressure: Haarlem and Amsterdam will be relieved by Kennemerland, Amsterdam also by the polder scheme, Het Gooi by the polders and by the expansion of Amersfoort, Utrecht by Amersfoort and the Gelderse Valley, Rotterdam by the delta scheme. But a problem remains: the cities of the Hague, Leiden and Delft, forming an agglomeration with a population of about 900,000 in 1970, and a potential overspill by 1980 of 120,000, are hemmed in on three sides by water or by existing urban development. Here outward expansion is not possible, and development will have to take place within the 'Little Randstad' which the three cities form. At one time a new town seemed likely, but during the late 1960s priority was being given to a new town development attached to the village of Zoetermeer, east of the Hague.

Government and the Randstad: The Second Report

Policy for the Randstad, then, is based on two suppositions: one, that net migration into the west can be reduced roughly to zero; two, that the growth of the Randstad itself can be channelled into certain areas and out of certain other areas. The question is whether these suppositions can be made real. This depends on the effectiveness of government policy, both at central and at local level.

These outgrowths make it all the more necessary to protect carefully the intervening rural land. So the Second Report on Physical Planning in the Netherlands, published in 1966, calls for an extension of protection policies from the green heart of the Randstad to other belts of open land outside the Randstad proper, but likely to be affected by its planned outward spread; they include the open land along the Rhine waterway, the heart of the delta region and the wooded Peel region around Breda and Tilburg. At the same time, the report stresses, the buffer zones which separate the Randstad cities must be carefully preserved; to this end, the government offers subsidies to local authorities to buy up threatened land.

The Second Report goes much further, though; in some detail, albeit diagrammatically, it sketches out a planned structure for the urban areas of the Netherlands around the year 2000. This structure is based on the principle of concentrated deconcentration: strong concentrations of people, homes, services and jobs at the city regional scale are internally decentralised into a variety of grouped sub-units of different sizes. The diagram shows four of these basic building blocks, ranging from a village unit of 5,000 people to a city of 250,000, with intermediate units of 15,000 and 60,000 people. Such a structure, the report claims, has a number of advantages. First, it is almost inevitable because of the constraints on further development; people are showing that they prefer a more dispersed form of living than in the past, but unlimited dispersion would be impossible in a country as densely populated as the Netherlands is likely to be by 2000. Secondly, the scheme provides for a variety of different styles of living to suit different tastes, ranging from the city to the village but with a major emphasis on small scale units at fairly low residential densities, which many people appear to want. Thirdly, it provides fairly short work journeys to major concentrations and employment. And fourthly, it provides good levels of services, either locally or via good transport to higher order centres nearby (map. 4.5).

The broad regional policy must be the responsibility of the central government in the Hague. Here the critical question is whether to rely on positive measures of attraction and inducement in the underdeveloped areas of the north and the east; or whether restrictive measures are not also needed in the west. Up to the early 1970s the government have remained convinced that the problem of the Randstad is not serious enough to merit restrictions on industrial location like those adopted in the London region since 1945 and in the Paris region since 1955. They prefer to use the possibility of restrictions, in the words of the 1956 report, 'as a stick behind the door' in case gentler measures fail. And they rely on government aid to the unfortunate regions of the Netherlands: 130 million guilders, or £13 million, were reserved for the improvement of the infrastructure of these regions by the Economic Ministry in their 1960–4 plan, as well as 60 million guilders (£6 million) for transport improvements; 20 million guilders (£2 million) were being provided in 1961 for contributions to firms decentralising out of the congested areas to the problem regions. In addition they rely on the direction of public investment having an important regional effect: the decision, in the late 1950s, to drain the South Flevoland polder before Markerwaard, was taken deliberately with the idea of improving access to the problem region of the northern Netherlands. The experience of the 1960s, with the net migration flow *out of* the west, seems to justify government policy.

The planned growth of the Randstad itself, on the other hand, involves close co-operation among different levels of government – national, provincial or regional, and local. And difficult problems of conflict of interest inevitably arise. The philosophy of the Netherlands government, as expressed in the Planning Law of 1962, is to give the maximum possible planning power to the municipalities. Under the 1962 Act, regional plans, showing broad land uses, will still be made by planning offices of the provincial government, and broad national lines of planning policy will be laid down in the Hague. But only the municipal plans will be legally binding, though the provincial authorities' regional plans may restrict building where 'extra-municipal' forces are involved. Yet the regional plans have clearly a critical role to play in guiding the growth of the Randstad, as the government recognised when they asked for plans for certain

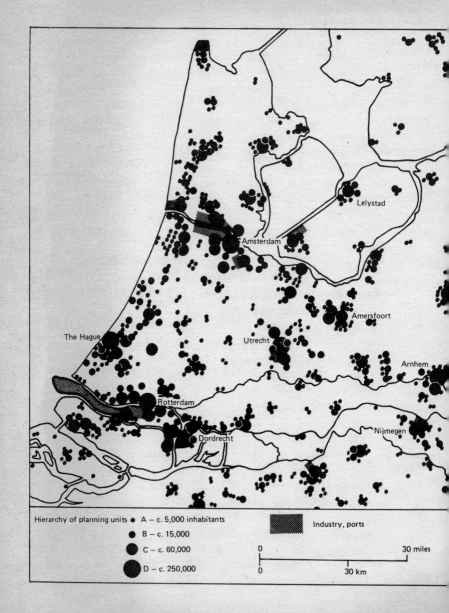

critical areas to be prepared as a matter of priority; they include northern Kennemerland, where it is critical to provide for a rapid growth of population north of IJmuiden and the North Sea Canal, and the Utrecht Hills, where it is necessary to protect the area as an agricultural and recreational zone for the benefit of the people of the Randstad. The test will be whether the municipal plans follow reasonably faithfully the guiding lines laid down in national and regional plans. And here there is room for doubt. The municipalities of the Netherlands are small, as were the planning authorities in England until the 1947 Act gave power to bigger authorities. In 1959 no less than 246 out of 994 municipalities had less than 2,000 people each, and 127 of these were in the west where the problems were most pressing. Only the most minor changes in this situation took place during the 1960s. The danger will be that many will see only their own problems in isolation, and will be tempted to allow urban expansion where it should not occur, or to prohibit it where it should be encouraged. And it is doubtful either whether they can pursue an active land policy, as is already practised by the larger municipalities, so as to prevent speculation in development land.

The problems here are intimately bound up with the existing structure of local government in the Netherlands, which – as so often the world over – is failing to keep pace with the rapid growth of urban populations. Thus in Amsterdam it was agreed that there should be a large-scale extension out from the south-east corner of the city, but building – and hence the renewal programme in the inner city – was held up while it was determined whether the city boundaries should be extended, or whether a completely new municipality should be created out of the small authorities at present governing the area. (Finally, in the late 1960s and early 1970s, the new town of Bijlermeer was built outside the city boundaries.) Many smaller towns, both within the agricultural heart of the Randstad and outside it, are finding difficulty in getting boundary extensions, and this is preventing them from performing their proper function of taking overspill population from the bigger cities. The government, in their 1960 report, frankly said that boundary reform must be speeded up.

4.5   *The principle of concentrated deconcentration in the Randstad:* The *Second Report on Physical Planning* (1966) suggested local groupings of differently-sized settlements to give a choice of residential lifestyles within limited commuting range. Unfortunately, in practice decentralization proved more explosive.

They stressed also the need for inter-municipal co-operation and even perhaps eventually for super-municipal authorities.

The truth is that many important jobs in the growing Randstad cannot be performed adequately by the existing authorities. Two important cases are the protection of the buffer zones, and the provision of urban transport over wide suburban areas. In the first case, the government recognise that the sums involved are beyond the purses of local authorities, and that the government in the Hague must provide them. The same goes for much of the investment that will be necessary to provide adequate planned recreation areas, such as the proposed park running through the heart of the Randstad between Amsterdam and Rotterdam. With transport, the steady growth in commuting from suburbs beyond city limits has caused the Dutch planners to look with favour at the idea of a supra-municipal authority on the model of London Transport.

By the early 1970s, in fact, it was embarassingly evident that the government's broad regional planning objectives were endangered by weakness in local implementation. The green heart of the Randstad was in danger of being progressively built over; during the 1960s, it had actually experienced higher rates of population growth than the nation as a whole, as the pressures for low density living proved too strong for the local municipalities' planning controls. Professor Steigenga, one of the most distinguished Dutch urban planners, was writing in 1972 that the urban areas of the Randstad were in danger of turning inside out on the American model, thus making of the Randstad a vast, highly dispersed, non-hierarchical structure: the very antithesis of what the official government planners had proposed in their Second Report on Physical Planning.

The Third Report: Planning for a Changed World

By the early 1970s, it was plain in the Netherlands – as elsewhere in western Europe – that the policies of the mid-1960s were in important respects no longer relevant. On the one hand, certain basic assumptions had ceased to apply. Thus the Randstad was no longer expected to grow rapidly; there was strong out-migration from it to the south and east, and its cities were losing people; contrary to expectations, long-distance commuting was on the increase as people travelled from their new homes in the south and east to jobs in the Randstad; car ownership had risen five fold during the 1970s; there had been an evident failure to apply the policies of concentrated deconcentration at the local level, and the green heart of the Randstad had been massively invaded. Yet, on the other hand, the energy crisis and the new strength of ecological arguments both suggested a planning policy that moved in different directions: towards conservation of energy and land, protection of the natural environment, reduction of the need for mobility, and greater concern to reduce social inequality.

Thus the Third Report on Physical Planning, published in 1974–6, is forced into a quite radical reappraisal of the policies of the 1960s. One major casualty is the idea of large-scale planned movement from the Randstad; developments like the decentralisation of government offices from the Hague, the new report suggests, have taken this quite far enough. Instead, the first aim should be to encourage a good urban structure within the Randstad itself, and at its edges. To that end, the green heart should be resolutely protected, as should the buffer zones that separate the Randstad on its outer sides – especially to the south, against the rapidly growing towns of North Brabant, and eastwards, towards Amersfoort and Arnhem. Yet, at the same time, planners must recognise that there is basic uncertainty about many important variables: the rate and nature of economic growth, the location preferences of industrialists and homeowners, the future role of the city. So planning has to be based on flexibility.

Tentatively, the Third Report looks at alternative models of development. One concentrates development in certain areas at a rather high density (22 dwellings to the acre net), with most travel by foot, bicycle and bus; most of the housing would be near city centres; there would be an emphasis on rehabilitation, and large amounts of open space; planning would be based on small city regions with short travel distances. This might be a good alternative where it is still feasible; but in the Randstad, generally, it is not.

A second alternative spreads the population more widely over the western Netherlands, with net densities around 14 dwellings to the acre, and travel times to work of up to 25–30 minutes by public transport. Some new residential areas would be developed in attractive recreational zones; the existing residential function in urban areas would be preserved. A third alternative would closely resemble this, but with higher densities (22 dwellings to the net acre, even higher in cities), concentrated near urban centres, and with a great deal of rehabilitation. The Third Report tentatively suggests that in the Randstad these two alternatives may be most appropriate:

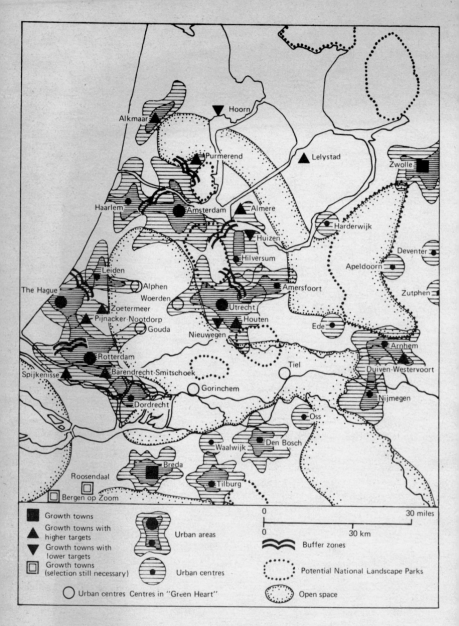

Growth towns

■ Growth towns

▲ Growth towns with higher targets

▼ Growth towns with lower targets

☐ Growth towns (selection still necessary)

○ Urban centres Centres in "Green Heart"

Urban areas

Urban centres

0 — 30 miles
0 — 30 km

〰 Buffer zones

⋯ Potential National Landscape Parks

◯ Open space

4.6 Principles of urban development in the Third Report: The *Third Report on Physical Planning* (1973–6) suggests that provision must be made for continued decentralization from the Randstad Cities, particularly by growth centres on the outsides of the two urbanized 'wings'. Buffer zones will separate the major cities within the wings.

the higher density variant in and around the largest cities, the lower density variant elsewhere.

The last alternative follows the trends of recent years. New residential areas are built at low densities; there is widespread urban renewal in the towns; open space norms are not very stringently applied; there is widespread commuting by private car over distances up to twenty miles; in consequence the larger cities have to adopt drastic measures to control traffic. The government planners clearly consider that this alternative, if continued, would place intolerable strain on city centres and would threaten to destroy both the green heart of the Randstad and its external buffer zones.

So the stress is on a city region solution, with growth centres close to the bigger cities to provide homes and some local services within easy daily reach. Many of these will be on the outer sides of the main north and south wings of the Randstad. Each of these centres should be under a single municipal control, with a single development agency; to that end transfers of territory may be necessary. The government would supply subsidies for land purchase, infrastructure development, and other essential purposes. Within the cities the emphasis would be on selective renewal or rehabilitation to improve the quality of the housing stock, but undertaken so as not to threaten the existing lower-income inhabitants; the main emphasis would be on preserving the human activities and the unique character of the city. Densities would be up to 32–40 dwellings to the net acre in the largest cities, 16–24 elsewhere; commuting distances would be kept below 35–40 minutes by the development of new public transport links, including railways and light railways (map 4.6).

The main emphasis of the 1970s, therefore, is not outward from the Randstad, but inward (map 4.6). The cities must be protected from decay; their centres must be encouraged, new residential areas must be provided close to jobs, both in the older inner urban areas and in new districts within easy reach. Therefore, the cities and the areas around them must be planned as integral city-regional wholes. To provide for new households and improve living standards, 195,000 extra homes will be needed in the Randstad between 1980 and 2000: the report suggests that the great majority will be provided in so-called growth centres close to the cities of the north and south wings of the Randstad, such as Zoetermeer, Pijnacker, Voorhout, Capelle an der Ijssel and the Drecht towns in the south, and Biljermeer, Purmerend, Almere and Lelystad in the north.

To develop these, agreements will be necessary between the different levels of government – national, provincial and local. And almost certainly there will be a need for administrative reform, including the creation of new-style provincial governments with greater powers vis-à-vis the multitude of small municipalities. Lastly, the government will need to be ready with subsidies for development on expensive land and for urban renewal. The Physical Planning Act will have to be reformed, with better defined powers given to the Minister to make directives; amendments will be required in the legislation on matters such as urban renewal, soil conservation and water supply. And the planning process will need to become more flexible and responsive to changing conditions, with broad structure plans (*Streekplannen*) showing the basic distribution of activities and land uses in outline diagrammatic form.

Thus, in important respects, the evolution of Dutch planning in the 1970s follows a model that earlier emerged in London. The fall in population growth, coupled with the flight from the cities, forces a radical reorientation of policy. No longer is the emphasis on longer-distance regional dispersal to the far peripheries of the country. Instead, the concern is to try to save the great cities from continued decline and eventual decay. To that end, resources and physical plans are focused on maintaining a balanced population and a wide range of jobs and services close to the city's heart. But in the Netherlands, as in the London region, there is no evidence at all that government determination can by itself turn the tide.

Moral of the Randstad

Has the Dutch experience any moral for the planners and citizens of urban giants like London, Paris or New York? The unique advantage of the Randstad is its *polycentric* quality. If Britain or France also had developed their government and commercial and financial functions in separate but nearby cities, they would suffer less intractable problems today; but history decided otherwise. Yet it must be remembered that history is always on the move. The central areas of London and Paris have seen profound changes since 1900, both in form and function; they will see more yet, and it is not beyond the ability of government to make these changes radical ones. If only a part of the British or French government machine was decentralised to a site within an hour's journey of the capital, there seems little doubt that a certain re-orientation of the London or Paris regions would result; they could eventually become, to a limited extent, more like the Randstad in form.

The Netherlands offer another moral, especially for the British, who have led Europe in many aspects of physical planning. The British early grasped the problem of metropolitan growth, and their answer was the green belt. But the green belt is admirably adapted to a city with a static population; as we have already seen in London, with a rapidly-growing population it creates many problems and is subject to serious pressures. Coming later to the problem, and faced with the necessity to plan for growth, the Dutch have rejected the belt in favour of the linear extension and the green wedge: a solution which allows unlimited extension along the transport lines, where much of the existing development has taken place, while keeping all the advantages of open country between those lines. There seems little doubt that for most of the still growing world cities of the present time, the Dutch solution is the right model.

The principle of concentrated deconcentration, too, demonstrates the hard-headed realism of Dutch city regional planning. It accepts the social trend towards greater dispersal of the population in search of space and more tranquil living conditions, but attempts to balance this by good accessibility to nearby urban jobs and services. It promises maximum choice of living environments, of job opportunities, and of services of all kinds. It is a model well worth study by other nations.

One final word of doubt must enter in; it concerns implementation. Paper plans may be admired, but the final test must be whether they can be made to work on the ground. Up to now, Dutch urban planning has been stronger at the high conceptual level than at the mundane level of effective enforcement. It would be a pity indeed if such essentially realistic, flexible plans were finally frustrated by failures at the local government level. But that, in the late 1970s, is too clearly the danger.

5 Rhine-Ruhr

From the Randstad, the E36 motorway joins the Netherlands to the heart of Europe, running at first eastwards through the heathlands between Utrecht and Arnhem. This country seems still almost unpopulated; yet only a few miles to the south, in the woods where the Airborne division landed for the tragic 1944 campaign, the villas and shops and petrol stations are sprouting in the 1960s and 1970s: here the Randstad is spreading fast, and threatening to encompass Arnhem itself. If and when this happens, there will remain 70 miles of open land along the E36 to separate two of the greatest urban agglomerations of continental Europe: Randstad and Ruhr. This frontier zone between the Netherlands and Germany has remained relatively undeveloped for centuries; the E36 motorway was completed here only in the mid-1960s. But Dutch geographers and planners are watching the buffer zone anxiously. They see a real danger that, by 1980 or 1990, the Dutch Randstad and the cities of the German Rhine and Ruhr will have coalesced into a single gigantic urban region: a European megalopolis, 180 miles long, stretching down the river Rhine from Bonn to the Hook of Holland.

As it is, the journey from Arnhem across the frontier station at Emmerich and into the Ruhr takes little more than an hour. The E36 Autobahn, or *Hollandelinie*, is joined by the east–west Autobahn from Berlin, Hanover and the eastern Ruhr, to make perhaps the greatest commercial artery in continental Europe, running south to Cologne, Frankfurt and south Germany. About half-way from this point to Cologne, off the Autobahn, lies the *Raststätte Düsseldorf-nord*: and within a radius of 40 miles of this point live well over 10 million people – the greatest concentration of people on the European continent, including the USSR, and only exceeded in all Europe by the area within 40 miles of central London.

This tremendous coalescence of people poses a particularly acute problem of definition. It is difficult enough to delimit a meaningful urban agglomeration around a single city centre, such as London or Paris. But here, within the 40-mile radius, are twelve cities with over 200,000 people apiece, and another ten with between 100,000 and 200,000; around most of these, suburbs extend far beyond the formal limits, in many cases effectively joining one city to the next. What then is the meaningful urban region? Several separate pieces of research have attacked this problem and have emerged with remarkably similar results. In 1957 Gerhard Isenberg defined a 'Rhine–Ruhr agglomeration' with a population in 1955 of 10·01 million and a 1961 Census population of 10·51 million; in 1959 International Urban Research, working mainly on the basis of commuter flows, defined seven distinct but contiguous 'metropolitan areas', with a combined 1961 Census population of 10,265,000. Isenberg's work was refined by other researchers; and, based on all this work, an official definition of densely populated agglomerations was agreed by a Ministerial Conference for Regional Planning in 1968. This gave a 1967 population for the Rhine–Ruhr agglomeration of 10,412,000. Meanwhile, a revised 1970 Census figure based on the definitions of International Urban Research gives a total of 10,924,000 in eight metropolitan areas – a separate area based on Leverkusen having been defined since the earlier exercise (map 5.1).

This complex metropolitan agglomeration, thus defined, occupies a triangular area, each side of which runs a few miles outside the triangular Autobahn network of the area. The west side runs just west of the Rhine from Bonn through Cologne to Xanten, parallel to the main north–south Autobahn; the north side runs from Xanten to Unna at the eastern end of the Ruhr, parallel to the east–west Autobahn; the third side runs from Unna back to Bonn, parallel to the diagonal Autobahn from the eastern Ruhr to Leverkusen north of Cologne. At the Federal German Census of 1970, the region contained ten and three-quarter million people, nearly one in five of the total population of the Federal Republic. Between the 1950 and 1961 Censuses, it had added 2·1 million, or 25 per cent, to its population; a figure which represented one-third of the total net increase of population in the Republic. Well over two-thirds of this increase was due to net migration; well over one-third came from outside the Federal German Republic, mainly from the communist east. This last migration, which was stopped two months after the

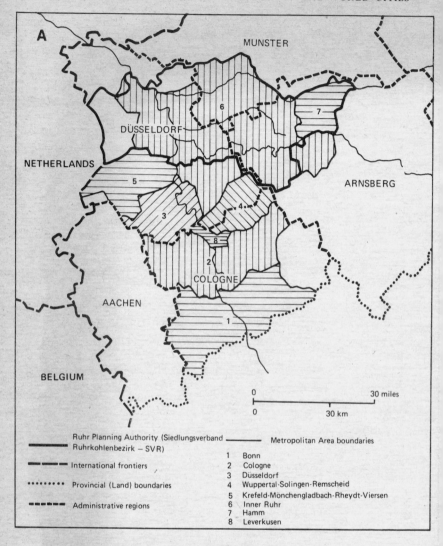

5.1 *The Rhine–Ruhr agglomeration.* Like the Dutch Randstad, Rhine–Ruhr is a complex, multi-centred urban agglomeration. The effective metropolitan region of post-1945 Federal Germany, it extends over five of the administrative regions (*Regierungsbezirke*) of the *Land* of Nordrhein-Westfalen, and two regional planning bodies are concerned with the major part of it. Functionally, the agglomeration may be broken down into eight metropolitan regions, several of which are themselves exceptionally complex in form.

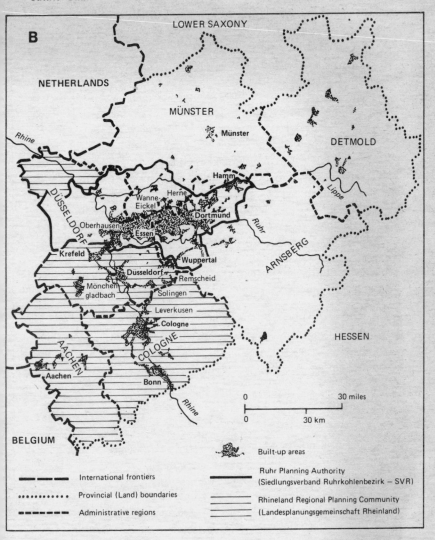

1961 Census by the Berlin wall, is undoubtedly the most important single factor in the extraordinary growth of the Rhine–Ruhr cities since the Second World War – a growth unparallelled elsewhere in western Europe. After it ceased, growth in Rhine–Ruhr plummeted – to a mere 659,000, or 6 per cent, between 1961 and 1970, 12 per cent of the national growth.

The Rhine–Ruhr region dominates Federal Germany in many other ways. In the 1970s, it was producing over four-fifths of its hard coal and three-fifths of its steel. It contained Bonn, the political capital; Cologne, headquarters of several Federal departments and one of the country's leading financial centres; Düsseldorf, capital of the *Land* of Nordrhein–Westfalen – the richest and most populous of the provinces of Federal Germany – and home of the administrative offices of many of its most powerful industrial enterprises; and Essen, traditional 'capital of the Ruhr', with the headquarters of many individual mining and steel firms as well as of workers', employers' and technical organisations. With only a limited degree of competition from Frankfurt and Hamburg in the financial sphere, from Hamburg in the trading sphere, and from the various *Land* capitals in the political and cultural sphere, this is evidently the region of postwar Federal Germany in which the distinctively metropolitan functions are concentrated. The Rhine–Ruhr cities are to modern Germany what the Randstad is to the Netherlands, Paris to France, London to Britain: they form post-1945 Germany's world city.

Rhine–Ruhr in history

This conclusion may puzzle some and infuriate others, especially in Germany; for since its inception in 1949 the Federal Republic has never recognised the division of Germany, and the capital at Bonn is a provisional one pending a return to Berlin. Yet in 1977 West Berlin remains separate from the Federal Republic by 110 miles of foreign territory, accessible from it by only three roads, three railways and three air corridors; it is not politically part of the Republic. True, with the aid of subventions from outside it had rebuilt itself brilliantly, retained many industries and kept a powerful hold over much of its former educational and cultural life. Yet in 1970 its population was below that in 1939; its industrial production index had climed during the 1950s significantly more slowly than the Federal Republic's; most critically, it has lost its essential *raison d'être*, the varied public activities that depend on the presence of government. For the affairs of Germany are no longer decided in Berlin. The focus of power – political, commercial, financial, industrial – has shifted decisively to the west.

It can be argued indeed that this shift represents merely a reversion to an older, more abiding German tradition, which was merely obscured in the short period of German unity from 1871 to 1945.

Many of the greatest Rhine–Ruhr cities date from the early middle ages and even from Roman times; Berlin in comparison is a relative newcomer. In the later Middle Ages the Rhine–Ruhr cities flourished, as they flourish today, because they stand at the junction-point of many of the most important trading routes of western Europe. From 1500 to 1800 trade stagnated and so did the cities. But the intense political fragmentation of Germany made several of them minor capitals, like Düsseldorf or Bonn, or even virtually independent empires, like Dortmund or Cologne. Yet in 1815, at the Treaty of Vienna, the Rhine–Ruhr region passed to Prussia. Henceforth, Prussian Germany had two seats of power: administrative power in Berlin, industrial and commercial power in Rhine–Ruhr. They increased together, and the achievement of German unity in 1871 was merely a stage in the process.

But old as the cities of the region are, their growth into major centres, within a complex urban region, was relatively late. The first deep coal shaft was not sunk through the overburden into the rich concealed coalfield of the central Ruhr until 1837; the first railway did not arrive in the Ruhr till 1847; Ruhr coal was not coked for iron-making until 1849; even in 1871, at the first census of the united German Reich, no Ruhr city had as many as 60,000 people, while many of today's major cities were still villages – Gelsenkirchen had 11,000 people, Oberhausen 15,000. But then the cities mushroomed. Those of the southern Ruhr, along the old medieval trade route of the Hellweg, expanded their old commercial functions and added the iron and steel works of the Ruhr tycoons: Krupp in Essen, Horter and Höesch in Dortmund, Thyssen in Mülheim and Hamborn. The villages of the northern Ruhr grew into enormous loose conglomerations of miners' cottages, which received the title of 'city' for administrative convenience. After 1890 the chemical industry developed, especially along the Rhine front: when Friedrich Bayer moved his works to Leverkusen in 1891 it was a village of 9,000 people; by 1961 the works employed 25,000 and Leverkusen was a city of 94,000 people. The population of the entire Ruhr coalfield, only 913,000 in 1871, rose to 3,521,000 in 1910 and then more slowly to 4,324,000 in 1939. Such growth of course reflects extraordinary physical advantages: the ready supplies of coal and brown coal within the region or nearby; the unrivalled water transport along the Rhine, and later by the ship canal system from the North Sea coast of Germany; the concentration of overland routes. But against this there were grave political handicaps. The area was peripheral to Bismarck's Germany, as to Hitler's; it was vulnerable to enemy attack, as the heavy defences of Cologne reminded Germans up to 1914 and as air bombardment reminded them between 1939 and 1945; between the two world wars the region was under Allied occupation until 1923, and remained demilitarised until Hitler marched his troops into it in 1936. Yet in the very different political circumstances of Europe after 1945, a liability has become an asset; less peripheral in the Federal Republic than ever in the *Reich*, the Rhine–Ruhr region is now the natural centre of the European Economic Community.

The multi-centred metropolis

With an urban region like London or Paris it is conventional and logical to begin analysis by looking at the centre, for the heart of the city commonly contains the economic *raison d'être* of the whole region around; but it is already evident that Rhine–Ruhr is an extreme case of a phenomenon already visited in Randstad Holland – the *polycentric* urban region. Not only does the region contain a score of cities: it has half a dozen regional centres, no one of which can be said to dominate the others, and each of which is surrounded by its distinct tributary area. The easiest way to penetrate the complexities of Rhine–Ruhr, then, is to distinguish the main urban *clusters* of the region; and the simplest way to do this is by looking at the eight metropolitan areas of International Urban Research.

In the extreme south the Bonn metropolitan area, with 651,000 people in 1970, is itself a union of opposites. On the left, or west, bank of the river, Bonn itself: Roman camp, medieval trading town, princely capital in the eighteenth century, Prussian university and residential town in the nineteenth. In 1949 its position, its historic and artistic associations, its broad leafy avenues and solid bourgeois houses made it an excellent choice for the Federal German capital, and the constellation of embassies and federal ministries has caused its population to mushroom. Opposite, on the east bank, is a different world: the heavy chemical plants and engineering works of Siegburg and Troisdorf, established in desolate heath country in the nineteenth century, and now benefiting from their excellent communications via the Cologne–Frankfurt Autobahn, which was routed this way in the late 1930s.

Immediately to the north the Cologne agglomeration, with 1·5 million people in 1970, is equally complex in function and form. The ancient Roman and medieval core of the city has emerged from wartime devastation, and is today a more powerful shopping and financial centre than ever; in particular it is important for insurance, for overseas organisations, for the German Federation of Industry and for wholesaling organisations, and it contains several departments of the Federal Government. Outside the centre is industrial Cologne: factories of very varied character break into the residential suburbs of the city along the railway lines, but the heaviest industry, dependent on waterborne materials, congregates along the river both north and south of the city, and in the right bank suburbs of Mülheim, Deutz and Poll. The fastest-growing and most obtrusive member of these concentrations is the chemical industry: its main centres are the vast Bayer works at Leverkusen on the east bank some 8 miles north of Cologne, and the new refining and petro-chemical complex at Wesseling on the west bank some 5 miles south of the city. Leverkusen's postwar growth has been so rapid that by 1970, with a population of over 100,000, it was recognised by International Urban Research as a separate metropolitan area.

North from Leverkusen, along the crowded Ruhr–Cologne Autobahn, there is hardly a break between the northward spread of the Leverkusen agglomeration and the southward expansion of the Düsseldorf metropolitan area, which had over 1 million people at the 1970 Census. Düsseldorf owes its celebrated elegance to its history as a minor political capital in the Age of Absolutism. Its importance as a regional centre stems from the luxury shops of its Königsallee; from its history as an administrative centre under Prussian and then German government, from 1815 to 1945; then from its critical choice as capital of the *Land* of Nordrhein–Westfalen, in 1946; and from the location nearby of the international airport for the whole region. Since then it has naturally attracted the headquarters offices of many of the Ruhr industries, whose skyscrapers give another distinction to its skyline; and it has become a major banking centre. Away from the centre, though, the other face of Düsseldorf is soon seen: for here is the home of one of the great iron and steel complexes of the entire Rhine–Ruhr region, that of Mannesmann, and the city's industrial structure closely resembles those of the big Ruhr cities to the north.

Two smaller agglomerations are somewhat isolated from the others, and are less markedly metropolitan, more exclusively industrial. They are the *Wuppertal–Solingen–Remscheid* group, with close on 1 million people in 1970, and with cutlery and engineering and textile industries whose craft origins go back to the Middle Ages; and the textile and engineering group of *Krefeld–Mönchengladbach–Rheydt–Viersen*, with a combined population of 730,000, on the west bank of the Rhine.

This leaves the gigantic Inner Ruhr agglomeration, with the very small and almost contiguous metropolitan area of Hamm (207,000 people in 1970) at its eastern end. The Inner Ruhr region itself presents a complex enough problem of analysis. In 1970 it contained some 5·7 million people, more than half the whole population of the Rhine–Ruhr area; or 10 per cent of that of the Federal Republic, living on 2 per cent of its area. Within a thirty-mile journey from east to west are found two cities of over half a million people and another three of between a quarter and half a million. These cities, and many smaller ones, have very different characters, some concerned predominantly with mining, others with manufacture, yet others with retail and other service trades. And a fundamental distinction must be made between the old cities of the Hellweg route, in the south, and the newer cities of the Emscher valley and the low plateaux to the north of it.

Like Düsseldorf, the Hellweg cities show two faces. Alike in Duisburg, Essen, Bochum and Dortmund, there is the striking juxtaposition of the old medieval city core, where shops and business still concentrate, with offices perhaps just beyond the line of the former wall; and not far away, the big heavy industrial works which arrived in the early or middle nineteenth century. Because industry arrived later here than in Britain or Belgium, because German industrialists inherited a tradition of paternal responsibility to their workers, the working-class housing areas of the Hellweg cities were always among the best of an industrial area in Europe, and the Second World War took away most of the inadequate housing that did remain. Today the industrial areas of the Hellweg cities are dominated by cheerful if not very imaginative flats nearer the centres, and by estates of houses with gardens in the suburbs; the middle classes tend to live in separate villas on the higher wooded slopes which lie to the south of the city centres. On the extreme southern edge of each city, the Ruhr river valley is almost completely rural: long deserted by coal-miners and iron-smelters, it serves as a gigantic reservoir and park for the cities just to the north.

The cities of the northern Ruhr present a different and a simpler face. These are one-industry and one-class towns, which grew from insignificant origins between 1870 and 1914 to house the vast coal-mining population that flooded into the Ruhr. Towns like Bottrop, Gladbeck or Castrop-Rauxel had over 60 per cent of their industrial workforce in coal-mining in the mid-1960s, though this proportion was declining. The Hellweg towns are distinguished by the size and vigour of their city centres; the northern towns by the absence or inadequacy of theirs. This marks a structural deficiency in the functions which central areas perform: the less regular, more specialised shopping functions, wholesale trade, finance, and the higher administrative, professional and cultural functions. Middle-class housing is hardly to be found; the towns consist of a series of miners' estates, built by the colliery companies, and each accompanied by shops, beer halls, schools and welfare services. Some towns are merely administrative marriages of formerly separate nuclei, as names like Castrop-Rauxel and Wanne-Eickel testify. The idea of the separate unitary city with the strong centre, so true of much German urban life, accords ill with economic and social reality in the northern Ruhr.

Space: the central problem

The basic problem of this vast and complex agglomeration is basic to all agglomerations the world over: it is growing demand on limited space. Since 1945, because of rapid population growth and the demand for more space per person, the cities of Rhine–Ruhr have spread physically at an unprecedented pace. In the Ruhr alone, between 1937 and 1955, the area developed for building and transport purposes increased from 24·8 per cent to 34·8 per cent of the total, mainly at the expense of agricultural land. Up to 1939 the population of the big Ruhr cities still tended to live fairly closely, in tenements close to the city centres. But in 1945 these areas lay destroyed. In many cases shops and offices were developed in these areas, while the new houses were built at the periphery. As a result, towns like Gelsenkirchen, Oberhausen and Duisburg actually doubled their built-up areas between 1937 and 1955. The most serious problem is found in the zone of these great cities – which the Ruhr planners distinguish as the 'core area' (map 5.2). Here, 85·5 per cent of the land was still under agriculture and woodland in 1893; by 1960 the proportion had fallen to 47·7 per cent. Even in the short period from 1949 to 1960, the core area lost 32 square miles of open

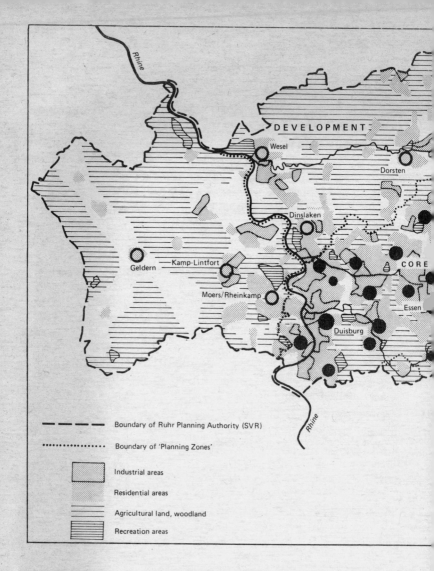

Rhine

DEVELOPMENT

Wesel

Dorsten

Dinslaken

Kamp·Lintfort

CORE

Geldern

Essen

Moers/Rheinkamp

Duisburg

Rhine

- – – – Boundary of Ruhr Planning Authority (SVR)

••••••••••••••• Boundary of 'Planning Zones'

Industrial areas

Residential areas

Agricultural land, woodland

Recreation areas

5.2 *The 1966 General Development Plan for the Ruhr.* The core area containing the main cities is to be stabilised; main growth of population and industry will take place to the north in the Development Zone, especially north of the River Lippe. A hierarchy of growth centres, mostly in the core area, will provide services and will be linked by rapid transit. *Inset* (right) shows main principles of the plan.

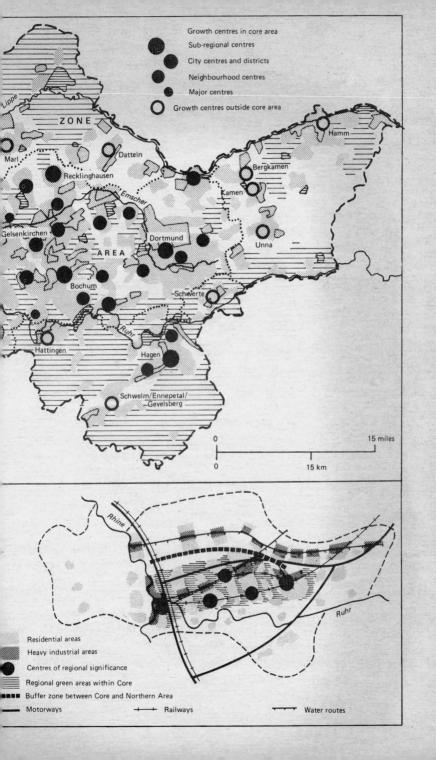

Growth centres in core area
Sub-regional centres
City centres and districts
Neighbourhood centres
Major centres
Growth centres outside core area

Lippe

ZONE

Marl
Datteln
Recklinghausen
Emscher
Gelsenkirchen
AREA
Dortmund
Bochum
Schwerte
Ruhr
Hattingen
Hagen
Schwelm/Ennepetal/
-Gevelsberg

Hamm
Bergkamen
Kamen
Unna

0   15 miles
0   15 km

Rhine
Ruhr

Residential areas
Heavy industrial areas
Centres of regional significance
Regional green areas within Core
Buffer zone between Core and Northern Area
Motorways   Railways   Water routes

land – approximately the area of the City of Mülheim; the whole Ruhr planning area lost 89 square miles, roughly the area of Dortmund.

The same process is recorded near Cologne. Here, building, industry and transport together appropriated over 50,000 acres in the years between 1900 and 1955 – close on one-fifth of the total area of the region. Since 1955 the petro-chemical industry has made further large demands in the river-front zone. And since 1950, growing vehicle ownership has caused the particularly rapid spread of low-density suburbs at some distance from the centre of the city; while the inner suburbs are static or even declining slightly in population. In the more distant right-bank suburbs, Cologne commuters are moving into areas formerly occupied only by local industrial workers. Further south, Bonn is still surrounded by an agricultural belt at about three miles from the centre; but the clear distinction between town and country is becoming increasingly obscured. This is particularly noticeable in the west, where the 'green fingers' of open land, which were formerly so typical in the suburban zones of Bonn and Godesberg, are disappearing very quickly.

Even in the Ruhr, this still leaves much open land. The trouble, especially in the Ruhr, is that much of the new development has not been adequately grouped and concentrated. After 1945 the critical priority was to get the cities working again quickly; this was accomplished by rebuilding on the old street lines and by allowing peripheral development at the edge of each city. Any attempt to secure a better distribution of population on a regional scale was perhaps bound to founder, because of the fact that many municipalities lacked the financial resources to undertake large-scale development.

Leverkusen is the classic example of rapid twentieth-century growth without adequate plan. It had developed round several separate village nuclei; the most important shopping street is the village street next to the original Bayer works, which is a virtual cul-de-sac leading to the Rhine front and completely peripheral to the modern town; the whole town is cut through by three pre-existing railways, and by the Autobahn which was actually built through the rapidly growing town in the 1930s. As a result the town has long suffered very poor internal communications, which are being slowly and expensively improved; it is relatively poor in shops and other services and depends greatly for these on Cologne, though this will be partly remedied by a massive redevelopment of the main commercial centre, the biggest of its kind in the Federal Republic in the early 1970s. The new petro-chemical centre at Wesseling, south of Cologne, seems only too likely to follow this unfortunate model of development.

The structural problem of the Ruhr

In many parts of Rhine–Ruhr, space will remain the dominant problem for years to come. True, it may not prove as acute as between 1945 and 1960: natural population increase in the Federal Republic is stagnant, migration from the east has been cut virtually to zero since August 1961, and the flows from other parts of the Federal Republic, and from southern Europe, may be diverted to other urban regions of Germany. Gerhard Isenberg showed in 1957 that between 1939 and 1955, the population of the Rhine–Ruhr agglomeration had grown slowly compared with some other agglomerations; and that during the early 1950s its increase in industrial workers was in fact the lowest of any major agglomeration of Federal Germany. It seems clear that some of the most dynamic areas of the German economy lie in the south, around provincial capitals like Stuttgart, Nuremberg and Munich. These areas benefit from improved transport, improved economies in power transmission, and from a large and willing labour force. The southern provinces of Bavaria and Baden-Württemberg have long been distinguished by their small, rather inefficient farms, with much underemployment. But since 1955 the Federal Government have sought to rationalise agriculture, and thousands of workers have left the land. Today, around the south German cities, works buses travel far into the countryside to bring this cheap, adaptable labour into the factories. Such workers live more cheaply, and almost certainly more pleasantly, than their compatriots in the Ruhr. And the cities in which they work are more attractive to industrialists than many of the congested, obsolescent and ugly heavy-industry towns of the Ruhr.

The result, already, is a sharp differentiation within the Rhine–Ruhr region, which will continue and may intensify. Those parts which perform truly metropolitan functions – the administrative, commercial and financial cities – will continue to attract workers, and their major planning problem will continue to be the effective use of space. But the purely industrial towns and cities, especially in the northern Ruhr, may face a heavy problem of structural adaptation and even of depopulation.

The fact that the Ruhr had an economic problem emerged very suddenly and sharply in the early 1960s. Population growth in the Ruhr, between the Censuses of 1950 and 1961, averaged out at over 100,000 a year. But this average conceals the fact that, after 1959, the population hardly increased at all. Between the 1961 and 1970 Censuses, a loss of 20,000 people was recorded. Thenceforth, the decline accelerated: between 1972 and 1974 there was a loss of 47,000. And in the coal districts, indeed, there was noticeable outward migration in these latter years. The reason was the sudden crisis in the coal industry, which occurred in the face of all economic prognostication in the late 1950s. Between 1957 and the beginning of 1963, the Ruhr coal industry lost 160,000 men; and by 1963–4 the rate of loss was some 2,500–3,000 a month. In towns with a high proportion of uneconomic pits, such as Bochum, the drop in coal-mining employment has been of the order of 50 per cent. As a result the entire industrial labour force increased much more slowly in the Ruhr, between 1950 and 1962, than in the Federal Republic as a whole; and since 1958 it has actually decreased. During the 1960s total employment rose slightly due to the growth of the service industries. But the decline of coal-mining employment was so rapid after 1965 – 70,000, or over 30 per cent, between 1967 and 1973 – that the rise in non-coal employment could not compensate.

The Ruhr, like north east England or southern Belgium, is thus faced with a problem of massive structural change in its economy. The proportion of workers in the growing service industries is lower than the national average; and within the manufacturing sector, much too high a proportion is concentrated in the declining basic industries – 25·3 per cent in mining, 23 per cent in iron, steel and metal processing in 1970. The fast-growing industries – electrical goods, vehicles, synthetic chemicals – are historically weak in the Ruhr. As in similar problem areas elsewhere, the problem is locally concentrated. It is not so serious in the Hellweg cities, where new industrial traditions are being established; it is very serious indeed in the one-industry towns of the northern Ruhr. While nearly every area in the Ruhr suffered a net loss of industrial workers between 1958 and 1962, the loss mounted to over 16 per cent in mining communities like Herne and Castrop-Rauxel. All the main coal-mining communities showed losses of more than 10 per cent of the population by migration over the four years 1959–62. And it is precisely these communities whose financial strength, in terms of their tax base, has traditionally been weak. Bottrop is a typical case: the coal industry obviously provides a weak basis for industrial taxation, and the property tax, from a town of small miners' houses, yields poor results. In 1964 the real tax yield of the town, per capita of population, was DM 171,00 (approximately £15·50 at the rate of exchange then) after the operation of the Nordrhein–Westfalen government's equalisation scheme, compared with DM 243,00 (£22·10) in Essen or DM 288,00 (£26·20) in Duisburg.

In spring 1964 the crisis of adaptation brought forth a detailed report from the Government of Nordrhein–Westfalen. Most of the measures recommended there were devoted to improving the infrastructure of public services, in which the Ruhr still lags badly behind Germany's other industrial areas. But the report stressed also that new industrial growth should be injected into the areas where the crisis was most severe. Indiscriminate encouragement of new industry was to be avoided, because the heavily congested inner Ruhr should not receive a net increase in employment potential. Instead, extra employment, especially in the growing service industries, should replace industry with weak prospects, especially coal-mining and metal-working. Some of this growth could provide for commuter employment from the towns of the north, because there was no point in encouraging those types of employment in areas where there was no real prospect for them. In the northern towns themselves, the emphasis would be on providing extra employment in manufacturing, especially in those lines employing a high proportion of female labour; for in these towns a much lower-than-average proportion of the female population had been drawn into the labour force.

Another report from the Land government – the Ruhr Development Programme for the period 1968–73 – had very much the same objectives. New industry should be encouraged to take the place of existing plants which shut down or contracted; new jobs should be provided for those ready and willing to take them; and direct public investment in new industry should be available. Retraining centres formed a specially important part of the programme, and new jobs would be provided with financial help from a great variety of agencies, including the European Recovery Programme, the European Coal and Steel Community, the Federal and the Land government. All these would be necessary, the report stressed, to fill the gap caused by an estimated loss of 60,000 coal and steel jobs within two or three years from 1968.

These reports outline the strategy for dealing with the new problem of the Ruhr, but only in broad terms. If experience in other European countries and in the United States offers any guide, parts of the coalfield may suffer heavy losses of population before official policies bring any result. And in consequence the entire metropolitan region is unlikely to dominate the pattern of German growth in the 1970s to anything like the same extent as in the period between 1945 and 1961.

The problem of obsolescence: transport in Rhine–Ruhr

Closely linked to the problems of space and adaptation are those of physical obsolescence. In some spheres – housing for instance – war removed much of the region's obsolescent physical plant. But in others, no renewal took place. Transport, especially in the Ruhr, is an acute case.

The road system of the Rhine–Ruhr region was fashioned in the late eighteenth and early nineteenth centuries to serve light traffic between small market towns. Now it must carry the commercial and industrial traffic of a great urban region – traffic which is exceptionally high because of the polycentric form of development. Meanwhile, not only has it not been fundamentally improved; unplanned ribbon development has actually made it less efficient as a means of carrying traffic. In the twentieth century, only two changes have come over the system. One is the *Ruhrschnellweg*, or Express Highway, begun in 1925 as a comprehensive improvement of the existing main east–west road connecting the Hellweg cities, with some new stretches; in the half-century up to 1973, mainly in the period since 1955, major reconstruction had converted this into an express highway. The other event was the arrival of the Autobahn or motorway network. Opened in 1932, the Cologne–Bonn Autobahn was the first inter-urban motorway in Germany; but the main bulk of the Nazi government's national programme did not come until the later 1930s, and was completed during the war. Even then, gaps remained: the Cologne–Aachen Autobahn was completed in 1961 and the so-called Ruhr Tangent, from Wuppertal to the east of Dortmund, only in 1962.

Apart from the motorways, the road system is demonstrably incapable of carrying the burdens put on it, especially in the zone of the Hellweg cities and around Cologne. With 10 per cent of the people of the Federal Republic (and a slightly lower ratio of vehicles to people than in the Republic as a whole, 194 vehicles per 1,000 people against 242 in 1968) the Ruhr coalfield area has only 4 per cent of the total length of roads and just under 3 per cent of the total length of the main (Federal) roads. Partly for this reason its motorways attract much local traffic for which they were never designed, and even stretches of the motorways are working dangerously near their physical capacity – particularly the north–south Ruhr–Cologne Autobahn, which was carrying 50,000 vehicles per day by 1963; parts of this highway were subsequently widened to give increased capacity.

The inadequacy of the road system is most marked within the cities. After 1945 parts of the Rhine–Ruhr cities were rebult piecemeal on their old street lines – which in most cases were medieval. The effective result, though it does not seem to have been consciously planned, is to keep the motor vehicle out of the central business districts of the cities. One element of deliberate planning was to seal off certain streets, such as Cologne's Hohe Strasse and Essen's Kettwiger Strasse, to vehicles altogether. (In Cologne this had been done before the Second World War.) The increasing numbers of vehicles are therefore found parked in the streets all around the inaccessible core-areas.

The region must therefore still depend to a considerable degree on the public transport system. It might be thought that high-speed rail transport would be ideally suited to the multi-centred pattern of the agglomeration. But the rail network of the Ruhr is singularly ill-adapted to the demands of today. Built mainly between 1847 and 1880, it was designed primarily to carry freight and long-distance passengers; it does not cater at all adequately for the modern commuter. Particularly notable is the relative lack of lines running north to south, which could take commuters from the one-industry towns of the northern Ruhr to the broader-based service centres along the Hellweg.

Because of the paucity of north–south rail routes, passenger traffic is channelled on to streetcar and bus; in the mid-1960s 26 per cent of all the streetcar mileage of the Federal Republic was in the Ruhr, and there the streetcars were especially important for journeys of 2 to 5 miles. But since they must frequently share the narrow and congested street network, they are themselves a cause of further delays.

Up to 1955 the transport problem of Rhine–Ruhr was notably less

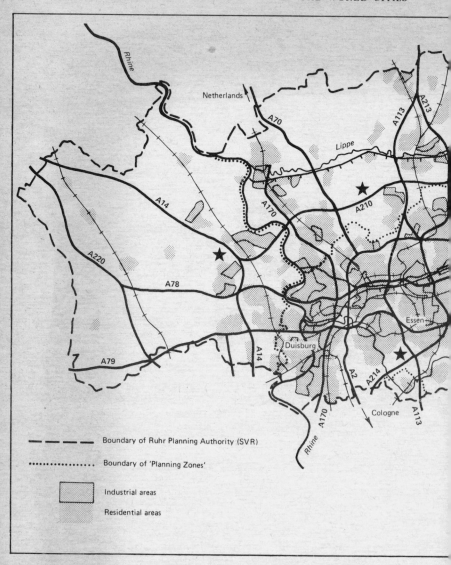

- - - - - -   Boundary of Ruhr Planning Authority (SVR)

....   Boundary of 'Planning Zones'

Industrial areas

Residential areas

serious than in the more centralised metropolitan regions of Europe; at that date, a survey showed that average time for all commuter journeys in the Ruhr was under 30 minutes, while two-thirds of these journeys were made on foot. Despite the explosion in car ownership after that date, the average commuter journey was still under 20

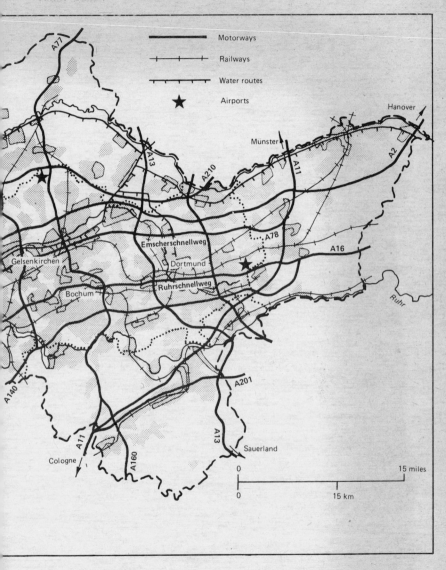

5.3 *The Ruhr: transport proposals.* The growth centres (map 5.2) are to be linked by a whole series of new east-west and north-south *Autobahnen*, running through the buffer zones between the cities. A new rapid transit system will connect the centres, giving access from one level of the hierarchy to another.

minutes in the late 1960s, and 25–30 minutes could be regarded as a maximum. But with the increasing spread of suburban homes and the growth of vehicle ownership, this may change. In Cologne in 1950, 86 per cent of workers still lived within the city; but between then and 1956 there was an increase of 15,000, or nearly one-third, in the commuters from outside. The result of such changes must be increasing dependence on the transport modes suited to longer-distance commuting: the train and the private car.

The planning machine

These are some of the major problems. The administrative machine for dealing with them is a divided affair. Under the fundamental 1960 town planning and building law of the Federal Republic, local land use planning is the concern of the separate municipalities or *Gemeinden*; regional plans, which lay down the general guide-lines for each province, are the responsibility of the *Land* or provincial governments. The *Land* government of Nordrhein–Westfalen has a development plan for the whole province, of which the first version appeared in 1966 and the second in 1970; these lay down a system of urban nodes or service centres connected by preferential development axes or corridors, some of the most important of which are naturally in the Rhine–Ruhr area. But at a more detailed scale of regional planning, according to *Land* Acts of 1962 and 1972, the *Land* government of Nordrhein–Westfalen delegates the preparation of regional plans to regional associations: the Regional Planning Communities or *Landesplanungsgemeinschaften*, which contain representatives of both the local authorities and the *Land* government. Thus the Rhine part of the Rhine–Ruhr region, from Bonn downstream to beyond Düsseldorf, is the province of the *Landesplanungsgemeinschaft Rheinland*. But the planning of the Ruhr is in the hands of a body unique in German experience, and unusual enough anywhere in the world. It is called literally the Ruhr Coal District Settlement Association – the *Siedlungsverband Ruhrkohlenbezirk*, or SVR – and it celebrated its fiftieth anniversary in 1970.

The SVR was founded by a special Prussian law of 5 May 1920, which recognised that the acute problems of the Ruhr could no longer be met adequately by an existing medley of ill-conceived and often contradictory plans prepared by individual towns. Under this law the local authorities or *Gemeinden* yielded up to the *Verband* those powers which it was necessary to centralise in the interests of the development of the region. They included the right to co-operate in the preparation of town plans; planning of roads and railways; giving subsidies and loans to individual local authorities for road-building, afforestation and planning; and buying land which it is decided to protect in the public interest. But under later laws – of 1936, 1950, 1962 and 1972 – the SVR became more than a confederation of authorities; it is now a regional planning association, whose overall regional policies must be respected by the individual authorities in the preparation of their local plans. Though the number of these authorities was cut by nearly half between 1967 and 1970, at the latter date there were still over 1,200 of them in the SVR area; the local government reorganisation of 1975 drastically reduced this number.

The SVR is managed by an Assembly, with eighty-eight members in 1969 – 60 per cent from the *Gemeinden* and 40 per cent drawn from the economic institutions in the region (20 per cent trades unions, 20 per cent employers) – plus a Council of seventeen members. It is responsible to the Minister for Planning, Housing and Public Works of the *Land* Government of Nordrhein–Westfalen in Düsseldorf. It is financially supported by the *Gemeinden* and it also has the right to raise loans. It covers an area of 4,592 square kilometres, or 1,773 square miles, with a 1970 population of 5,599,530 (map 5.1).

The basis of the work of the SVR is the so-called General Settlement Plan, which is in effect a regional plan for the Ruhr. It outlines the broad distribution of industrial and residential land, green space, and regional traffic lines for roads and railways. The SVR has the right to establish legal plans for areas of green space and traffic lines, and for future development if two *Gemeinden* are concerned. The *Gemeinden* have the right to comment on these plans before they are confirmed. Planning by individual *Gemeinden* is co-ordinated by the SVR. The fundamental law of 1920 also gives the SVR certain rights to build roads, operate railways and create green spaces itself. But in practice it has used such powers sparingly, preferring to work through subsidies and advice to the *Gemeinden*. The SVR is, however, concerned (through its membership of a special development corporation) with the building of a new town for 50,000 people, in connection with a new deep coal-mining development, at Wulfen, north of the Lippe Valley on the northern edge of the Ruhr.

The strategy of Ruhr planning

The most basic planning assumption of all has recently been upset in the Ruhr. In 1960, in its *Planning Atlas*, the SVR was still reckoning with a possible long-term population growth from a little over 5·5 million to 8 million. But the coal crisis was even then dramatically reducing the rate of population increase: never less than 100,000 a year from 1950 to 1957, it fell to some 30,000 in 1960 and then, after a temporary upswing, to 14,000 in 1963. Thereafter, actual net population loss set in; over the whole period between the 1961 and 1970 Censuses, the population of the SVR area fell by 100,000. Nevertheless, the Regional Development Plan of the SVR, published in 1966 after extensive discussion with local authorities and institutions, and formally approved by the Planning Office of *Land* Nordrhein-Westfalen, retains the 8 million population figure; it is taken as the limit of population growth if good planning principles are to be maintained. The Plan discusses how long it may take to reach the 8 million limit: on the basis that in the long term the birth rate remains fixed at the average of 1959–64, while in- and out-migration remain in balance, it will take until AD 2020. Because the birth rate in the Ruhr is below the average for the Federal Republic, this implies a progressive fall in the Ruhr's share of the total population of the country. But in absolute terms, it will mean a 2·4 million increase of population over a sixty year period from 1960 to 2020.

Seen against the existing background of congestion and lack of planning in the past, such an increase of population clearly calls for a regional strategy of control and limitation in some areas, development and growth in others. This strategy was formulated in the 1960 Planning Atlas, and was further developed in the 1966 Development Plan. It depends on a division of the territory of the SVR into areas with different problems and development potentials (map 5.2).

The 1960 strategy is based on a threefold division. *Zone one* is the *saturation zone* of the south, especially the valley of the river Ruhr. Here is an area which experienced very early industrial development and mining colonisation, but which was already being deserted by the northern movement of development by the mid-nineteenth century. Today, mining has disappeared or is much diminished; the economic structure is fairly well-balanced, with a mixture of industrial workers and of people who live here and commute into the Hellweg cities. This area presents few problems, and existing development is to be stabilised.

Zone two is the *replanning zone* – the core of the Ruhr which contains the most serious social and economic problems. This zone embraces the major cities and towns of the Ruhr – both the old Hellweg cities and the newer Emscher mining and heavy industrial towns. Fundamentally it is already overcrowded and must not experience further increase of population. *Zone three* is a *development zone* in the west, east and north – especially the last.

The 1966 Development Plan – the first legally effective regional development plan in the Federal Republic – modifies somewhat the division. The replanning zone is greatly enlarged into the *core area*, which contains 4·2 million out of a total of 5·6 million people (in 1970) and the most intense problems of the Ruhr: congestion, unplanned mixture of land uses, lack of open space, polluted air. The 1966 plan postulates that the core's share of the population of the Ruhr will fall from 75 per cent (in 1970) to 70 per cent in the future. Further development is needed, but it should consist of replacement of obsolescent structures. In a few places only is there some potential for new development. But industrial diversification is critically necessary, especially in the mining towns of the northern core. New residential areas for the big cities will have to be built just outside the core, especially in the attractive hilly areas to the South. The Ruhr Valley, and parts of the hills around, must be kept open for recreational purposes.

But the main opportunity for positive planning comes in the *peripheral zone* – the wide and still almost open area in the north, west and east, which is expected in the future to increase its share of the Ruhr's total population from 1·18 million or 21 per cent (in 1970) to an eventual 25 per cent. Here, the 1966 Plan chooses four major growth points where further development will be mainly concentrated: some are already being colonised by the coal mining industry, in its steady northward migration, but above all these sites are exceptionally well sited in relation to the natural lines of easy transportation. They are all sited on or near the canal which runs beside the river Lippe, and their links with the core area to the south will be improved by new and reconstructed north–south roads. They will become the foci of a balanced industrial development, for it is essential that these centres do not follow the unfortunate one-sided development of the mining towns in the core area to the south. The Rhine Valley itself, separating the northern from the western sector of the development zone, is to be kept largely open, and a green barrier south of the Lippe Valley will separate the northern sector from the core area; while the attractive sandy area around Haltern, in the extreme north, will be preserved as an important recreation zone for the crowded populations of the Inner Ruhr.

The location of centres of employment growth must be the basic element in any regional plan; all other elements hinge on it. So a supplementary report to the 1966 Plan, published in 1969, identifies 41 major centres (*Siedlungsschwerpunkte*) with good communications, infra structure and social facilities. If required, they should each be capable of housing 50,000 extra people, thus increasing their total population from 1·5 million to 3·2 million; an extra 1·1 million will be within easy access via the planned rapid transit system that will link the centres. Thus, connected with each other and with their hinterlands, the centres will develop as primary locations for central services and facilities. Most of them – 26 out of the 41 – are in the core; 14 are in the peripheral zone of the agglomeration and only one is in the rural zone outside. 7 out of the 41 are classed as regional sub-centres, performing a wide range of services for an entire subdivision of the Ruhr area; they are the centres of the largest cities. Below them in the hierarchy come city, district and local centres. So cities like Duisburg, Essen or Dortmund have four or five such centres each (map 5.2). But two other elements in the 1966 plan deserve particular attention, because they will help provide an adequate economic and social environment for further development. One is the transport net; the other is the provision of open space.

For transport planning the basic law gives the SVR a unique power, denied even to the Federal Ministry of Transport: the power, upon agreement of the *Gemeinden*, to establish the line of a future road development, which is then kept open for an indefinite time. So the SVR can plan a future road network in the sure knowledge that future development will not set the plan at nought. What has hindered the SVR in the past is not lack of power but lack of financial means. The original plan, conceived in the mid-1920s, was never carried out save for a few stretches of the *Ruhrschnellweg*; in 1958 it was replaced by a new transport plan, drawn up after detailed survey and after extensive consultations with all interested parties and with neighbouring planning associations (map 5.3). A survivor from the 1920s appears in the 1958 plan: it is the *Ruhrschnellweg*, now to be built to motorway standards to connect the great Hellweg cities. (Much of this work was actually completed during the 1960s, including the construction of complex and costly stretches of expressway within the cities.) The *Emscherschnellweg* would perform a similar function for the line of cities a few miles to the north; it would be built to similar standards. Another new east–west road, a motorway, would follow the line of the Lippe in the 'development zone' of the far north. The most important new feature of the 1958 plan, though, was the eleven new or improved north–south roads, which would play an important part in linking the development zone of the north with the core area. They include a new motorway to relieve the congested Federal Highway 51 through the central Ruhr east of Bochum – to be the new central axis of the Ruhr; a new link from Essen south-westwards to the main north–south Autobahn; a new north–south motorway to the west of Dortmund, leading to the recreation areas of the southern highlands; and an improvement of the north–south road through Duisburg in the west of the Ruhr, including a new urban motorway. Most of these roads were completed by the early 1970s. But, to deal with an anticipated growth of private car ownership which would almost double the ratio of cars to people between 1965 and 1980, the 1970 evaluation report on the General Traffic Plan for Nordrhein Westfalen envisages a massive further construction programme within the *Land* which would produce 8,700 km (5,500 miles) of improvements and 7,700 km (4,600 miles) of new road construction.

Public transport also receives a high priority in the work of the SVR and of the planners at *Land* level. Here the ambitious objective is to create an integrated system comprising the electrified S-Bahn network of the German Federal Railways, lining the major centres of the whole Rhine–Ruhr agglomeration, together with more local urban railways (some of them underground), with a total length of 1,100 km or 700 miles. The interchanges between the two systems, which will also link with bus systems, will involve ambitious and costly investments. Here the objective is to try and create local concentrations of employment, services, and high-density residential areas around the transportation nodes, thus bringing as many people as possible within easy access to the public transport system.

The other element in the plan is the critical 'green land' which will provide barriers guiding new development into the right places (map 5.4). The protection of this land has indeed for years been one of the outstanding achievements of the SVR, especially in the period of rapid suburban growth after the Second World War; as late as 1960

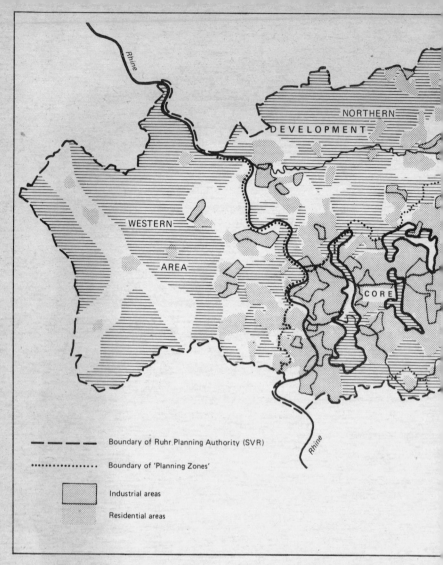

– – – – –	Boundary of Ruhr Planning Authority (SVR)
··············	Boundary of 'Planning Zones'
▨	Industrial areas
▦	Residential areas

only 22·0 per cent of the SVR area was built over (or 23·8 per cent including parks and playing fields), while no less than 71·1 per cent was still in agriculture or woodland. (The corresponding figure for the more densely developed core area was 47·7 per cent.) The green spaces, which have to be re-determined every three years, are based as far as possible on the surviving agricultural and woodland areas. They are designed so as to separate the major communities and to provide large recreation spaces next to the big cities. In the central highly congested zone, the policy is 'linkage': existing areas of open

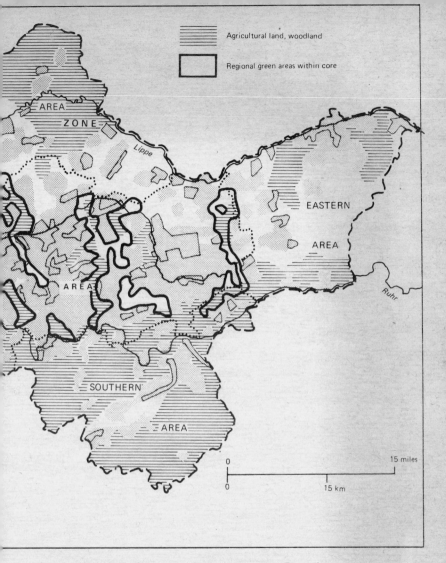

AREA
ZONE
Lippe
AREA
EASTERN
AREA
Ruhr
SOUTHERN
AREA

Agricultural land, woodland

Regional green areas within core

0   15 miles

0   15 km

5.4   *Ruhr development plan 1966: proposals for open space*. Protection
of open space against urban encroachment has long been one of the
most successful features of the Ruhr Planning Authority's regional
programme. Two main types of open land are especially important for
the regional plan. The first is the main north-south green wedges within
the congested core area, which separate the major cities and prevent
their sprawling into each other. They are based on existing woodland
and agricultural land and by running mainly north-south they will help
reduce air pollution. The second element is the large areas of open
recreational land which will be preserved in the more attractive areas of
the northern and southern periphery of the Ruhr region, including the
Ruhr Valley and the Rhine highlands to the south of it, and the fine
sandy heathlands around Haltern in the north.

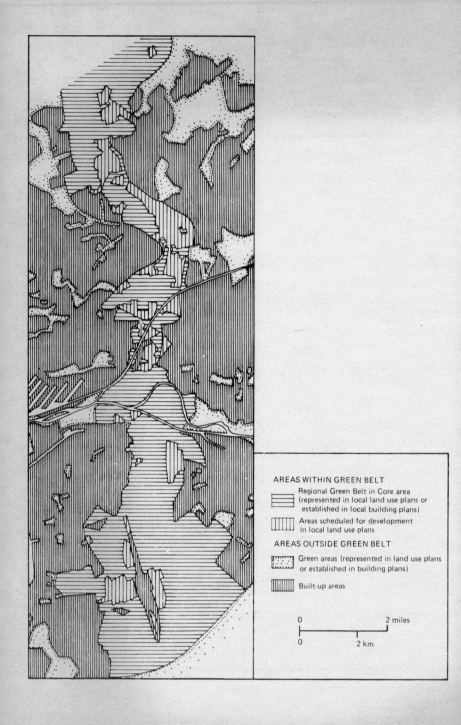

AREAS WITHIN GREEN BELT

Regional Green Belt in Core area
(represented in local land use plans or
established in local building plans)

Areas scheduled for development
in local land use plans

AREAS OUTSIDE GREEN BELT

Green areas (represented in land use plans
or established in building plans)

Built-up areas

0   2 miles

0   2 km

space are to be joined together in a north–south direction in order to separate one major city from the next, with east–west cross-links where feasible. The north–south barriers will run at right angles across the prevailing winds, and so help reduce the air pollution which is one of the most serious public health problems in the Ruhr (map 5.5). As far as possible they will include the existing recreation areas. Finally, large areas will be reserved for recreation in the more attractive parts of the peripheral zone of the Ruhr.

A very important element in the continuing work of the SVR following the 1966 Plan, in fact, is the implementation of these policies. In the period 1965–9 alone, 36 plan proposals were made and 28 approved, and by the end of that time some 29 square miles of green areas were legally established. They included the so-called *Revierparks* constructed and operated jointly by the SVR and individual Ruhr cities, of which the first opened in 1970. Another major proposal, for a regional leisure centre over 1 square mile in extent based on a reservoir behind a dam on the river Ruhr at Kemnade, was supported both by the *Land* government and an SVR-cities joint fund. In pursuit of these proposals the SVR has the power not merely to prevent new building but also to buy and demolish existing development; but the compensation involved is necessarily heavy, and this power is used sparingly.

The green belts in the Ruhr plan, however, will not deal with the problem of air pollution at source. This problem, as the 1968 Development Programme of the *Land* government stresses, is highly concentrated in the heavy industrial areas of Duisburg–Dinslaken–Oberhausen in the western Ruhr, Bottrop–Herne in the centre, and Dortmund–Lünen in the east. An ambitious and costly programme aims at the eradication, or substantial reduction, of emissions from about eighty of the worst offenders in these areas by 1973. There is also to be a major attack on pollution in the rivers – particularly the Emscher and Ruhr – through the construction of new purification plants.

5.5   *Ruhr development plan 1966 : green belt in the core area.*
A representative example of a north-south regional green belt which separates Duisburg (left) from Mülheim (right) in the southern (lower) half of the map, and Ruhrort-Hamborn (left) from Oberhausen (right) in the northern half. The plans referred to in the key are local development plans which are framed within the regional plan laid down by the Ruhr Planning Authority.

Some lessons from the Rhine–Ruhr cities

Of all the metropolitan regions described in this book, Rhine–Ruhr is the most heterogeneous and therefore the most difficult to describe within a small compass. Nevertheless, from this account some important points have emerged.

The first is that within any metropolitan region, the economic elements are apt to be very mixed indeed. One central characteristic of all world cities is their economic diversity, their lack of any single dominant economic base. Most of the varied economic elements contain the seeds of further growth; a few seem destined to decline. Therefore at any time some sectors of the metropolitan economy will grow, and with them the areas where they are concentrated; other sectors and areas will contract. Rhine–Ruhr is admittedly an extreme case, for no other metropolitan region contains a major coalfield in decline. But the same problem of decay-within-growth is seen on a less spectacular scale in many small-workshop industries of inner London, Paris or New York.

The second point concerns the inner form of Rhine–Ruhr. Here as in the Randstad is a multi-centred, or polycentric, metropolis. No single city in Randstad or Ruhr, in the early 1970s, contained as many as one million people; many major cities were much smaller, smaller even indeed than the leading provincial cities of other countries. (1970: Amsterdam 820,000, Rotterdam 679,000, the Hague 538,000; Cologne 848,000, Essen 698,000, Düsseldorf 664,000, Dortmund 640,000; 1971: Birmingham, England 1,015,000; 1968: Marseilles 889,000.) The polycentric form may seem strange to those people, especially those Europeans who live in countries dominated by a single metropolitan city. But not only is the polycentric metropolis a perfectly natural form, which has evolved over a period of history quite as long as the single metropolitan centre; in many respects, it appears a more viable form for the mid-twentieth century. Though Rhine–Ruhr and Randstad have traffic problems and journey-to-work problems, they are small compared with those of London, Paris or New York. Though they have problems of congestion of people and competition for scarce space, still it appears that they are much more capable of holding comfortably a large and sustained increase in population than the single-centred urban region. A region like Randstad or Rhine–Ruhr presents a tremendous challenge to the regional planner; but it is an exhilarating challenge, because there is a chance of a really satisfactory solution.

The third conclusion concerns the role of the metropolitan region in comparison with the country of which it forms a part. Comparisons of this sort are notoriously difficult because they depend on the definition of the metropolitan region; in Germany it is arguable that part of the population of the Ruhr coalfield is not 'metropolitan' in the strict sense at all. If this is accepted, it could be argued that the metropolitan region of Federal Germany is less prominent, in the size of its population and its share in the highest types of service industry, than are the London or Paris regions: that its role is diminished by the presence of great provincial capitals like Hamburg, Frankfurt, Stuttgart and Munich. Like the polycentric form, this importance of the provincial capitals stems from Germany's long tradition of political fragmentation; it has been fortified, since 1949, by the federal form of government. More centralised European countries may find it difficult to emulate the German example; but experience shows that such a radical change may be the only way in which planning can break the increasing hold of the centralised metropolis over national life.

A fourth conclusion concerns the machinery of regional planning. The SVR is unique not merely in Germany, but virtually in the world. Though other large metropolitan areas have regional planning commissions, hardly any other has one which covers such a wide area – incorporating not merely urban areas, but the surrounding recreational and environmental protection zones as well as land for future development – and which at the same time has really effective powers of development control over the constituent local authorities. So widely is the SVR regarded as a model in Germany that in 1968, a Ministerial Commission of the *Land* government of Nordrhein–Westfalen suggested that it be enlarged to cover the whole Rhine–Ruhr area of this chapter, with increased responsibilities. Though the proposal was rejected on the ground that the new authority would be too large and remote, it did recognise that for many planning purposes, Rhine–Ruhr is now a single planning whole.

6 Moscow

London, Paris, the Randstad, Rhine–Ruhr: all these great metropolitan regions belong to the world which, for lack of a more accurate and meaningful title, we call the capitalist world. The socio-economic historian might well conclude that in some way, they were a product of the evolution of capitalism. As chapter 1 has already argued, that view would not take account of the fundamental causes of modern urban growth. For the communist world has its giant metropolitan cities too; and no better example exists than the city which (despite Peking's insistent rival claims) may fairly be called the World City of communism. The city of Moscow, in 1970, had a population of over seven million; and it was the centre of a great urban complex containing satellite cities and towns, which altogether numbered well over nine million people. Thus after Rhine–Ruhr, Moscow is the greatest urban complex of continental Europe, and it is certainly the biggest complex based on a single city centre.

This fact may surprise western observers. But more surprising is Moscow's growth. The city's population was 360,000 in 1860, the year before Tsar Alexander II abolished serfdom, and 1·7 million in 1917, the year of the October revolution; by 1935, helped by the transfer of capital functions from Leningrad, it had risen to 3·66 million. At this point the authorities acted. The Central Committee of the Communist Party of the USSR had, in 1931, already declared itself against the further growth of big cities and from 1932 the policy was to restrict further industrial growth in Moscow and Leningrad. In the 1935 General Plan of Reconstruction for the City of Moscow, limitation of the city's growth was made into a central planning objective, perhaps for the first time in city planning history anywhere. The future population target was to be five million, which the city would reach eventually by natural increase alone; net immigration was to be cut to zero.

Table 11 The Moscow Region

	area square miles	population 1959	population 1970	population change 1959–70
City of Moscow (as enlarged 1960)	201	6,044,000	7,061,000	+ 1,017,000
40-mile ring*	5,328	3,033,000	3,656,600	+ 623,600
City plus 40-mile ring*	5,666	9,077,000	10,717,600	+ 1,630,600
Outside 40-mile ring*		1,872,700	2,117,900	+ 245,200
Moscow Oblast		4,905,700	5,774,500	+ 868,800
Moscow City plus Oblast		10,949,700	12,835,500	+ 1,885,800

* Involves estimates.

Even by the Census of 1939, despite close attempts to limit migration into Moscow for work, the city's population had reached 4·14 million – 80 per cent of the ultimate planning limit. The war undoubtedly brought some relief, because many activities and people were evacuated eastwards; yet by the first postwar Census of the Soviet Union, in 1959, Moscow's population had risen to 5,046,000 – a figure already above the ultimate 1935 limit. Nor was this any longer a meaningful figure; for on 18 August 1960 a decree more than doubled the area of the city, to incorporate the suburban areas which had grown up outside the former limits. Thus, by a stroke of the pen, nearly one million people were added to the city's population; and it became quite clear that the 'ultimate' target figure of 1935 had long been passed. By the 1970 Census the population of the extended city had reached 7,061,000, having added over one million in the eleven years since the previous census – a rate comparable with that of many western European capitals. Though much of it may well represent natural increase of the city's own population, in most years there has been a balance of in-migration which has made Moscow a city of young, working-age people. And this seems to have been unplanned and unexpected, to judge by the fact that only a year before the Census an official population estimate gave a total over 400,000 fewer.

However, even this extended City of Moscow is only part of a much larger urban whole (map 6.1). According to the Soviet geographer Mischenko, in 1959 no fewer than nine million people lived in the

region within about 40 miles of central Moscow; by 1970 this total
had swollen to 10·7 million (see table 11). Of course not all these
people have a functional relationship with Moscow. The Soviet
geographer Davidovich, in 1961, made a careful estimate of the
population of the Soviet 'satellite cities' (*goroda-sputniki*), defined as:

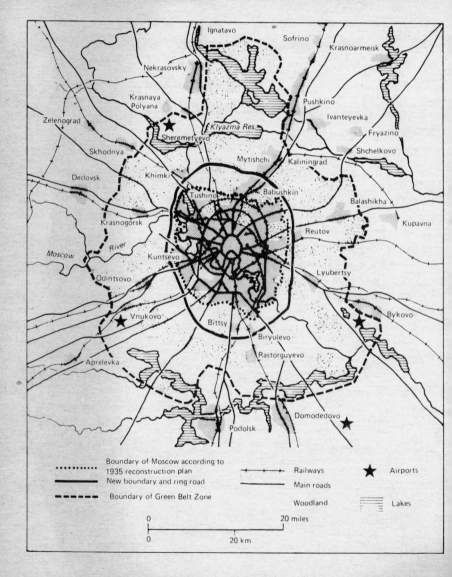

'those cities, towns and villages that develop around a large central city and are related to it by common features in the life of the population – commuting to places of employment and for cultural and other service purposes (the second order satellites)'. It is clear that this definition is very close to that used by International Urban Research to delimit their functional metropolitan area, which gave a 1959 population of 7,884,000. Within the 40-mile ring virtually all the growth of 1,631,000 since 1959 had been in the satellite towns. The *sputniki* should not be regarded as planned satellites like the British new towns – though some of the most recent of them do serve a similar function. The older ones were developed immediately after the 1935 plan, as part of the limitation of the city's growth. Many are one-industry towns specialising in a single branch of engineering.

Some *sputniki* are considerable towns in their own right: for instance Mytishchi (119,000 in 1970) and Lyubertsy (139,000), which are part of the Green Belt ring, and Podolsk (169,000), Elektrostal (123,000) and Noginsk (104,000), outside it. They are grouped along the main railway lines, and some even merge together, especially along the earliest-electrified lines. The nearest of them – towns within 20 miles from the centre, and only 50–55 minutes' travelling time away – are, many of them, big commuter towns: Odintsovo, Balaskikha, Pushkino. They send 600,000 commuters into Moscow every working day. But, by the late 1960s, the commuting ring had broadened to take in towns like Serpukhov, Mozhaisk and Kashira – up to 60 miles distant and up to 2 hours' travelling time away. In fact, by 1970 it could be said that the satellite ring was becoming co-terminous with the Moscow administrative unit, or oblast; this, together with the city, had a 1970 Census population of no less than 12,835,000, representing an increase of no less than 1,886,000 since 1959. Again, virtually all the growth had occurred in the *sputniki*.

Moscow's future

Official Soviet policy is still to restrain city growth – Moscow's in particular. But that limitation does not extend to the surrounding

6.1 *Moscow: the city and the region.* Moscow's city limits were extended in 1960 up to the ring motorway, then under construction. The population of the extended city was then over 6 million. But outside this, within the 10-mile-wide Green Belt zone and beyond, the satellite towns (*goroda-sputniki*) had close commuting and other ties with the city, and brought the population of the functional urban region up to about 8 million.

suburban ring, where extensions of existing towns, and the development of new *sputniki*, are seen as ways of channelling city growth outside the city limits. Soviet planners do not see the continued growth of the capital region as somehow perilous to the nation's economic and social health, as British or French planners might. Metropolitan congestion, which obsesses west European planners, is a barely comprehensible idea in a country as big as the Soviet Union; the aim is rather to channel more people and resources into the still phenomenally underdeveloped east. This aim has been pursued with some success, for between the 1939 and 1970 Censuses virtually the whole of the net population increase of Soviet Russia occurred east of the Urals. But between 1959 and 1970, this eastern area accounted for only 2·8 million of the 32·9 million net national increase; the industrialised west recorded a 12·9 million growth and the warmer climatic areas of the south west no less than 17·2 million. In the USSR as in the USA, it seemed, population growth was following the sun.

But broad regional analysis omits what is perhaps the most significant feature of Soviet population growth: the growth of the cities. In 1939, 32 per cent of the Soviet Union, 60·4 million, was classed as urban; in 1959, 48 per cent, 99·8 million; in 1970, 56 per cent, 136·0 million. The biggest cities, those with over 100,000 people, accounted for 75 per cent of the total urban population growth in this latter period. Further, despite the creation during the 1960s of some 800 new communities, five-sixths of the urban increase of 36 million took place in older cities.

Some three-fifths of the total increase in urban population, between 1939 and 1959, represented migrants from the countryside; in the period 1959–70 natural increase and migration were more evenly balanced. This great shift out of agriculture is common to all peasant or ex-peasant countries, in both eastern and western Europe; it has contributed to the growth of Paris, the Randstad, and Rhine–Ruhr too; and in the USSR as elsewhere, it will continue – at least up to 1980 when it is expected that the same percentage of the labour force will work in agriculture as in the USA. (In 1968, 29 per cent of the total labour force was still in agriculture and forestry: a very high proportion by western standards.) This shift will benefit all other sectors, including manufacturing and construction, but above all the service industries like education and public health, or trade, public catering and supply. Here today there is a sharp divergence between American and Soviet employment patterns: the United States employs 20 per cent of its labour force in the distributive sector, the Soviet Union (in 1968) 7 per cent. The Soviet planners claim that the American figures represent a waste of labour resources, but they are providing for a rapid increase in their own figures; for the distributive system is on their own admission still inadequate, and consumption was supposed to increase by nearly two-thirds in the 1959–65 Plan period alone. According to documents prepared for the 22nd Party Congress in 1961, the net increase in the able-bodied population of working age up to 1980 would be almost wholly swallowed up by increases in so-called 'non-productive' employment like education, public health and other public utilities. (The terms 'productive' and 'non-productive' refer to a distinction in Marxist economics; roughly, any activity leading to the consumption of *goods* – including many commercial activities – is 'productive'.) In 1976, it was stated that about half of total employment in Moscow was in the 'non-productive' sector; in fact 1970 statistics showed that close on 70 per cent was in service industries, though these included some ancillary service workers in manufacturing plants.

In the capitalist west observers are all too aware of the fact that many service trades tend to be disproportionately concentrated in the metropolitan cities. It is difficult to discover how far this is also true of the Soviet Union; but there are some pointers. One concerns the administrative machine. Up to 1957 the vast Soviet planning apparatus was highly centralised in Moscow. Then, a fundamental reversal took place: major economic planning went to the economic planning regions, originally sixteen in number but then increased to eighteen. Of course many of these regions are concentrated in the Moscow area and the areas around it, especially to the south; for this central region contains almost one-fifth of the population of the USSR and more than one-quarter of its industry. But the net effect has been to take many administrative planning decisions out of Moscow, and to put them in the provincial cities.

In other activities within the service sector, possibilities for decentralisation may be more limited. Moscow remains the main transport focus of Soviet Russia, with eleven main radiating railways and two major airports – Vnukovo and Sheremetyevo (which supplanted Vnukovo as the international airport in 1960), supplemented since March 1964 by a new airport, one of the world's biggest, at Domodedovo. Moscow is the centre of all forms of entertainment, from the Moscow Arts Theatre and the Bolshoi Ballet to the great new all-Union television station at Ostankino, which was started in August 1963 and completed in 1967. This station not only provides the central technical link between the existing television networks in the USSR; it contains also a large administrative building, to house all the editorial offices of the USSR central television system. Moscow is also the unquestioned centre of the USSR's developing tourist trade, with an ambitious programme of hotel construction, including one 6,000-guest hotel – the Rossya, Europe's biggest – completed in 1967. The USSR's very extensive range of higher educational institutions also shows a pronounced clustering in Moscow – especially the higher research institutions. Here are found the USSR Academy of Sciences with its many specialised sections, the Lenin Library (largest in the USSR and in the world), the Moscow University with 40,000 students, more than fifty specialised institutes of higher education, three hundred scientific research institutes, and the Lenin Museum. Altogether, scientific workers numbered 233,000 in 1971; one-quarter of the total for the USSR. There were also 600,000 students in higher education. In 1962 the chief city architect of Moscow, M.Posokhin, admitted that although industry could develop technologically with an actual reduction in the labour force, the chief problem in controlling Moscow's growth lay with the research institutions, design organisations and bureaux.

In factory industry Moscow's attractive power is less sure, though in the late 1950s the Moscow region still accounted for 20 per cent of the total industrial output of the USSR – Moscow city alone for 16 per cent. The traditional industry of the Moscow region, textiles, has been somewhat displaced since the October revolution by the engineering group of industries – the most characteristic growth industry of modern metropolitan cities the world over. By 1970 over 55 per cent of total manufacturing employment was in the engineering and metal processing group. These industries have shown the largest increases in volume of production of all industrial groups in the USSR since 1917. Especially during their period of rapid growth under the early Five-Year Plans, skilled labour proved to be the limiting factor in their development; and in so far as this labour existed, it was concentrated in the Moscow region. So, critical decisions were taken to set up plants here; the existence of the plants created complexes of component suppliers (thirty-four factories in the Moscow area produce components for the Gorki motor-car plant, 400 miles away), and the complexes cannot now easily be shifted. Besides vehicle and vehicle component manufacture, which are still disproportionately concentrated in the Moscow–Gorki region, other important Moscow industries include machine tools, precision instruments like watches and calculating machines, and consumer goods like refrigerators and sewing machines. Of these, machine tools employed most workers in 1970, though instrument-making had grown fastest in the previous decade – indicating the increasingly science-based character of Moscow industry.

Admittedly, industrial expansion has occurred rapidly east of the Urals. By 1960, for instance, well over one-third of all Soviet machinery was produced there. But it appears that a great deal of this activity represents the production of heavy goods which incorporate local raw material and which may be uneconomic to send over long distances – construction equipment, power station equipment, mining and chemical plant. The same goes for other types of industry. Current Soviet plans for the development of the eastern regions – eastern Siberia for instance – visualise them chiefly, for a long time ahead, as producers of cheap fuel and power and of products incorporating that fuel and power: steel, ferro-alloys and synthetic chemicals. Industries needing a great deal of skilled labour, including many of the fastest-growing science-based assembly industries, will continue to grow in the Moscow area – especially in the satellite towns outside the city, but within about 30 miles. And it will be a long time before eastern Siberia takes over traditional Muscovite staples like printing and publishing.

These principles of planned location are still highly generalised. It cannot be said that up to now Soviet planners have evolved any more sophisticated and precise theory of the economics of industrial location. Indeed, the Head of the Department for the Study of Productive Forces in the USSR State Planning Commission, A. Probst, declared in 1963 that: 'the level of substantiating the most rational location is still low ... the economic aspects of planning should be improved'. The main reason for the failing was 'the weak development of the theory of the location of socialist production, from the fact that economic science lags behind the practice of socialist construction'. Papers on the subject of location, Probst complained, were too often hopelessly generalised and diffuse; precise studies of the factors of location, which attempted to analyse quantitatively the interdependence of the factors of location, were extremely scarce. Probst's attack reflects the Soviet economic planners' new awareness of the possibilities of close statistical and mathematical analysis, with the aid of computers, of problems such as location. Eventually these methods may have spectacular results, in the form of global analyses of the total costs and benefits of location in big cities. But it will be some years before they can begin to have a noticeable effect on actual planning decisions. Until then, Soviet industrial managements in a wide range of processing industry will doubtless find it to their private advantage to expand production in the big urban centres if they can, whatever the social costs that have to be paid by the rest of the community. Repeated complaints occur in the Soviet press, not least in Moscow, about the cavalier way in which big industrial enterprises ignore planning and architectural requirements. Undoubtedly many features of Soviet economy and society contribute to this: the tremendous premium put until recently on production at the expense of almost any other consideration; the division of responsibility for many aspects of urban construction between different ministries and authorities, frequently with contradictory interests; and the relative weakness of the city planning organisations themselves. Since 1957, with the movement towards more effective regional devolution and co-ordination of powers, matters seem to have improved somewhat; but progress is still slow. In 1962 the Moscow Chief City Architect was still complaining that many industrial enterprises in the city had no long-range general plan for development; though an integral plan for modernisation and development of industry should be linked with a city reconstruction plan, departmental barriers still blocked co-ordination.

Planning within the Moscow region: the housing drive

Within the Moscow region, planning is the responsibility of a special organisation: the Institute of the General Plan (GLAV APU MOSKVA). In west European or North American terms, the Institute is a regional planning organisation. It is concerned with the broad problems of employment, population, housing, communications, open space and the green belt, and the planning of satellite towns within the Moscow region. It works through plans on a scale of 1:10,000 – roughly equivalent to the six-inch scale on which town maps are drawn in the British development planning process – which are monitored by a state planning agency

(GOSGRAJDANSTROI, the Committee of State for Civil Construction and Architecture); after approval the plans are handed over for detailed development to a building organisation, MOSSTROI, organised in thirteen sections covering various sectors of the city. The Institute uses varied skills: it employs economists, geographers, demographers, engineers and architects.

The broad objectives of planning are clear. Within the city limits as extended in 1960 – that is within the belt motorway, which was opened in 1962 and which completely encircles the city at a radius of about eleven miles from the centre – the intention (not realised in the event) has been to stabilise population, and the emphasis is on a re-housing programme of awe-inspiring scale, and speed of execution. It is clear that during the Stalinist period, despite the ambitious schemes outlined in the 1935 Moscow Plan, housing took a low priority behind military needs and the development of industry. As a result, after the Second World War the USSR suffered from an acute deficiency of urban housing: Maurice F. Parkins has estimated that on average there were 4·02 persons to each habitable room in 1950. But in 1956 the Twentieth Congress of the Communist Party of the Soviet Union decreed an end to the housing shortage within twenty years – thereby marking, perhaps, the first significant shift in emphasis towards consumer goods in Soviet planning. Overall, throughout the whole period 1956–70, housing production was remarkably even at around 2·3 million dwellings per year, of an average size of 42–42·5 m^2 (452–7 square feet), making the USSR the world's most prolific housebuilder. In Moscow alone 3,793,000 Muscovites were housed in new flats in the decade 1961–71, the flats being completed at the rate of 120,000 per year; by 1970 54 per cent of families lived in housing completed after 1960; the total floorspace doubled between 1965 and 1975. Most of this new housing was in the outermost zone annexed in 1959.

This extraordinary rate of progress was largely made possible by the development of industrialised building techniques using factory-built parts, assembled on site. By the end of the Seven-Year Plan in 1965 it was intended that 70 per cent of all construction in the Soviet Union would be of this type; and that 40 per cent would consist of large-panel assembly housing, which was introduced in 1959 and which represents the most radical example of assembly methods so far.

Soviet cities contain a mixture of public and private housing, and the private sector is larger than one might think: in 1957 almost exactly one-third of the total floorspace of urban housing consisted of individually built homes, and in 1959 slightly more than one-third of completed space came from the private source. Indeed Article 10 of the Soviet constitution specifically protects the rights of individual ownership, though the law specifies also that this right extends only to personal consumption: property cannot be used to derive an unearned income. But in practice, almost inevitably perhaps, there has been much violation of this rule, so that individual housing has run into disfavour with the authorities. In addition, private housing is condemned as wasteful of land; it is said to take three to five times as much land to house an equivalent number of people compared with four- or five-storey flats, with a consequent steep rise in servicing costs. In August 1962, therefore, the Central Committee of the Communist Party of the USSR and the Council of Ministers adopted a resolution which aimed at replacing the construction of individual housing, progressively, by multi-storey co-operative buildings. This applied to all towns and cities – beginning with the biggest cities where the problem of space was most acute. The co-operatives will be financed by a mixture of contributions from their members and state loans.

The aim of Soviet housing policy has been to eliminate the worst aspects of the housing shortage by 1970; by then, all families in overcrowded and substandard housing were to be rehoused. In order to fulfil the first stage of the programme, however, standards of space were deliberately cut to the minimum in 1958, so as to reduce the costs of construction per dwelling by up to 30 per cent and thus make possible an increase within the budget of nearly one-third in the number of dwellings built. This necessarily meant flats, during the 1959–65 planning period, with small halls, combined bathroom and lavatory, and some rooms reached only through other rooms. Space norms in Moscow in 1970 averaged 3 rooms totalling 60 m^2 (646 square feet) for a family of four; actual averages were much lower, less than 10 m^2 (108 square feet) per person. It is now planned to raise norms rapidly, to reach 1 room per person (22 m^2, or 240 square feet) by 1990; this is especially important for housing the bigger families, for whom the standard designs seem to provide rather inadequately at present.

The overriding need for economy has also produced an extraordinary degree of standardisation in the design and layout of the big new housing developments like the south-western district of

Moscow. More than 50 per cent of state housing in the early sixties, rising to between 70 and 75 per cent by the end of the seven-year planning period in 1965, consisted of four- and five-storey flats without lifts, which were said to be most economical. But already by the early 1960s in Moscow experiments were made with more varied designs – notably in the celebrated block 9 of the Noviye Cheremushki area of south-west Moscow, where four- and five-storey housing was laid out in an open design. And mixed developments, with some nine- and twelve-storey blocks for single people and childless couples, were being built. Higher buildings, with lifts, are particularly justified in the biggest cities like Moscow because of the higher costs of servicing the land; in Moscow it would be economical to put up fourteen-, fifteen-, and sixteen-storey buildings.

By the early 1970s this argument was generally accepted. By then the main emphasis was moving from construction of new housing areas on the Moscow outskirts, to urban renewal of older housing areas nearer the centre; and this was taking the form of high-rise blocks (15 storeys), rising from podia with shops and services, and leaving 80 per cent of the ground space open. In other sections, massive prefabricated blocks up to 30 storeys were planned with underground vehicle circulation and servicing. Ironically, this trend towards construction of architectural megastructures was occurring just at the point when in western countries – such as Britain and the United States – architectural ideas were moving in the opposite direction.

The residential areas: failure in planning

Detailed planning of Soviet residential areas is based on the fundamental concept of the 'micro-district' (*mikrorayon*). The Russian word *rayon* means a 'district'; it is also used to indicate an administrative district, roughly of the same order as a 'borough' in British or American practice. The city of Moscow has 29 such *rayons*; the new town of Zelenograd makes a thirtieth. Because of this the word *mikrorayon* is sometimes translated, misleadingly, as 'micro-borough'.) These areas are ideally between 75 and 125 acres in size, housing between five and fifteen thousand people, together with necessary community services like public restaurants, nurseries, kindergartens, club rooms, public workshops, a library, a swimming pool and a park. The service radius of a micro-district is normally not more than 1,000–1,300 feet. Because most necessary everyday services can be found there, the city centre then has to provide merely specialised services – a department store, a cinema, a hotel, a car rental centre, higher grade schools and specialised cultural facilities. Clearly the essential idea of the micro-district is the same as that of the 'neighbourhood' in western planning practice: it is that of a unit of life based on local shopping and public services. But as too often in the west also, it appears that there is often a failure to develop the micro-districts as coherent wholes. Thus in Moscow the chief city architect has complained that areas are opened up without landscaping, site improvement work, sports facilities, or even sufficient shops, schools, nurseries or kindergartens. The root of the trouble, as a writer form Kharkov has explained, is the division of finance for different parts of the project among different enterprises – the Ministry of Education for schools and children's institutions, the Ministry of Public Health for hospitals and clinics, the Ministry of Communal Economy for public services and the Ministry of Communications for telephones. In 1963 it was agreed that the Moscow Inspection Service of the State Architectural and Construction control Corporation would not accept projects for use until all construction and landscaping work was finished.

The point about public services may be more important for Soviet planners than for western ones. For in the relatively near future, according to some Soviet ideologists, the transition to fully fledged communism will sharply reduce the traditional role of the family. Children will be brought up communally from an early age; and most meals will be taken not round the family table, but in a communal dining room. These ideas have been strongly put by the veteran economist, S.Strumilin; but it appears that there are strong social pressures from the younger generation for bigger flats with more private services. The debate is not yet over, either among Soviet architects or in the councils of the Communist party. In any event, Soviet planning philosophy is internally quite consistent: collective dwellings, public rather than private open space, public transport.

Though the concept of the micro-district has remained basic to Soviet ideas of planning since the 1930s, its physical expression has recently changed. The micro-district of the mid-1950s was still typically built in the form of blocks arranged round a closed rectangular courtyard, a type of planning all too familiar from many western housing schemes of pre-1939 vintage. In the USSR, combined with standardised building types and the pseudo-classicist architectural excesses inherited from the Stalin period, it produced an effect of crushing monotony and oppressiveness in some of Moscow's biggest housing projects, notably the enormous development on the Lenin Hills in south-west Moscow, which was being severely criticised in the Moscow press by 1960. Here, despite the hilly nature of the relief, the same rigid geometrical layout was followed everywhere, with only the most minor concessions to the nature of the terrain. Instead of being placed in separate buildings, the shops were put in the ground floors of the residential blocks, so that goods loading often had to take place via the central courtyards, and columns and service ducts within the shops got in the way of staff and customers. It was mistakes like these that led to the new emphasis in the late 1960s on 'three dimensional' planning of massive integrated structures in which servicing functions were buried underground.

Soviet traffic planning

The story of Soviet urban traffic planning is a curiously mixed one: a story of gigantic achievement and of equally colossal failure to seize opportunities. Ever since the 1935 plan, a major concern of Moscow's planners has been the recasting of the transport net. Moscow in 1935 had a typically continental European street plan, composed of straight radial roads, formal squares and ring boulevards. But many of the streets were narrow by twentieth-century standards. The 1935 plan therefore provided a scheme of street widenings and of new arteries which rivalled Haussmann's grandiose projects in nineteenth-century Paris. Though execution of the schemes was delayed by the war, it is evident that during most of Stalin's lifetime they took a much higher priority than more banal programmes like the provision of housing. The central area of Moscow is surrounded by a ring boulevard – the Sadovoye Ring – which was widened so that it rivals in scale many of the great *Ringstrassen* of Habsburg or Prussian capitals. It was lined by commercial and residential blocks. The radial streets which cut through the older (pre-1917) areas of housing, immediately outside the Sadovoye Ring, were similarly widened: the most notable was Gorki Street, which was transformed over a forty-year period from 1917 to 1958. Then, as an integral part of the suburban extension of Moscow in the postwar period, a number of the existing radial highways were developed as extensions of the inner street improvements. In this way Gorki Street was continued to the north west by an improvement of the Leningrad

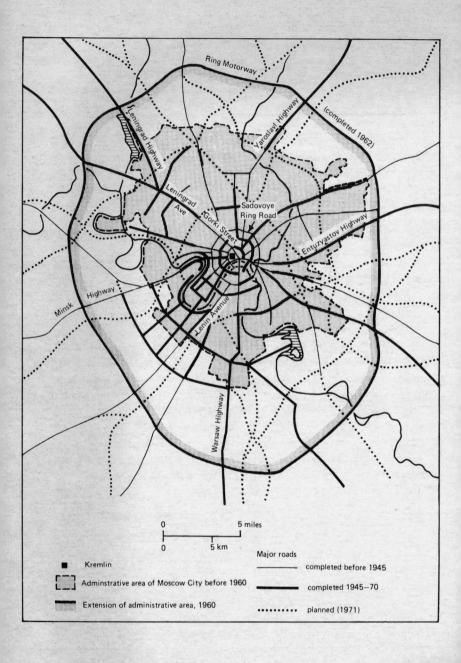

Ring Motorway

Leningrad Highway

Iaroslavl Highway

(completed 1962)

Leningrad Ave

Gorki Street

Sadovoye Ring Road

Entuzyastov Highway

Minsk Highway

Lenin Avenue

Warsaw Highway

0   5 miles
0   5 km

■ Kremlin

▨ Adminstrative area of Moscow City before 1960

▨ Extension of administrative area, 1960

Major roads

—————— completed before 1945

▬▬▬▬▬ completed 1945–70

••••••••• planned (1971)

Highway, partly renamed Leningrad Avenue, between 1945 and 1960. To the south west a completely new radial road, the Lenin Avenue, was developed in similar fashion across the Lenin Hills to serve as the central artery of the great south-western housing development (map 6.2).

Like Haussmann's planning, these developments were fundamentally monumental in their conception. There was little or no apparent understanding of the character of traffic, or of the needs of people who were to live or work or shop in such close proximity to the great radial traffic flows to and from the city. Despite the great width of the streets – over 300 feet from pavement to pavement – many intersections are simple signal-controlled crossroads, and there are delays at some of them. In the residential areas the new avenues are lined by residential blocks which are thus exposed to the maximum noise, dust and fumes. The monumental approach betrays itself also here in the exaggerated scale and heavy design of the façades, which derives from the mistakes made in the design for the Moscow University and other public buildings of the early 1950s. Although 'excesses' in architecture were condemned by a resolution of 1955, following the resolution of an all-Union architects' congress in 1954, they continued to persist in designs up to 1960 and perhaps even later.

The call in the Soviet Union in the 1960s – it was repeated again and again in the press – was for free planning of the residential blocks themselves around their service cores and their open spaces. Through traffic will be segregated on express arteries, with separation of different types of traffic at different levels, and with no direct frontage development. These roads will separate the residential districts, and will run through open land between them; the housing areas will be reached by distributor roads, which will separate each micro-district from the next. In the inner areas two-level intersections have been built at the most important points of traffic conflict, as along the Sadovoye Ring and at Red Square. New roads like Leningrad Avenue are being similarly improved. There is a new concern about the right relation between land use and traffic generation: press

6.2 *Moscow: road planning.* From 1935 until the late 1950s, with a break only during the war, the Moscow authorities carried through a prodigious programme of road improvements, widening the old streets to create a network of broad arterial boulevards. But traffic engineering was often sacrificed to monumental effort, and the main effort in the 1960s and 1970s has been to improve traffic flow by building two-level intersections. A start has been made on a middle ring road connecting the main railway stations and industrial areas.

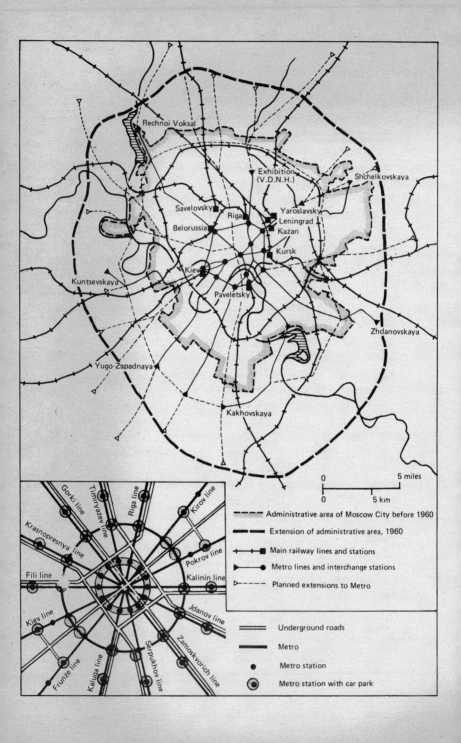

Rechnoi Voksal

Exhibition
(V.D.N.H.)

Shchelkovskaya

Savelovsky
Riga
Yaroslavsky
Leningrad
Belorussia
Kazan

Kursk

Kiev

Kuntsevskaya

Paveletsky

Zhdanovskaya

Yugo-Zapadnaya

Kakhovskaya

0   5 miles

0   5 km

▨▨▨▨ Administrative area of Moscow City before 1960

━ ━ ━ Extension of administrative area, 1960

+━┿━■ Main railway lines and stations

▶━━● Metro lines and interchange stations

▽- - - Planned extensions to Metro

═══ Underground roads

━━━ Metro

● Metro station

◉ Metro station with car park

Gorki line
Timiryazev line
Riga line
Kirov line
Krasnopresnya line
Pokrov line
Fili line
Kalinin line
Kiev line
Jdanov line
Frunze line
Zamoskvorich line
Serpukhov line
Kaluga line

criticism is directed at the narrow streets and the lack of parking spaces around the big central Moscow department stores, or at the bad siting of the Dynamo Stadium next to the Leningrad Avenue. Some of these mistakes, though, are not likely to be corrected easily. For the future, Moscow traffic planners have developed some extraordinarily advanced ideas, with deep level traffic tunnels connecting the city centre to the main district centres, linked to underground garages and to sub-surface highways which will relieve the existing rings and radials (map 6.2a).

It is evident that in recent years Soviet planners have begun to face the consequences of an automobile revolution. If so, they are doing so well in advance. In 1969, the total number of cars in Moscow was only 100,000, or one for each 730 of the population; this rose to 250,000 (1 in 290) by 1974 and is planned to rise to 1 million (1 in 70) by 1990. The Soviet idea of a 'reasonable' future proportion was one car to ten to fifteen people, or three to five families. This is a low ratio compared with western projections; but the Soviet planners claimed that it will be adequate because they planned to introduce popular motoring, probably between 1970 and 1980, not by private ownership but through the very extensive development of car-hire schemes and taxi pools. The Moscow car-hire service already had eleven thousand subscribers in 1960, and was developing rapidly. But then came a major policy reversal, with the decision to speed up production of private cars and to build a gigantic Fiat plant at Togliatti on the Volga. By 1975 it was expected that production of private cars would reach up to 1,300,000 a year – nearly four times the 1970 total. As a result, it has been estimated that rush hour traffic flows might rise by 50–100 per cent.

For the great majority of journeys, especially work journeys but including many leisure-time journeys, Soviet thinking is still in terms of generous investment in a cheap and efficient public transport system. Most observers seem to agree that at present, the Moscow city transport system justifies the claims made for it. By the standards of most western cities, investment in the Moscow Metro system for

6.3   *Moscow: railways.* The Metro system will be rapidly extended to 350 km (220 miles) by the mid-1980s, while the suburban railways will be upgraded by express tracks and connected to the Metro at new interchanges in the outer parts of the city. *Inset: Moscow: future Metro development, and the underground road net.* Plans for 2000 include connecting the new peripheral district centres with the inner ring road (Sadovoye Ring).

instance is prodigious. By 1971, 170 kilometres were complete; it was proposed to increase this to 350 kilometres by the mid-1980s and then to build a second system of similar proportions, linked to the first at key interchanges (map 6.3).

The Metro is fundamentally a city service; it provides a system that is very frequent (every 80 seconds at peak hours), very capacious (70,000 passengers an hour in one direction at the peak) and very cheap (maximum fare 4p). But it extends only some 18 kilometres (12 miles) from the centre, within the city limits. Beyond this, for the wider zone of the green belt and the satellites there are commuter services from the main-line terminal stations, which have been completely electrified and which are serious contenders for the title of the world's best commuter service. One such service, between Yaroslavl station and Mytishchi (eleven miles), runs for all but ninety minutes of a twenty-four hour day, with an on-peak service of twenty-two or twenty-three trains per hour and an off-peak service of fifteen per hour. Of course, 'on-peak' and 'off-peak' are relative terms in the Soviet Union: because of frequent shift working and staggered hours, even during daytime off-peak hours about one-half of the seats are occupied at the Moscow end of the trip. These lines carry very heavy commuter flows – 600,000 a day from the satellite ring into Moscow – and commuting times are long, averaging 77 minutes. Plans provide for extra tracks to give express services, cutting typical journey times to 40 minutes; there will be 22 direct interchanges with the Metro system in the outer parts of the city, of which 7 had been completed in the early 1970s. Latterly the idea has been mooted of linking Metro lines, in the suburbs, with surface railway stations, so as to provide direct and easy interchange in the inner suburbs.

The Green Belt and the satellites

The great housing areas of the Moscow suburbs are all found within the 66-mile-long belt motorway, which was opened in 1962 and which rings the city at a radius of about 11 miles from the centre. This is the city boundary against the Moscow district (*oblast*); it forms the inner boundary of the Green Belt, which was first proposed in the 1935 Plan as a ring 6 miles wide, surrounding the city. Since 1960 work has proceeded rapidly to develop this belt into a readily accessible recreation area for the city, a project warmly urged by Mr Khrushchev. The particular concern of the Soviet planners in this zone is that continued pressure for the construction of individual summer *dachas* would eat rapidly into the available green land. It has been calculated that if every Muscovite received land to build a *dacha*, the result would mean building over an area four times that of the present city. Current policy, therefore, is to prohibit further *dacha* construction in the Green Belt, but instead to develop a variety of public accommodation, ranging from hotels through hostels to simple camps, with public restaurants as well as kitchens for families who want to cook their own food. Also available will be a wide range of services – kindergartens, athletic grounds, boat and yacht cruises, dance halls and parking lots. In keeping with the Soviet emphasis, the areas will be connected by frequent public transport services from central Moscow; there will be Metro extensions, special high-speed electric trains, and even express boats. In one such centre, the Klyazma Reservoir north of Moscow, the first hotel opened in summer 1963, and was immediately followed by two others. A hutted summer camp, nearby, costs only one-quarter as much to live in as the hotel. Eventually all the developments at this centre will hold up to 200,000 visitors a day.

But the future of the Green Belt is still a matter of concern. In 1962 Moscow's chief architect. M.Posokhin, was still having to demand that construction must be strictly controlled, and prohibited on undeveloped land; and that the existing satellite towns within the Belt, which send 400,000 commuters a day into central Moscow, must be reconstructed so as to introduce more work opportunities. In particular, the many old houses in these towns could be reconstructed to house research and design organisations. Evidently, then, office decentralisation is not merely a concern of the western world.

These *goroda-sputniki* do not lie only within the Green Belt zone; most of them are beyond its outer edge. The term, as the Russians use it, is ambiguous. Most of the satellites are not planned: they grew up first in the pre-revolutionary period, as part of the nineteenth-century industrial development of the wider Moscow region, but then expanded prodigiously after 1917, particularly as a result of the growth of the engineering industries. A few were consciously created by the Soviets themselves as part of the policy of relieving the pressure of industry and population within the city itself. These include Elektrostal, Khimki and Krasnogorsk. Most interesting of all is the new planned satellite town of Zelenograd, eighteen miles north west of Moscow on the main railway line to Kalinin and Leningrad, and just beyond the main international airport of Sheremetyevo, which was started in 1960. The basic idea here is the same as that behind London's New Towns, in the immediate post-1945 period: industry and population are being developed together in a self-contained community. The industries that have come here are high-technology ones like electronics, radio and precision engineering; they have close links with the city itself, so they cannot be moved far, but it is undesirable to leave them to grow within the congested city.

Zelenograd is planned in micro-districts which in concept closely resemble the neighbourhoods of the older British New Towns. Each is based on a school which provides the basic eight years of Soviet education: other, more specialised education is provided on a whole-town basis. The green spaces between the blocks open out into the garden of the micro-district, which in turn merges with the forest outside the town. Schools and kindergartens and nurseries are at the forest edge, farthest from the road. The housing is of various types to suit the needs of different family groups. The net residential density of population in the residential areas is 180 people on each acre, more than double the 'higher densities' which were being recommended for British New Towns in the early sixties.

Zelenograd was originally planned with a target population of 65,000; by 1975 the total had already reached 120,000 and was growing at 10,000 a year. The new target was 200,000, with the possibility of creating a polycentric 'social city' on the lines that Ebenezer Howard suggested in his pioneer work on garden cities.

Moscow 2000: the 1971 and 1973 Plans

Despite a fundamental difference of philosophy, Moscow's planners face many of the same problems and uncertainties as their western counterparts. They are unsure about future population growth, including both natural increase (which is among the lowest in the world) and migration to the Moscow region; about the type of economic growth, in particular the development of the service sector in which the Soviet Union still lags; about conflicts between economic growth and environmental protection; about the balance between wholesale urban renewal and conservation of the city's historic fabric.

Most of all, they are concerned for the future form and internal coherence of their vast urban region. Soviet urban planning dogma has always accepted the radial-concentric form of development – though the green belt itself, a borrowing from British planning principles of the 1930s, disturbs the principle. Continuing growth of population and employment, albeit more slowly than in other parts of the Soviet Union, means that increasing numbers of Muscovites must find homes and jobs outside the city limits – a majority, in fact, by the year 2000. So the future organisation of this growth is a matter for intense debate.

Within the city limits, the problem is easier: growth by the mid 1970s was largely over, the inner and parts of the middle ring were declining in population, and the future intention was first to stabilise population at around 7·3 million, then to allow slow decline. Here, therefore, the main future emphasis is on restructuring.The 1971 General Plan for the Development of Moscow, approved by the Central Committee of the Communist Party and the Council of Ministers, starts from the position that decentralisation from the city will continue. Progressively, the city will be developed in a polycentric way: the city centre will be balanced by seven peripheral centres, each serving a sector of the city with between 600,000 and 1,200,000 people, which are in turn subdivided into districts of 200,000–400,000 people. These centres will provide the higher order services, which at present are unduly concentrated in the city centre – and thus will permit the evolution of the service sector of Moscow's economy while conserving much of the historic centre's urban fabric. The centres themselves will be located astride major transportation junctions, where the suburban commuter railways make direct connections with the city Metro system; in future, they will be directly linked to a deep-level highway system which will provide direct access to the city centre. Around them, the city sectors will be demarcated and divided by green belts and wedges, which will follow natural lines – especially the Moscow river and its tributaries – to penetrate right in to the heart of the city (map 6.4).

But it is in the zone outside the city limits – in the belt of satellite towns, and beyond – that the major future choices lie. Consequently, the 1971 city plan was followed in 1973 by a plan for the entire region. This considered four major alternatives for future growth (map 6.5 a–d). One would consist of more or less spontaneous growth in the form of concentric rings round the city, which would lead to erosion of the green belt. A second would be based on preservation of the green belt plus the creation of satellite towns within about thirty miles of the centre, on the model of Abercrombie's 1944 plan for London. A third would be based on the development of preferential axes

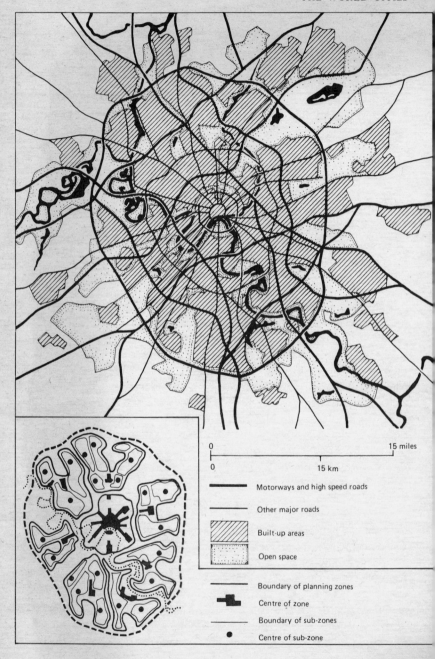

0 ————————————————————————— 15 miles

0 ————————————————————————— 15 km

——————— Motorways and high speed roads

——————— Other major roads

▨▨▨ Built-up areas

▧▧▧ Open space

——————— Boundary of planning zones

◆ Centre of zone

——————— Boundary of sub-zones

● Centre of sub-zone

outside the green belt, based on major transportation lines. A fourth would develop large growth centres, housing 400,000 or 500,000 people apiece, at distances of about thirty miles from the centre; this last, which has clear affinities to the Paris plan of 1965 and the British South East strategy of 1970, is the preferred solution. Particularly good possibilities for such centres exist in the north-west, west, south-east and south sectors; and only four or five such major centres would be needed to house the expected growth in this ring down to the end of the century.

Table 12 Growth of the Moscow region, in the 1973 Regional Plan

	1973	1985/90	2000
Moscow City	7·4	7·5	6·5
Green Belt ring	1·7	1·8	1·8
Internal (satellite) zone	2·0	2·9	3·8
External zone	2·3	3·3	4·5
Regional Total	13·4	15·5	16·6

Farther out still, in the external zone between 40 and 60 miles from the centre, there will be even more rapid growth as the medium-sized towns receive 1,000 industrial plants, decentralised from the city itself. But here a flexible kind of planning will suffice, based on the orderly growth of these towns; for open land will predominate well after the end of the century. Nevertheless, the preferred axes of growth – especially north-westwards (towards Klin and Voloko-lamsk), southwards (towards Serpoukov and Toula) and to the south-east (towards Kolomina and Riazan) – will receive a substantial share of the growth. Elsewhere, the existence of reservoirs, airports and other open land will limit the possibilities of growth – and thus the application of radial-concentric dogma.

The future of Soviet planning

For a verdict on Soviet urban planning so far, it is perhaps fairest to turn to the Soviets themselves. From the Soviet press the outsider receives an extraordinarily powerful impression of legitimate pride in

6.4 *Moscow: The 1971 Plan.* The city is to be restructured through the development of seven major district centres at major transport interchanges in the outer parts of the city, dividing the entire city into sectors separated by green wedges which will penetrate (especially along river valleys) into the heart of the system.

achievement, coupled with savage public criticism. Of course the
tradition of criticism, including self-criticism, is deeply rooted both in
the Russian character and in the Soviet way of life; for in a society
where almost everything is publicly managed, it is natural that

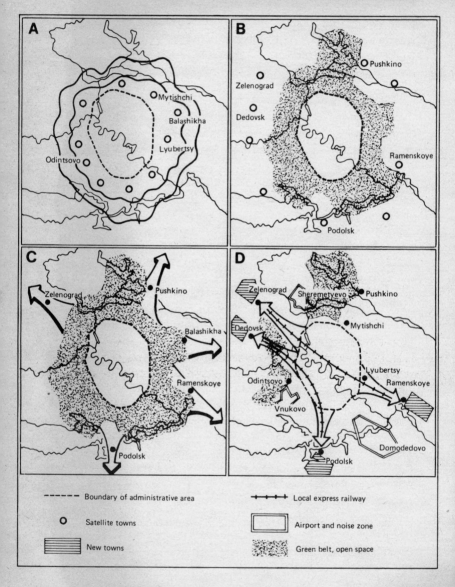

everything is publicly criticised. In the western world, if you do not like your grocer, you go to another grocer; in the Soviet Union, you write to *Izvestia* about him, and in a surprising number of cases *Izvestia* publishes your letter. The same goes naturally, on an even larger scale, for housing and urban planning, in which everyone has a lively interest.

From this debate two major weaknesses in Soviet planning had been exposed by the early sixties. One was the relatively poor quality of detailed development design, especially in the big housing projects. One of the major reasons, astonishingly, is that in most big city design workshops the overall design has been relegated to the most menial members of the staff. This in turn relates to a remarkable indifference to practical town planning within the Soviet Union itself, despite official enthusiasm and despite some notable pioneering examples such as the design for Volgograd (Stalingrad) in the early thirties. It is small wonder that outside the biggest cities there were not enough general plans, and that they were specially lacking in the fast-developing suburban zones outside the major cities. Thus industrial enterprises sprout on land that should have been used for recreation, large areas near the city are occupied by individual low-density housing, while often unplanned sand and gravel workings take place nearby. It is no wonder that in 1960 V.A.Kucherenko, Chairman of the USSR State Construction Committee, was calling for an immediate increase in the number of specialists – architects, landscape architects, civil engineers and economists – specialising in city planning.

The other weakness is perhaps even more serious: it is the apparent failure to develop adequate regional planning policies relating industrial growth, infrastructure services, and the development of old and new communities, for the regions embracing the major cities. In 1959 V.A.Kucherenko noted the continued growth of New York to thirteen and a half million people and of London to more than eleven million; 'no restrictive legislation,' he said, 'can curb the spontaneous growth of capitalist cities.' Under the conditions of the 'construction

6.5   *Moscow: 1973 Regional Plan Alternatives.* **A** Concentric growth (the 'oil splash' principle) invades the green belt. **B** Green belt and satellites, following the 1944 London plan. **C** Axial development along preferred transportation corridors. **D** Major growth centres along preferred corridors, at distances more than 50 km (30 miles) from the centre.

of communism', of course, problems of city growth were quite soluble, 'but in practice we do not always exploit the advantages that lie in the fact that ours is a planned state'. Despite the decrees issued by the Party Central Committee and the USSR Council of Ministers, the number of large cities with more than half a million people continued to grow. The general plans of many large cities still provided for 'unfounded' population growth; and the work being done in regional planning, in 1959, was 'quite feeble'. Work was being undertaken in thirty-seven areas but it was needed in at least eighty; Moscow is again a shining exception.

The big question concerns future urban scale. Soviet planners are currently exercised to discover the most economic size of urban unit – taking into account not only construction costs, but also the wider costs of servicing. Their studies, and practical experience, indicate that the optimum is in the range between two hundred and fifty and three hundred thousand people. This figure, much higher than that of the English New Towns, may arise from the high average Soviet densities, which make it possible to service a much bigger population within a given radius. At the same time, Soviet planners recognise the advantages of the very big city: better education and technical training, better cultural facilities, linkages between industries and services. They see the creation of satellites as the only way of retaining these advantages while avoiding suburban sprawl. There is general agreement on the siting of the satellites: they should be not less than 40–60 miles from the city, so that a generous Green Belt may ring the city itself, but not much farther, or they will lose their economic and cultural ties with the city. (On these criteria, Zelenograd is too near its parent city.)

Certainly, Moscow planners themselves do not think that the 1973 regional plan has fully resolved major outstanding issues. Unless a very rapid and smooth transfer of industrial plants out of the city can be engineered, there will soon be a problem of housing the workers; for the city is full up, and will soon have a declining population. More effective commuter rail services might delay the crisis, but not for long. The call then might be to allow further building close to the city – even in the green belt. Another question is how the traditional radial-concentric dogma can be modified to fit the different circumstances of a vast and complex city region, for which some form of polycentric solution is clearly appropriate. Related to this is a third unresolved problem: that of the connections between the city and its surrounding area, which daily become more frequent and more complex.

One point is evident: as in other great world cities, the administrative structures are no longer adequate. Only since 1973 have the city planners had any rights over development in the green belt and the internal ring. Some experts now think that there should be a regional authority responsible for all development in the region, and charged with responsibility for a regional plan. With the prospect of 100,000 hectares (nearly 250,000 acres) of new development down to the end of the century, some effective overall control is surely needed.

Soviet planning has clearly made mistakes in the past, and these are freely admitted. It could continue to do so in the future, but there is frank realisation of the scale of the problems – and also a large and enthusiastic cadre of specialists. The need now is for more effective regional integration of the economic and physical plans made by separate authorities. Given these, and given certain likely structural changes in the economy described earlier, it is likely that Soviet cities may increasingly resemble their better-planned western European counterparts, with some significant differences in social life. What seems certain, even if the Soviets do limit net immigration into the cities of European Russia, is that natural increase of urban population alone will lead to the further development of great and complex city regions, each embracing a central city, a Green Belt and a system of satellite towns bound by a variety of social, economic and cultural ties to the central city. Such giant urban areas are already a feature of Soviet life, as of life in the industrialised west; planners, of whatever political persuasion, are having to come to terms with the fact.

7 New York

Among the great urban agglomerations of the world, New York is second only to Tokyo. Its unique interest does not stem from that alone, but also from the fact that it is American: as the average income of the Metropolitan area is above that of the United States as a whole, it can demonstrate to other city-dwellers the sorts of problem which they may experience if they achieve American mass living standards. Thus it provides Europeans, in particular, with a sort of social laboratory where they can test both their assumptions about the cities they can expect in the future, and their plans for shaping these cities.

But the size is the most immediately striking feature. The United States Census of 1970 recognises a *New York–Northeastern New Jersey Standard Consolidated Area* – a union of no less than four contiguous Standard Metropolitan Statistical Areas, which are the units used to define comparable functional urban areas in the United States, plus two suburban counties in New Jersey. This Consolidated Area embraces seventeen counties in the States of New York and New Jersey, with an area of 3,931 square miles and a 1970 population of 16,178,700. A yet bigger area is the unit adopted for the study of transport problems by the *Tri-State Transportation Committee* – an area covering 7,912 square miles with a 1970 population of 18,980,457. Lastly, an even bigger area for analysing socio-economic trends and problems is the *Tri-State New York Metropolitan Region*, devised as long ago as 1922 by the Regional Plan Association of New York – a private association which in the 1970s was still the only body, official or unofficial, taking a serious and continuous look at the planning problems of the New York region as a whole. Their area stretches on average up to 100 miles from Times Square, conventional centre of the region; it embraces 12,928 square miles in 31 counties (three of which are in the State of Connecticut), and had a 1970 Census population of 19,747,964 (map 7.1).

Most of the problems of this vast region stem, paradoxically, from rapid economic and social advance. They spring from the increasingly complex nature of the United States economy, which causes large and rapid shifts in the composition of the labour force; from the high living standards which this economy guarantees for the great majority of Americans; from the social strains set up by the continuing existence of an undereducated, underskilled, underpaid and underprivileged minority, which is a particularly acute problem in New York; from the failure of local administration to evolve in line with the rapidly changing social and economic structure of the region. These problems will most readily emerge from a bird's eye view of the entire region, working outwards from centre to periphery.

Manhattan: congestion at the centre

Of the world's great metropolitan cities, two alone are distinguished by being centred upon an island. They are New York and Hong Kong, and both these cities draw an extraordinary combination of advantages and disadvantages from the fact. It was no accident that both became great world ports – New York the world's greatest. The southern tip of Manhattan Island between the Hudson and the East rivers – the area first occupied by the Dutch in 1615 – was bounded on two sides by open water, offering unsurpassed facilities for loading and unloading ships. Logically, warehousing and wholesale trade gathered in this tiny triangular area; with equal logic, risk-bearing finance developed in the same place to serve the shipping men; and even before the revolution of 1776, New York's 'Downtown' was established. Today, some 400,000 workers still congregate, every working day, in the three-fifths of a square mile of skyscrapers which cluster between the cavernous streets of the Wall Street area. Some wholesalers still remain in this colony; but those requiring space, for the storage of bulky goods, have been forced out by steadily rising rents, and Wall Street is dominated above all by banking and by certain types of insurance.

Up to about 1880, finance and wholesaling were the most characteristic activities of any commercial metropolis. But then, rapidly, American cities were transformed by the 'bureaucratic revolution' which has already been described in chapter 1 of this book. About 1880, railroads and financial trusts began to set up

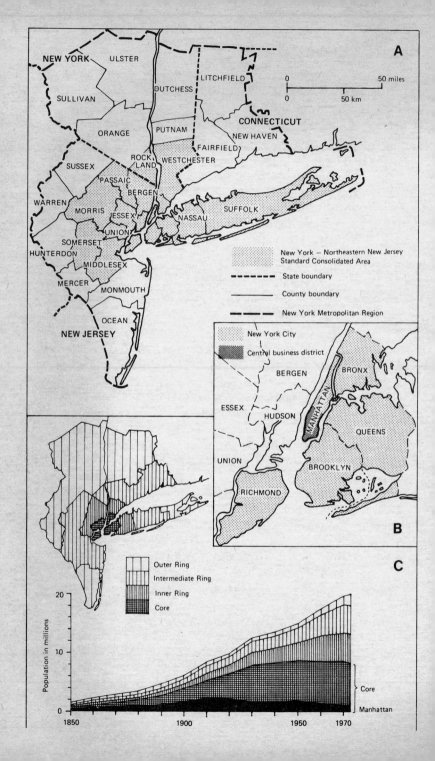

NEW YORK
ULSTER
SULLIVAN
ORANGE
SUSSEX
PASSAIC
BERGEN
WARREN
MORRIS
ESSEX
UNION
SOMERSET
HUNTERDON
MIDDLESEX
MERCER
MONMOUTH
OCEAN
NEW JERSEY

DUTCHESS
LITCHFIELD
PUTNAM
CONNECTICUT
NEW HAVEN
FAIRFIELD
ROCK-LAND
WESTCHESTER
NASSAU
SUFFOLK

A

0   50 miles
0   50 km

New York − Northeastern New Jersey
Standard Consolidated Area

- - - -   State boundary
───────   County boundary
━ ━ ━   New York Metropolitan Region

New York City
Central business district

BERGEN
ESSEX
HUDSON
UNION
RICHMOND

BRONX
MANHATTAN
QUEENS
BROOKLYN

B

C

Outer Ring
Intermediate Ring
Inner Ring
Core

20

10

0

Population in millions

1850   1900   1950   1970

Core
Manhattan

offices in New York. They chose not to locate in the Downtown financial district or in the densely populated and highly industrialised area to the north of it – the so-called 'loft district' between Chambers and Houston streets, which between 1880 and 1910 became the leading reception area for immigrants from southern and eastern Europe. Instead they built their new offices in what was then the luxury residential quarter of 'Midtown' Manhattan, north of 34th Street. (Similarly in London offices colonised the West End; and in Paris the Grands Boulevards and the Champs Elysées.) Other types of office – especially the head offices of the big new industrial combines – followed suit. In the twentieth century they were followed by a host of non-profit making organisations like trades unions, research institutes and professional bodies, as well as government which extended its operations enormously. Around them, a host of special services progressively developed to minister to them – real estate experts, advertising, taxation experts, engineers, designers, draughtsmen and operational research consultants. Many of these professions changed from small-scale ancillary factory activities into large-scale, full-time office jobs. Other activities shifted relatively. Some insurance head offices began to find Midtown Manhattan a more attractive site than congested Downtown. The growth of business was so great that by the 1950s the banks also were beginning to set up second head offices to tap the Midtown trade.

Other types of central employment have seen a similarly rapid growth, though yet others have been displaced in the competition for land. Midtown had been traditionally the home of luxury specialised shopping. As a mass market developed, the specialised shops steadily broadened their market; after 1880, the new department stores settled in the same area to tap the available shoppers. An important segment of manufacturing industry, working rapidly to unpredictable orders, had also to locate on Manhattan: thus the women's

7.1 *New York: definition of a metropolis.* **A** The urban region of New York exceeds the City, with its five boroughs having a 1970 population of 7,894,692. The Standard Consolidated Metropolitan Area of the Census had 16,178,700 people in 1970; the larger New York Metropolitan Region, defined by the Regional Plan Association, had 31 counties with a total population of 19,747,964. **B** The CBD of this vast area, covering only 9 square miles of Manhattan Island, had one-quarter of its total employment. **C** But residential population has been decentralising from the core counties to the intermediate and outer rings of the region.

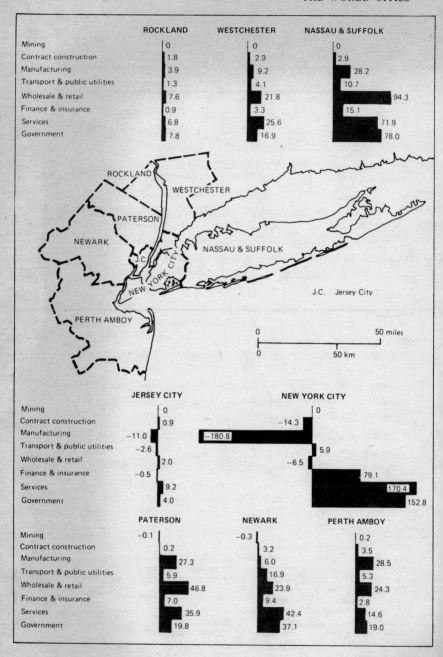

ROCKLAND   WESTCHESTER   NASSAU & SUFFOLK

	ROCKLAND	WESTCHESTER	NASSAU & SUFFOLK
Mining	0	0	0
Contract construction	1.8	2.9	2.9
Manufacturing	3.9	9.2	28.2
Transport & public utilities	1.3	4.1	10.7
Wholesale & retail	7.6	21.8	94.3
Finance & insurance	0.9	3.3	15.1
Services	6.8	25.6	71.9
Government	7.8	16.9	78.0

ROCKLAND
WESTCHESTER
PATERSON
NEWARK
J.C.
NASSAU & SUFFOLK
NEW YORK CITY
PERTH AMBOY

J.C.   Jersey City

0   50 miles
0   50 km

JERSEY CITY   NEW YORK CITY

	JERSEY CITY	NEW YORK CITY
Mining	0	0
Contract construction	0.9	−14.3
Manufacturing	−11.0	−180.8
Transport & public utilities	−2.6	5.9
Wholesale & retail	2.0	−6.5
Finance & insurance	−0.5	79.1
Services	9.2	170.4
Government	4.0	152.8

PATERSON   NEWARK   PERTH AMBOY

	PATERSON	NEWARK	PERTH AMBOY
Mining	−0.1	−0.3	0.2
Contract construction	0.2	3.2	3.5
Manufacturing	27.3	6.0	28.5
Transport & public utilities	5.9	16.9	5.3
Wholesale & retail	46.8	23.9	24.3
Finance & insurance	7.0	9.4	2.8
Services	35.9	42.4	14.6
Government	19.8	37.1	19.0

fashion industry, in the Garment Centre on the lower middle West Side, and various types of specialised printing.

In the middle 1970s, Manhattan's central business district runs up from the Battery in the south to a conventional boundary along 61st Street – that is about two-fifths of the way up the island and just above the southern end of Central Park (map 7.1 inset). Since 1900 it has shown a strong tendency to migrate steadily northwards. The big department stores have shifted progressively from the northern edge of the financial district to 34th Street; the specialised luxury shops have moved north of 42nd Street; since the Second World War the new industrial headquarters offices – Seagram, Lever, Pepsi-Cola – have been built on Park Avenue between 46th and 59th Streets. There were signs in the early 1960s that the CBD might spread further north – signs like the establishment of the Lincoln Center for the Performing Arts, in the middle 1960s of the West Side. But by the early 1970s the main movement seemed to be westward and southward. The City Plan Commission had encouraged the redevelopment of the western part of the Midtown district, between 40th and 57th Street and west of the Avenue of the Americas; the first stage involved new office space plus redevelopment of the live theatres for which this district is renowned, while a second stage will create a combination of offices, homes, an exhibition centre and a new ocean liner terminal on the Hudson River, with extensive pedestrian ways. A key to this development is the planned 48th Street crosstown subway, which will bring new accessibility to this part of Manhattan Island. But down at the island's southern tip, even more dramatic developments were taking place in the early 1970s, following publication of the City's Lower Manhattan Plan. This involves extensive decking over the peripheral highways which surround the island's lower end, coupled with extension of the land area into the rivers by landfilling. The spectacular Port of New York Authority's World Trade Centre, with its twin 110 storey towers – the highest in the world, with a total office space of over 7 million square feet – was a first stage in this development, completed in 1973; the

7.2 *New York region: employment changes, 1960–70.* (All figures in thousands.) New York City suffered massive declines in manufacturing, countered by large increases in tertiary (especially office) industry. (After 1970 these failed to compensate, and total city employment declined.) In the suburbs, both manufacturing and local services showed gains as employment decentralised together with population.

excavation for the centre has been used as landfill for the even bigger development in front of it, the Battery Park City which will create 15,000 square feet of new office space and 15,000 apartments on reclaimed land. Notable in these developments is the careful integration with public transportation. The World Trade Center for instance is served by three subways and by the Cross–Hudson tubes from the New Jersey shore, which terminate underneath it.

Meanwhile, the nine and one third miles of Manhattan Island south of 61st Street – an area equivalent in size to Kennedy International Airport – had on an average 1967 weekday an estimated working population of 2 million: almost exactly one quarter of all the employees of the New York Region as defined by the Regional Plan Association. (A mere 3 per cent of the region's population, in contrast, lived here.) Of the total of 2 million, close on half – 950,000 – were office workers. And just under one half of the region's office employment was found in the CBD. Here too were 76 per cent of the live theatres, 26 per cent of the department store floorspace, 25 per cent of employment in manufacturing and warehousing, and 14 per cent of the region's college enrolment.

This concentration of workpeople – the greatest in the world – can be explained only by the extraordinary economic advantages which individual activities derive from location at the centre. The heart of Wall Street or Midtown is the small minority of the whole workforce – variously estimated at 1 in 10, or in 20, or in 50, or in 100 – who make decisions; the business and professional élite. Many of them are in the national headquarters offices that make up over 45 per cent of total CBD office employment. The executive's job essentially consists of taking rapid, informed decisions on a wide variety of new, unpredictable, non-standard problems. To do this, he must achieve quick person-to-person contact with a large number of other decision-takers, whether in his own business or outside it; he must be able to command also a wide range of specialised expertise. It is therefore almost impossible to conceive of the executive functions being shifted far from their present home. Technological developments, like teleprinters and closed-circuit television, will make some difference; but they are unlikely to provide an adequate substitute for person-to-person contact. True, a very large majority of the labour force cannot be classed as 'executive' and so are not tied to Manhattan; but for a variety of reasons most of them remain there. Too many of them are preparing and processing information which may be needed, at short call, by the executives. Too many more are being supervised in their routine work by the same executive. Though they do not constitute the élite, many of them have their special skills; and their employees find that these skills are available in greater variety here than elsewhere, because of the highly centralised transport system. Originally created in response to the existing centralisation of jobs, this system has now become an important factor working for further centralisation.

So the growth of Manhattan's office jobs showed little sign of slackening until the end of the 1960s (map 7.2). Between 1959 and 1965, office jobs in office buildings – about nine in ten of all office jobs – rose from 760,000 to 804,000, or nearly 1 per cent per year. But during this period CBD factory jobs fell by 50,000 while other jobs – in warehousing and retailing, for instance – rose; total CBD employment remained almost static, as it had since 1930, while in the rest of the region employment rapidly rose. But because office space standards are rising, these increases bring a much bigger increase in floorspace. Between 1950 and 1970 the total CBD floorspace rose from 128 to 226 million square feet, or by 77 per cent.

For the future, in the late 1960s Regional Plan Association have produced a detailed projection of employment in the New York region. They expect total employment to rise from 7·7 million in the mid-1960s to 13·2 million in 2000 – a growth of 71 per cent. This represents a marginal fall in the region's share of total United States employment, from 11 to 10 per cent. Whereas commodity production – basically manufacturing – is expected to employ a static number of the region's workers, other employment will nearly double, from 5·5 million (72 per cent of the total) to 10·9 million (83 per cent of the total). And while blue collar jobs will barely grow, white collar jobs will double, rising from 54 to 64 per cent of the workforce. Within this total, office jobs will rise from 29 per cent to 37 per cent of the regional workforce.

The critical question is how this employment growth will distribute itself within the region. Regional Plan Association believe that many of the new office jobs will need the unique advantages the Manhattan CBD offers – above all the top jobs in headquarters offices, which will form an increasing share of the total. Total CBD jobs may rise from 2·0 million to around 2·2–2·3 million between 1967 and 2000. There would be an increase in office jobs from 0·8 million to about 1·3 million, with headquarters jobs rising from 46 to 54 per cent of this

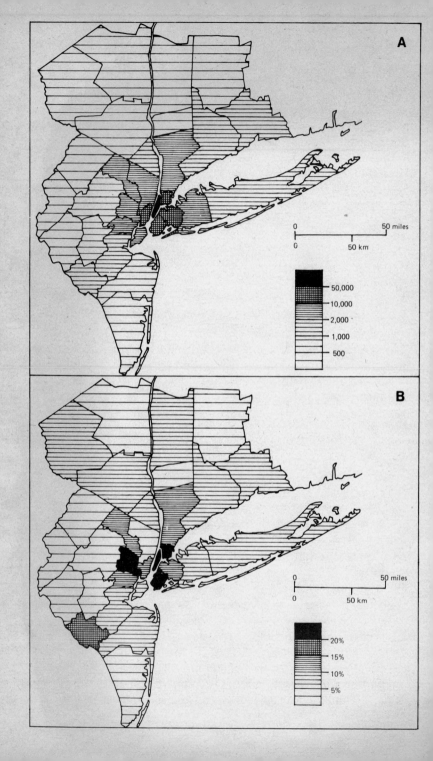

A

■	50,000
▦	10,000
≡	2,000
≡	1,000
	500

0 ————————— 50 miles
0 ————————— 50 km

B

■	20%
▦	15%
≡	10%
	5%

0 ————————— 50 miles
0 ————————— 50 km

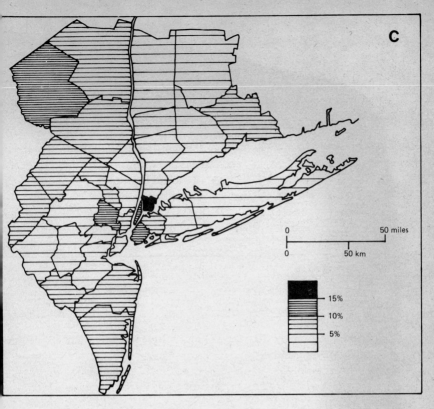

C

total; factory jobs might halve, to 0·3 million, while a range of other jobs might employ about 0·7 million. Space to accommodate the extra CBD office jobs would be no problem, since the decline in manufacturing would release more than enough land; though Regional Plan Association suggest grouping the new space above subway and other rail connections for greater efficiency of movement, with pedestrian and shopping space at below ground level linked directly to the subway access. The real problem is that the increase of about half a million CBD office jobs would be

7.3   *New York region: socio-economic indices, 1970.*
A Population density: densities decline from 50,000 to the square mile in the inner boroughs of New York City – exceptional by North American standards – to less than 500 per square mile at the periphery: the suburbs have very even densities of 1,000–2,000 per square mile.
B Per cent non-white: non-whites (and also Puerto Ricans, not shown here) form more than 20 per cent of total population in Manhattan, Brooklyn and Newark; elsewhere they make up a negligible proportion.
C Per cent below poverty line: there is a close correlation with the percentage of non-white population, with high concentrations in the inner urban areas; but low incomes are also a feature of parts of the rural periphery.

accompanied by steady dispersal of the region's resident workforce, coupled with lack of appropriate white collar job skills among the remaining inner city population. All in all, Regional Plan expect the number of CBD office commuters almost to double during this period, from 780,000 to 1,310,000, with an even bigger proportionate increase (220,000 to 570,000) in long distance commuters from outside New York City – a daunting prospect, when it is realised that already in 1960 the CBD took in a total of over 1·6 million commuters each workday. But it would still leave the great bulk of the new jobs – an expected 5 million, of which one half would be office jobs and one third in purpose built offices – to be housed outside Manhattan's CBD.

Harlem, West Side, Bronx: black belt and grey belt

Immediately outside the congested core lies another New York. The actual City of New York, which achieved its present size and form in 1898, still accounts for almost half the population of the whole Standard Consolidated Area: 7,894,862 people in 1970. 1,539,233 of them live in Manhattan, though relatively few of them are on the expensive acres south of Chambers Street or between 23rd and 61st streets; another 2,602,012 are in Brooklyn across the East River. Here, but above all in lower middle or northern Manhattan, is concentrated one of the most intractable problems facing New York – or any American city – in the 1970s.

These areas were developed during the great wave of late nineteenth-century immigration from eastern and southern Europe. They were built up quickly and poorly to an extraordinarily high density: in 1900, when half New York's population was foreign-born, parts of the lower East Side had densities of up to 640,000 on each square mile, the highest recorded density of population in world history. They have lost population for some decades now, but they still retain densities unusual by current American standards – 66,923 on average on each square mile of Manhattan in 1970, 37,172 in Brooklyn, 35,895 in the Bronx (map 7.3). Some of the older waves of immigrants, and their descendants, remain in the areas which they colonised before 1910. In lower midtown Manhattan, Delancey Street is still the main thoroughfare for the historic Jewish East Side; west of it is the Italian quarter; south west of it the Chinese quarter; north west the Polish and Ukrainian quarters. But most of the older waves of immigrants have left, to be replaced by new waves. Since the anti-immigration legislation of 1921 and 1924, most of New York's immigrants have been citizens of the United States. The 'non-white' – nearly all black – population of New York City was 60,000 in 1900, 776,000 in 1950, 1,141,000 in 1960 and 1,846,000 in 1970. Even more recent, dating from the 1940s, is the flow from the congested island of Puerto Rico in the Caribbean. By 1960 there were 613,000 people of 'Puerto Rican birth or descent' in New York City, an increase of 149 per cent over 1950; by 1970 there were 812,000, a 33 per cent increase. In total, it is estimated that between 1960 and 1970 New York City lost nearly 600,000 white people; it gained 705,000 non-whites and 199,000 Puerto Ricans.

The Jewish and Italian immigrants of 1900, in many cases, soon left the densely packed central ghettoes; the blacks and the Puerto Ricans find it harder to do so (map 7.3). Of the 2,900,000 non-whites recorded in the Regional Plan area at the 1970 Census, 1,846,000 or close on 64 per cent were in New York City and another 214,000 (7 per cent) in Newark. The bulk of the non-white population of New York City (23 per cent of the city's total population) and of the Puerto Ricans (12 per cent) are still concentrated in Harlem at the northern end of Manhattan and in the Bedford–Stuyvesant area of Brooklyn. And over one-third of the housing units in Manhattan were still recorded as 'not sound' by the 1960 Census. The black population of New York records a lower average income, a small percentage of owner-occupancy, a higher degree of overcrowding and a higher tendency to occupy old buildings than the population at large (map 7.3). In 1969, 19 per cent of non-white families in the city – as against 16 per cent of the white – were below official poverty levels, though the white/non-white differential in average income narrowed during the decade, partly because more non-whites have gone into white-collar jobs. It is thus no coincidence that New York City recorded 64 per cent of the region's non-white population and also 59 per cent – 1,165,000 – of those living on incomes below the official poverty line. In Harlem the red brick houses, built mostly to accommodate white middle-class citizens who left after 1890, have become one of the most concentrated areas of black population on the North American continent. Between 110th Street on the south and 155th Street on the north, between 8th Avenue on the west and the East and Harlem rivers to the east, live some quarter-million blacks. Here are found all the signs of extreme poverty and physical degradation: the pawnbrokers' shops, the horrifying advertisements for rodent and pest exterminators in every druggist's window, the aimless unemployed teenagers on the street corners. And, since 1940, the position of the blacks has relatively deteriorated. New waves of blacks and Puerto Ricans have arrived so quickly – attracted both by better employment prospects, and by much more generous welfare payments than in their areas of origin – that the city's housing stock was overwhelmed. Urban renewal, carried through under the 1949 Housing Act, has exacerbated the problem since it has been carried out by private developers on a commercial basis, with only limited procedures for public housing of low-income families. Typical ghetto schools have a fifth grade average reading score, over $1\frac{1}{2}$ years behind white schools. Out of 100 children entering ghetto schools, 55 will drop out before completing high school and only 13 will graduate with the academic diploma (as against 45 in a middle income neighbourhood) which is a prerequisite for a job with reasonable prospects; while three-quarters of New York city jobs are in the white collar or skilled craftsman categories, only 16 per cent of ghetto unemployed (in 1966) had these skills. And ghetto unemployment is well above average levels for the city – especially for teenagers, where it may reach 30 per cent and more. In the ghetto, too, are found a large part of the estimated 100,000 heroin addicts in the city – half the national total, and the greatest single factor in the crime rate.

The result of these forces is a staggering welfare burden. In 1971 the city had 1·2 million people on welfare – four times the 1960 figure, and 15 per cent of the population. The total bill – $2 billion (US) in 1971 – had more than doubled in four years; for the city, which bore one-third of the cost, welfare burdens represented 22 per cent of the budget against 12 per cent in 1965. One major problem, commentators agreed, was the 'poverty trap'; for many welfare recipients, it did not pay to work.

The blacks thus find themselves under almost impossible pressure. The white areas are closed to them, and give way slowly and reluctantly if at all. Any dispersion is apt to be into the immediately neighbouring blocks, which rapidly lose their white populations. As incidents during the summer of 1964 showed, black resentment is accumulating and may prove a potent force. The non-white population of the region, about 2·6 million in 1970, will grow, even though the increase may not be on the scale of the period 1940–60. Regional Plan Association estimated in 1968 that to keep the New York City and Newark ghettoes from growing, more than $1\frac{1}{4}$ million blacks and Puerto Ricans must find housing in other areas by 1985 – and this made no allowance for in-migration, which seems certain to continue. Unless dispersal occurred, the Association warned, then even without allowance for in-migration New York City's population could be 43 per cent black and Puerto Rican by 1985; in Newark the proportion could be 90 per cent. Meanwhile, the number of housing units in New York City actually fell after 1965 as apartment blocks began to be abandoned by their owners – who found it no longer worthwhile to maintain them in decayed or decaying areas. By the early 1970s, abandonment in the city was estimated to be running at 50,000 apartments a year. The causes were not easy to unravel, but one was undoubtedly rent control: a relic of World War Two Federal legislation, maintained here long after its disappearance from the rest of the United States. When the City took over administration of the scheme in 1962, almost by definition it found rent increases impossible because of the political power of the tenants – who comprise 80 per cent of households, against less than 40 per cent in the United States as a whole. At last, in 1971 a State law provided for decontrol of tenancies, and in 1972 the city introduced a system allowing rents to rise nearer to market levels. Nor did public agencies step in to the breach; in fact, Federal housing programmes virtually halted at the end of the 1960s, as construction costs exceeded budget limits.

One important basis for postulating a marked shift is the character of the areas just outside the Negro ghettoes. Here, in the Bronx and in outer Brooklyn and inner Queens, and in Hudson County on the New Jersey shore, are the grey areas of the New York region. They are the interwar suburbs: the creation of the subway and tube age. The New York subway opened its first line in 1904. By the mid-1920s it was throwing out long tentacles into the developing fringes of the city, five to ten miles from the centre, and it was carrying four million passengers a day. Similarly, the deep-level tubes under the Hudson opened up the New Jersey shore. Then, America was far from being the land of the universal automobile. In 1920, one family in three in the United States owned a car; in the mid-1920s, one in two. For work and for play, the most important consideration was access to the subway stations. So these areas (which Europeans would call suburbs, but which Americans do not), were built densely by later American standards: houses at 10 or 12 to the acre, houses mixed with apartments at up to 50 dwellings per acre. They were built and occupied quickly, for between 1910 and 1930 the population of the Metropolitan Region rose by 4,000,000. The people who settled here were America's new middle class, many of them the first-generation children of the Jewish and Italian immigrants of 1900, who were marrying and having children in the middle 1920s. By the 1960s, these people were old; their children had grown up, married and moved away, and areas like the Bronx lost population during the decade 1950–60. These older inhabitants were already dying or moving away from New York. And their houses do not prove fully acceptable to young people forming new families in the 1970s: they are small, with small gardens, with insufficient space for the two cars which many Americans are coming to regard as the essential standard, and because they were too quickly and speculatively built they often look tawdry, neglected and unattractive. The cheap building materials, the undeveloped weed-grown lots, the overhead railway tracks, the garish advertisements along the main avenues and the surrealist patterns of overhead cables make these areas singularly dispiriting and uninviting in comparison with most European counterparts; some of the neglected suburbs of northern Paris provide perhaps the closest parallel. From these areas the commuter travels by subway, which gives a cheap but slow and uncomfortable journey to Manhattan.

The result, in the late 1960s and early 1970s, is a big stock of available housing, forty or fifty years old and semi-obsolescent by modern middle-class American standards, in a wide belt between five and fifteen miles from Times Square. True, not every American family can afford the newest and best: five-sixths of Americans never earn sufficient income to buy a new house. But in this period, there will be relatively few families to take up the offer of rather cheap, slightly substandard housing; for these are the years when the poor crop of depression babies is passing into the housing market. Here is a paradox: for the statistics show that many Americans, and in particular many New Yorkers, are inadequately housed. The problem is that these people tend to be poor, unskilled, poorly educated – and black. What seems likely is that large tracts of the grey areas will pass to the blacks. Already by 1970, nearly 27 per cent of the population of the Bronx was non-white – a proportion almost equal to Manhattan and Brooklyn; in Queens nearly 15 per cent were non-white, and even suburban Westchester County recorded 10 per cent. Yet it seems doubtful whether the dispersal process can satisfy the pent-up demands of the densely packed inner areas.

A critical factor here will be the distribution of jobs in the zone of black ghettoes and in the grey belt. More than one-quarter of the New York region's jobs are concentrated in this zone – the so-called core of the region, excluding the CBD – stretching from three to thirteen miles from Times Square. Here are found the activities which need close contact with the centre but which cannot afford the highest central rents. They include many types of wholesaling and storage, distribution and service centres for the local market, and manufacturing industries like the production of the less fashion-conscious types of clothing, printing and specialised electronics. These industries need a great deal of unskilled labour which is increasingly drawn from the black and Puerto Rican populations. So they set up increasing flows of 'reverse commuters' out of Manhattan and inner Brooklyn, where much of the labour force still has to live (map 7.3). More and more, these people will try to find homes nearer their jobs. The same stimulus will come from the outward shift of the suburban population, generating a demand for local services which can often be kept going only with the help of the non-white population. And eventually, as the more dynamic types of industry grow in the outer suburbs, their demands too will influence the distribution of the black workforce.

Dispersal of the ghetto populations must, therefore, be one answer. But, as Regional Plan Association stress, it is not alone sufficient; the older cities, in this region as across the United States, must be spared the crushing burden of poverty-related public services, Federal funds need to be channelled into the cities, helping to reduce poverty and to release city funds for other urgently needed purposes, at the same time reducing the incentive to migrate. But the so-called Moynihan plan for guaranteed Federal welfare benefits, proposed by the 1968 Nixon administration, which would have achieved some of this, was rejected by Senate; though the new emphasis in the 1973 Budget on revenue-sharing may achieve a similar effect by giving massive Federal funds direct to the cities, which will themselves determine their use.

Suburbs and exurbs: Westchester, Nassau, Suffolk, Fairfield

Almost every part of any city was at one time a suburb. Fleet Street in London, the Châtelet in Paris, Unter den Linden in Berlin were all once *in suburbio*. In the United States, the word suburban connotes

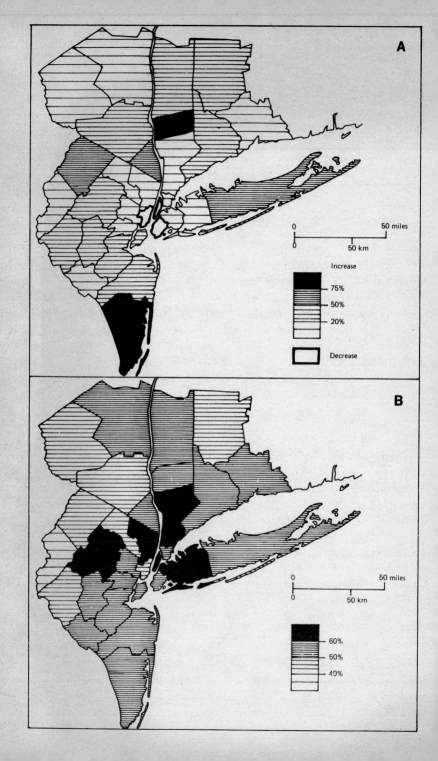

A

0 _____ 50 miles
0 _____ 50 km

Increase

75%
50%
20%

Decrease

B

0 _____ 50 miles
0 _____ 50 km

60%
50%
40%

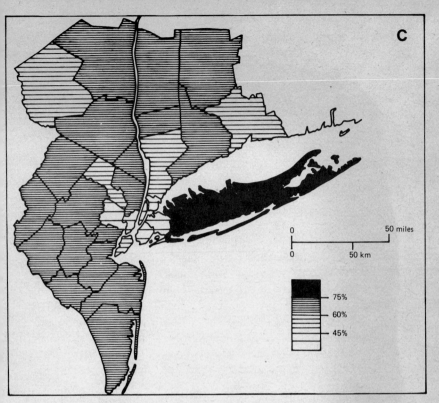

something different from the common European meaning. It refers directly to areas outside a city; it tends therefore to describe development in the recent past – since 1945; development based on the universal possession of the private automobile; development at a density which is extraordinarily low even by generous European standards.

So the interwar housing of the grey belt, the suburbs based on subway transportation and built at densities of ten to fifty dwellings on each acre, are not what New Yorkers mean by suburbs; suburbs start where the city ends. By 1945 the City area was more or less fully built-up, and suburban developments were started on a wide scale.

7.4 *New York region: socio-economic indices, 1970.*
A Per cent population change 1960–70: the most rapid increases have been in the belt 30–50 miles from Times Square, especially on Long Island, Putnam County (N.Y.) and the middle-distance New Jersey suburbs.
B Per cent white-collar: the proportion is highest in the inner suburbs; it is generally high throughout the suburbs, lower at the rural fringe.
C Per cent owner-occupied: the figures are uniformly high outside the inner city and certain older parts of the New Jersey shore; like other big cities, New York is distinguished by a high proportion of renters.

They were built at lower densities, averaging seven houses to each acre, which allowed generous garage and garden room: Levittown on Long Island, dating from the late 1940s and one of the classic homes of William H. Whyte's Organisation Man, is the model. Though almost all families in Levittown own cars, many of its commuters into Manhattan go by public (though privately owned) transportation. Just as the interwar suburbs depended on the subway, so the suburbs of 1945–70 – 15 to 45 miles from Times Square – depend on longer-distance commuter railroads like the Long Island, the New Haven and the Jersey Central (map 7.4).

But since the late 1950s a profound change has come over New York suburbs. As development progressed farther and farther from Manhattan, so the new houses were spaced farther and farther apart from each other. By 1962 some 200 municipalities had undeveloped land in the New York Metropolitan Region, and almost all were zoning it at fixed maximum densities. An analysis by Regional Plan Association showed that no less than 67·2 per cent of all the vacant residentially zoned land was zoned in lots of half an acre or more; 47·5 per cent in lots of one acre and more. Allowing for the usual tendency for some development to take place on lots bigger than the zoned minimum, the Association calculated that the average developed lot of the future might be over two-thirds of an acre. In 1950, by comparison, the average was less than one-quarter of an acre.

The result may already be seen in the most recent developments at the fringe of the present built-up area, some 25–30 miles from Times Square, in areas like northern Westchester County in New York or Fairfield County in Connecticut. Here is evolving a type of urban area without parallel in eastern North America: an importation from the universal urban sprawl of Los Angeles. It depends almost wholly on the automobile, for a finely developed railroad net, or even adequate express bus transportation, is no longer economic. The commuter bound for Manhattan must drive long distances to a suburban railhead; his wife needs a second car for the long journey to the shopping centre. The early developments are tending to cluster round the infrequent junctions on the freeways; but this will be possible only for a privileged few. And losing the traditional advantages of urban life, the new suburbanites will not gain complete rural seclusion either. True, they will not usually be able to glimpse their neighbours' houses through the trees; but they will still live at ten times rural densities. This new type of suburbia needs a new name. Some Americans call it 'exurbia'. The Regional Plan Association have christened it 'spread city'.

Exurbia tends to be occupied only by the most fortunate members of American society. The 1970 Census shows that here are the highest proportions of white-collar workers, of households with very high incomes, and of owner-occupancy (map 7.4). But rich as these people are, the communities they inhabit are in a chronic state of financial anxiety. They find it increasingly difficult to bear the heavy burden of local expenditure, especially school expenditure, which results from the immigration of young people with children. The structure of American government being what it is, they get relatively little help from State or Federal authorties in meeting these expenditures. And here, in pure anxiety, lies the origin of exurbia. It is not something that anyone appears to want; scatteration restricts choice even for the better-off, increases travel distance unnecessarily, and further raises the cost of essential public services. For fear that more families will strain municipal resources, the communities of exurbia create the zoning laws to limit the numbers of newcomers. The spread of light industry, research organisations and routine office functions into the suburbs helps; but many small municipalities do not get much benefit. Regional Plan Association has suggested ways out of this impasse – larger tax districts, to avoid the present highly localised tax burdens, and greater aid from the States. What is certain is that unless a change comes, spread city will go on spreading.

The implications of this are disturbing. In 1968, out of a total of 12,900 square miles in the New York Metropolitan Region, 2,350 were developed or committed to some public use like open space. Another 1,150 square miles were given over to parks, reservoirs and military camps, leaving 9,250 square miles – over 70 per cent – completely rural. At the space standards of recent development, by the end of the century the developed areas could cover 5,600 square miles and the open spaces 2,650 square miles, leaving only 4,500 square miles (35 per cent of the total) still open. But given the likely increase of population between 1960 and 1985, and given the present zoning arrangements, development could eat up another 2,800 square miles. Thus within thirty-five years the New York region could use up more land than in all the years since 1626, when Manhattan was bought from the Indians for $24. The result would be a continuous urban sprawl stretching on average forty-five to fifty

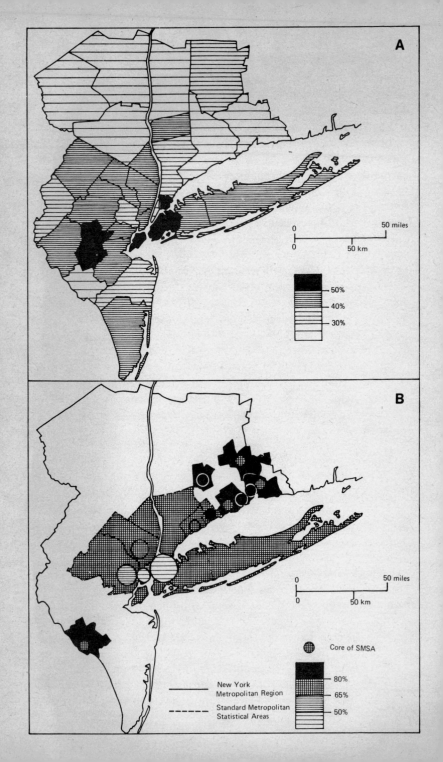

A

■	50%
▤	40%
☐	30%

50 miles

50 km

B

⊕	Core of SMSA
■	80%
▦	65%
▤	50%

50 miles

50 km

—— New York Metropolitan Region

---- Standard Metropolitan Statistical Areas

miles from Times Square – much farther than that along certain transport lines. Development will be exceptionally rapid after 1975, when the big immediate-postwar generation reaches marrying and childbearing age.

Then, the concept of the American Megalopolis will threaten to take on a new dimension. Megalopolis, in the description of the geographer Jean Gottmann, is 'an almost continuous stretch of urban and suburban areas from southern New Hampshire to northern Virginia' – a stretch of some 450 miles of Atlantic seaboard. But though over 30 million people lived here in 1960, in the greatest extended urban agglomeration in the world, they did so on only about 10,000 square miles, or 20 per cent of the land area of the region. If, however, the rest of Megalopolis proves as land-hungry in the coming decades as its New York regional heart threatens to, then there is a real prospect that by the end of the century a majority of the land area of Megalopolis will be urbanised.

Will the new pattern of living prove tolerable to the New Yorkers of 2000? The Regional Plan Association are reasonably sanguine – provided the spatial pattern of development is right. Much will depend on the location of jobs then. Exurbia will be occupied predominantly by decision-taking executives and their families. If in 1985 there are many more executive jobs in Manhattan, the length and strain of commuter journeys will surely increase. If there is rapid growth of decentralised office and laboratory jobs, the dweller in exurbia may make more cross-trips round the periphery to his work. And here the emphasis on the automobile, and the relatively low densities of people and jobs, may help – especially if the highway pattern is developed to provide better links around the edge of the region. The strong probability, according to the detailed projections made for Regional Plan Association, is that both trends will occur: alike in Manhattan, in the 10–25 mile ring and in exurbia, the highest-paid, most responsible white-collar jobs will grow. So it is likely that

7.5   *New York: commuting, 1970.*
A Per cent of resident workers commuting outside county of
   residence; the outer parts of New York City and suburbs are the
   principal dormitory areas, while Manhattan and rural fringe
   residents tend to find work locally.
B Per cent of resident workers in cores and rings of Standard
   Metropolitan Statistical Areas (SMSAs) commuting by car:
   generally, the great majority of workers in the rings of each SMSA
   (13 in the New York region) commute by car. For workers in the
   central cities, especially New York, the proportion is much lower.

some exurbanites will be comparatively badly served by the sort of city they have to inhabit; some less so. Nevertheless, it is fairly clear that intelligent planning could produce an arrangement which would suit almost everyone better. Regional Plan Association argue strongly for the build up of about two dozen major metropolitan centres throughout the region, containing concentrations of office jobs, college and hospital facilities, stores, museums and galleries, and high density apartments. They would thus house a substantial proportion of the big expected growth in white collar jobs. They could draw on big local labour pools because they would be strategically sited in relation to highways and at major public transportation nodes. First priority would go to centres in the core of the region just outside the CBD, which could hold residents who might otherwise move out: downtown Brooklyn, downtown Newark and above all the proposed major centre at Jamaica, on Long Island near Kennedy Airport within the New York City borough of Queens. This centre, astride the Long Island Rail Road and on the new subway connection from Manhattan to the airport, would draw on an estimated 285,000 white collar workers within half an hour by railroad or subway, as well as 700,000 potential shoppers within twenty minutes travel time; and it is only 12 minutes from midtown Manhattan by train. Such new centres could be coupled with more flexible zoning, so that the higher densities occurred closer to job or shopping opportunities, or at least closer to the transportation systems that would give access to them; in this way, the region's people could be offered a rational trade-off between better accessibility and more space. But, given present local government structures, the prospects seem questionable.

The basic problems: government

Underlying the particular problems in the different parts of the New York region, it now becomes evident that there are two deeper, extremely intractable problems. And one of these is in part an expression of the other. They are the government problem and the transportation problem: and of these that of government is the more basic.

In the Regional Plan Association Harvard Study of 1959–60, Professor Robert Wood described the system of government within the New York Metropolitan Region as perhaps the most complicated ever devised. At the last count, there were 1,467 governments each with the power to raise and spend money. That is not to say that the region is divided into 1,467 separate geographical units of government, for a feature of the American local government system is that it multiplies special-purpose or ad hoc authorities in addition to the normal units of local government. In fact at least three separate types of government may be distinguished. First, there are the elected local governments at several levels, including cities, counties, boroughs, towns and villages. The precise role of each of these units varies from State to State. In Connecticut, which follows the New England tradition, the town is the important unit; in New York the County is more important than in New Jersey. Secondly, there are the local ad hoc authorities which usually represent unions of several municipal governments, such as school districts, water supply districts and fire districts. Lastly, there are region-wide ad hoc authorities which have jurisdiction over a substantial part of the whole metropolitan region, such as the Triborough Bridge and Tunnel Authority within the City of New York, or the Port of New York Authority. This is quite apart from the State governments, whose departments play an important role in the performance of some functions.

This summary description merely concerns the forms of government. Their actual working is conditioned by government traditions, which vary greatly from State to State, and in particular between New York and New Jersey. New Jersey has an extremely restricted tax base with no personal income tax and in general much more restricted than that of New York State. Thus in 1966–7, in different school districts within the region, State aid for education varied from less than one-quarter to more than one-third of the total cost. Statewide, New York provided 40 per cent on average of local school costs, New Jersey 30 per cent and Connecticut less than 30 per cent. Within New York State, the city gets less than its needs would call for; so it relies on a variety of its own taxes, including sales and service taxes. But out of these, it has to bear a heavy burden of welfare and educational services for the poor. In 1966–7, out of New York City's total budget of $4·6 billion (US), $3·1 billion came from the city's own funds; within this total, the $1.5 billion spent on poverty-related services included $1·0 billion from State and Federal funds and $0·5 billion from the city treasury. Regional Plan Association suggested that to achieve needed improvements in services, the total budget should go up to $7·2 billion and the poverty-related budget to $3·0 billion; nearly half the former, and all the latter, should be met from outside funds. This would permit a marked improvement in the city's general, non-poverty-related spending programmes, making it a more attractive place to live in.

In practice the different major authorities find rich sources of conflict with each other. The State of New Jersey is at loggerheads with the State of New York, over the taxation of New Jersey residents who work in New York; New York State with New York City, over the allocation of State aid; New York City with the Port of New York Authority, over the failure to co-ordinate transport investments; the Port Authority with the State of New Jersey, over proposals to pool transit revenues. Pollution control is another rich source of confusion; most of New York City's effluent is treated before it goes into the Hudson, but a much higher proportion of New Jersey sewage is untreated; car emission control standards are in part a State matter; solid waste disposal, and the location of power stations, engender conflicts between the city and distant rural areas. Nevertheless, they find it possible to co-operate over some major metropolitan issues. The most outstanding case is perhaps the Tri-State Transportation Committee, set up by the governors of the three States in 1961, which has created a permanent system of regional transportation planning. The complaint is still that such examples of co-ordination are too belated and too few.

To non-American eyes, the most logical solution would be to create an effective unit of local government covering the developed area, like the Greater London Council in Britain. But this is hardly a realistic prospect in America, where one of the most persistent features of twentieth-century life is the apparent failure to reorganise metropolitan government in line with metropolitan development. Few major metropolitan areas have witnessed extensions of territory by their central cities since 1890. Meanwhile, especially since 1940, these central cities have become increasingly the home of the recent immigrant, who brings disproportionately great problems of housing, education and employment. Not surprisingly, the suburbs do not want to share these problems. And the Federal Government is powerless to intervene to force annexation through.

The likely trends are two. First, the Federal Government will play an increasing role, through its interest in a major spending programmes like transportation, mortgage financing, urban renewal, water supply and open space – and, from 1973 on, through its revenue-sharing programme. But the present weakness is the failure of local governments to shape the Federal programmes for regional ends. With 551 municipalities and county governments, possessing limited powers, Federal money may be uselessly dissipated. Federal government may therefore increasingly press for more effective region-wide special-purpose authorities to administer Federal or State aid. In the New York region there already exists the Metropolitan Regional Council, which was formed in 1956 and which could play an important role as a central co-ordinating council for such regional agencies.

Secondly, it seems certain that outside New York City the county governments will assume greater reponsibility, especially in co-ordinating arrangements for public health, welfare and correction. But existing county governments are poorly suited for this role: they are pure State agencies with limited powers, no right of special tax assessment, and governing bodies which are virtually impotent. To succeed in bigger roles they must have more effective governments, must be recognised by the State as municipal corporations and must be given power to make ordinances. Nassau and Westchester counties in New York State have gone some way towards this ideal: they are relatively free of routine administrative duties but they have greater legal powers than usual, and they are run by Boards of Supervisors which represent constituent towns and cities.

In this way, gradually and with the least possible violence to existing institutions, a more viable system of government may emerge. At the lower level, democratised counties could take a broader view of such problems as the rapid rise in suburban population, and the means of providing for it. They would be less readily stampeded into low-density zoning as an expedient to keep down school taxes. At the higher level, the counties could be associated in maintaining democratic region-wide control over special authorities receiving Federal and State aid to deal with problems like transportation planning, land use, water supply, water and air pollution, waste disposal, slum clearance and public housing, recreation and civil defence.

The basic problems: transportation

Transportation in the New York region is only one area where, apparently, the existing administrative machine is defective. But so important is transportation to the whole pattern of development of the region, that it is worthwhile to focus special attention upon it.

Like other major world cities, New York is an urban region with a highly centralised urban economy: more than one-third of all the workers of the Metropolitan Region find their living in Manhattan south of 61st Street. This labour force depends on the most highly developed system of public transportation in the United States. In 1963 on a typical working day, 1,627,000 people entered the Manhattan Central Business District to work. 111,000 or 7·1 per cent came by car; another 74,000 or 4·7 per cent came by miscellaneous modes (e.g. taxi, ferry or truck) and 73,000 (4·7 per cent) walked. That left 1,306,000, or 83·5 per cent, using public transportation – of whom 1,098,000 (70·2 per cent) used the subway, 63,000 (4·0 per cent) the railroad and 145,000 (9·3 per cent) the bus. In New York City, outside the CBD, the percentage of public transportation commuters fell to 43·4; in the Transportation Study area outside the city, it fell to 10·8 per cent, and here 76·5 per cent commuted by car. The dependence of the CBD on public transportation in fact has no parallel elsewhere in the United States; it reflects the much greater capacity of rail transport to carry big flows of people within a relatively short time to the same destination. It has been estimated that cars on a normal New York street can handle about 1,300 people in each lane, per hour (assuming an average of 1·75 people in each car), and cars on an urban motorway can handle 3,200 persons per lane, per hour on the same assumption; but a commuter railroad could theoretically carry 43,200 passengers per track per hour with all passengers seated, and the subway with its standing capacity could take 60,000 per track per hour. It is also estimated that if all Manhattan's commuters arrived by automobile, five levels of parking space would be required over all the usable land from the Bowery to 52nd Street. Whatever the future curve of Manhattan employment, it is certain that by 1985 the great majority of workers there will still rely on the public transportation system to get to work (map 7.5). But conversely, the more the hold of Manhattan is loosened, the more workers are likely to turn to their private cars for travel to work.

Yet within the New York region, until recently there has been no authority to see that the transport system, and investment in future transportation, make a coherent whole; still more seriously, there has been no body looking at the relation between transport and land use. Decisions on investment and charging have been taken independently by dozens of authorities, of which only the most important are the Port of New York Authority, the Triborough Bridge and Tunnel Authority, the State and Federal Highway Authorities, toll highway agencies, suburban railroads, private suburban bus lines, the New York City Transit Authority, the three State Transportation Regulation Authorities, the Interstate Commerce Commission, County and City public works officials and planners. Finally, at the instigation of the Regional Plan Association, the governors of the States of New York, New Jersey and Connecticut agreed in 1961 to set up the Tri-State Transportation Committee in order to consider the future development of the public transportation of the region. Though the Committee is strictly concerned only with public transport, it has published total transportation studies of its area. In a study of development alternatives for the region in 1985, the Tri-State planners have stressed the clear relationship between transportation and economic activity patterns. Since employment in Manhattan is expected to grow and the commuters' homes will be even more dispersed than now, heavy investment for better rail public transportation to the CBD must be a priority in all plans. But for the six in ten of the Tri-State region's workers who will find employment outside the CBD, much will depend on whether employment opportunities are strongly concentrated in a few major centres based on public transportation, or dispersed. The more concentrated alternatives would need good mass transit to be workable; but on the other hand they could exploit it more effectively.

Meanwhile, despite the planning studies of the Tri-State Committee, the making of transport policy is fragmented to an extreme degree. Despite the great preponderance of public transportation into Manhattan during working hours, all the major improvements in access to Manhattan since 1945 have been in the private sector: notably the opening of the third tube of the Lincoln vehicular tunnel from New Jersey in 1957, and the completion of the second deck of the George Washington Bridge, connecting the northern tip of Manhattan with the New Jersey shore, in 1962. Overall, during the period 1932–58 no less than 34 extra lanes of expressway were created into Manhattan, while little extra roadspace was created on the island itself and the rail capacity remained almost constant. No major improvement on the subway system was completed between 1932 and 1970; the express lines became seriously overcrowded, and there was a particular deficiency on the east side of

Manhattan, where much of the postwar office development has occurred. Paradoxically, road access to Manhattan is better than to the central districts of many smaller American cities, though Manhattan itself is almost without doubt the most congested American central business area. The reason is that the Manhattan street system is maintained by the City, and is open to all: the most important of the access ways have been constructed and are maintained by autonomous public corporations which charge for the facilities they provide. Thus the Port of New York Authority runs the George Washington Bridge and the Lincoln and Holland tunnels across the Hudson river, while the Triborough Bridge and Tunnel Authority runs the Triborough Bridge between the Bronx, Manhattan and Queens, and the Throgs Neck Bridge between the Bronx and Queens; both authorities also maintain the freeway approaches to these bridges and tunnels, and they charge user tolls to meet the cost of their construction and maintenance. Parking is in turn separately administered, mainly by private agencies, though the Department of Traffic regulates street parking and some facilities are provided by the Port of New York and Triborough Authorities. Thus while the system generously provides for the minority of automobile commuters, at a price, it actually acts to increase congestion on the city streets.

In the public sector the tradition has been quite opposite. American mass transportation was the product of an era of monopoly, before 1918. When the automobile arrived in large numbers on New York streets, in the 1920s, it ate into the public transportation system's off-peak revenues, making the highly concentrated peak-hour week-day commuting services less and less profitable. During this period, public service commissions circumscribed the freedom of action of the railroads and subways: they were not allowed to raise fares, so the quality of the services deteriorated as stations and rolling stock were under-maintained. After 1945 fares were allowed to rise at last, but it was by then impossible to save a good-quality service. By the mid-1950s, the whole public transportation sector was facing crisis. The 237-route-mile New York City subway system was taken over by the city in 1940; by 1953 it was losing over $100 million a year, and was transferred to the semi-autonomous New York City Transit Authority so as to relieve the city finances. In 1968 it was transferred to the Metropolitan Transit Authority. By this time the annual deficit was $132 million – all met by the city. The new arrangement made it possible to issue state bonds to cover almost half the cost of a $13 billion (US) construction programme, especially on the east side. New cross-Manhattan links were another priority; extensions in the outer boroughs, to serve a dispersing population, were another. But by 1972 eventual costs were estimated at $2·5 billion (US) of which the State contribution was fixed at $0·6 billion. Meanwhile ridership, stable throughout most of the 1960s, had begun to decline again.

The short but important Hudson and Manhattan Tube system, connecting the New Jersey railroads with the central district, went bankrupt in 1954 and by 1962 faced abandonment, though it carried 29 million passengers a year; in September 1962 it was taken over by a Port Authority subsidiary, the Port Authority Trans-Hudson Corporation or PATH, which has spent large sums on regeneration. The Long Island Rail Road, which carries heavy commuter loads from Nassau and Suffolk Counties, had long been a subject of bitter New York jokes; it went bankrupt in 1949 and by the early 1950s had reached a point of near-physical collapse. In 1954, a twelve-year rehabilitation programme was announced, based on help from all sides: tax concessions from the State, City and County governments; a waiver by the Pennsylvania Railroad (the parent company) of interest dividend and principal payments; and a $60 million investment programme. This work has continued, and the railroad is being extended into east midtown Manhattan to give direct access from Long Island to the new office concentrations there; in 1965 the system was brought under the control of the Metropolitan Transit Authority. The New York, New Haven and Hartford Railroad, bringing commuters from Westchester County and from Connecticut, was also bankrupt by 1961. On this system – part of the Penn Central Railroad, which is now part of the national AMTRAK system – the Metropolitan Transit Authority has now assumed responsibility. The New Jersey railroads can finance their commuter services from freight operations, but they suffer from lack of direct Manhattan access and from competition from long-distance buses which can use the Lincoln Tunnel; their total patronage fell catastrophically from 1951 onwards and several services are now being kept open only with the help of State subsidies.

The future outlook is confusing. The Federal Government has financed a 41,000-mile $41-billion (US) programme of Interstate and Defense Highways, to be completed by 1980; in the New York region some of the most important projects have given extra capacity in

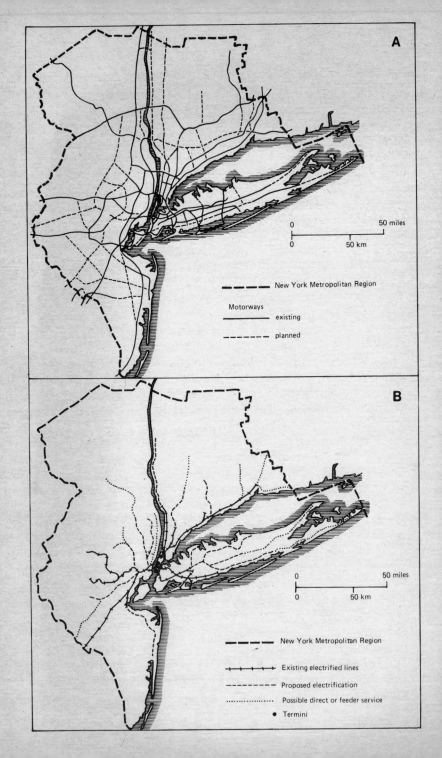

A

50 miles

50 km

New York Metropolitan Region

Motorways

——— existing

- - - - planned

B

50 miles

50 km

New York Metropolitan Region

+—+—+ Existing electrified lines

- - - - Proposed electrification

············ Possible direct or feeder service

● Termini

radial freeways like the New Jersey Turnpike or the Long Island Expressway, so bringing more automobile commuters to the Manhattan approaches. But it is now accepted policy that no extra highway capacity in the inner city should be provided, and plans for the cross-Brooklyn and Lower Manhattan Expressways, which were vigorously supported by the Tri-State planners, have been abandoned by the City. The big increase in population in the exurban zone, 25–50 miles from Manhattan, coupled with the growth of executive jobs in Manhattan, will throw an extra strain on the longer-distance commuter railroads – though the investments now in hand should help to cope.

In 1962, the local governments of the region spent 32 per cent of their capital budgets on highways and only 5 per cent on mass transit; the Tri-State interim transportation plan for 1985 would demand a shift in these proportions, with rail transit receiving one-third of the capital expenditure on transportation. Meanwhile, the Metropolitan Transit Agency's deficit escalated from $64 million in 1969–70 to $400 million in 1975. Only a small part would be met by Federal funds, through the 1974 Mass Transportation Assistance Act; and the danger was that the city would be tempted to fill the operating gap by raiding the available construction subsidy, thus postponing much needed developments like the Second Avenue subway and the 63rd Street tunnel. Yet the move towards transit is occurring: by 1972 the three States of New York, New Jersey and Connecticut had together devised programmes for spending $1·5 billion (US) on suburban railroads and $2·3 billion (US) on subways. The New York programme will involve modernisation and extension of the suburban railways; the New Jersey programme concentrates on the suburban railroads. And at last, on the New York side of the Hudson it seemed likely that the Metropolitan Transit Authority would take over all rail transit under unified management by the mid-1970s.

Overall, by the early 1970s there was a real determination to invest in extra and improved rail capacity into the Manhattan CBD. This

7.6 *New York region: transport projects.* The major expressways up to about 1970, mainly toll facilities built by the States or special agencies, improved access to Manhattan and thus increased congestion in the central area. In the 1960s the Interstate Highways (particularly 287) and the Verrazano-Narrows Bridge offered circumferential links aiding decentralisation of factory and office jobs. (This map shows only heavy freight-carrying Highways.) By the 1970s major rail projects were also under way on Manhattan.

should not only improve service levels for existing commuters; it should substantially increase the CBD's commuter field, allowing it to help cope with the expected increase in white-collar employment. But, according to Regional Plan Association, it will not by itself cope with the whole growth: for this some totally new mass transit technology will be needed, based on very rapid transit. The Gravity Vacuum Tube, with trains moving underground at several hundred miles an hour under the combined impact of vacuum and gravity, is one possibility.

The biggest question, however, concerns the increase in jobs outside the central core, especially the growth of factory and wholesale jobs in the outer suburbs. This must lead to a big increase in reverse commuting, against the main central tide, and even more to the growth of cross-trips round the periphery, which can be satisfactorily undertaken only by automobile. If this could be accompanied by a concentration of highway construction on concentric lines, round the edge of the region, it might be a wholesome trend. By the mid-1970s, there was a well-developed network of freeways which by-passed the congested core, such as the Garden State Parkway of New Jersey, the Cross–Bronx Expressway from the George Washington Bridge to the Throgs Neck Bridge, the Cross–Westchester Expressway farther north and above all the circumferential highway, Interstate 287, around the entire western periphery of the region from Perth Amboy on the Atlantic coast in the south to the New York State Thruway's Tappan Zee bridge in the north; it may be expected to attract fast-growing types of factory industry, just as the circumferential Route 128 has done so dramatically on the western side of Boston. A similar project is the Triborough Authority's Verrazano Narrows Bridge, which since 1964 has provided a critical link across the southern coastal periphery, linking Staten and Long Islands (map 7.6a).

The Tri-State plans provide for big extensions to the region's expressway network, which already totalled 1,100 miles in the late 1960s, to give better circumferential access from suburb to suburb. Many of these planned highways were in fact blocked by protest movements in the mid-1970s; some seemed unlikely ever to be built. In any case the extra non-CBD workplaces cannot and should not depend exclusively on the private car. Regional Plan Association call for their new planned metropolitan centres to be linked by efficient mass transit lines giving very rapid reverse commuting facilities from

Manhattan and Brooklyn. In many cases these would be the existing services which have spare capacity in the reverse direction to the peak flows. Centres nearer the Manhattan CBD would be served by rail; more distant centres would depend on buses (map 7.6b).

One feature of the New York pattern of transportation will not greatly change. Manhattan will still remain almost unbearably congested. Average traffic speeds there in working hours are estimated at 4–6 miles per hour; far below most European cities. It is calculated that even if 50 per cent of the present automobile commuters between New Jersey and New York shift to other means, the total street usage in Manhattan streets would drop by only about 3·5 per cent. For most Manhattan traffic is commercial traffic which is firmly rooted there. It could be displaced only if Manhattan were deserted by much of its present business activity; and that, we have already seen, seems an unlikely prospect.

The region's future: the 1960s view

In the late 1950s, Regional Plan Association took a pioneering world lead in analysing and forecasting the progress of an urban economy by commissioning a team of Harvard economists to study the main facets of the New York region's economy with a projection of employment and population down to 1985. Updated and extended in the late 1960s, these forecasts gave a picture of the growth of the region as far as the year 2000.

During the period from 1965 to 2000, the Association estimated (in 1967–8), employment in the region as they define it would nearly double, from 7·7 million to 13·2 million; this growth would be dominated by white collar jobs, already 55 per cent of total employment in 1965, which would double from 4·2 to 8·4 million. This growth of 5·7 million jobs would naturally trigger an even bigger population growth – an estimated increase of 11·2 million, from 19·0 to 30·2 million. Of this, a mere 13 per cent was expected to represent net immigration, as compared with 28 per cent for the quarter century 1940 to 1965. Much would depend here, of course, on the future characteristics of the New York labour market: the great majority of the black and Puerto Rican immigrants of the 1940s and 1950s were unskilled, but the needs of the regional economy for such labour now seems to have dried up for ever.

The population would divide itself into more and smaller households: there might be 9·7 million of them in 2000, compared with 6·0 million in the mid-1960s, and the average size would have fallen from 3·19 to 3·12, with a notable increase (from 43 to 49 per cent) in the percentage of one and two person households. This in itself was bound to generate a buoyant demand for new apartment construction. Households would be richer on average, with a dramatic increase – from 26 per cent to 71 per cent of all households – in the proportion with incomes over $10,000 a year in constant 1965 terms. But the poor, and above all the non-whites, might fail to share in this growing affluence – especially if they live in large households. Thus the problem of relative deprivation in comparison with the affluence of the majority, already glaringly evident in the New York of the 1960s and 1970s, might escalate in the last decades of the century. And affluence would bring with it problems of greater mobility, with total miles driven increasing by perhaps 85 per cent between 1965 and 2000.

For traditionally trained urban planners, perhaps the most spectacular resulting problem would be the implications for land development: as already shown, Regional Plan's own estimates suggest that open land may fall from over 70 per cent of the total area of the region in 1965, to only 35 per cent in the year 2000. Thus more land would be needed for the 11 million extra people expected between 1965 and 2000, than were required for the 19 million living in the region in the mid-1960s. Nevertheless, Regional Plan Association argued, with proper regional planning this would be acceptable. Without it, spread city would mean lengthening commuter journeys, a steadily more segregated society, lack of access to the services a large urban region like this ought to be able to provide, poor transportation services, a feeling of being shut off from nature and the countryside, and a lack of a clear community focus.

To counter these dangers, the Association's Second Regional Plan, published as a draft for discussion in 1968, suggests five basic principles of regional planning. First, as already outlined, is the creation of new major urban centres to provide for a lion's share of new jobs – above all in the white collar sector, where 65 per cent of new office jobs are expected to locate outside the Manhattan CBD – and provide needed concentrations of higher level community services – health, entertainment, retailing, the arts, education. They would cut the length and the strain of commuter journeys, provide better services to the growing suburbs, and provide an alternative location to the CBD for many employers and employees alike; they would convert the New York region into a polycentric metropolis, which has already been shown to offer such striking advantages in agglomerations such as Randstad and Rhine–Ruhr. Secondly, and associated with the first, zoning policies for new housing would be revised to provide a much greater variety of new housing types and densities. Above all, people would be given a better choice to trade off accessibility against space, and people of lower incomes would get better access to the general housing market.

Thirdly, Regional Plan Association suggest, the older cities must be relieved of the crushing burden of paying for poverty related public services so that they may spend necessary resources in raising their general level of service provision – thus, finally, improving their general environment so as to make the cities once again attractive to a mixture of income levels and social groups. At the same time, if welfare burdens were shouldered by the Federal government, the pressure of in-migration by further poor groups could be greatly eased. Training programmes should be developed to allow the poor to move up the ladder of skills; and more unskilled jobs need to be provided for the populations that could benefit from them, near the heart of the cities.

Fourthly, the new urban development should be channelled so as to keep substantial parts of the region still in a state of nature. About 10,000 square miles of the Appalachian Mountains, stretching from Vermont to Virginia, should be acquired as a vast regional park, while the remaining open coast and many river areas should also be reserved for recreation and conservation. It would be prudent, Regional Plan Association suggest, to buy this land now before the prospect of development raises land values.

Lastly, the draft Regional Plan makes important proposals for transportation. If the new major metropolitan centres are built as the Association suggest, then they will both demand much better public transportation if they are to work properly, but at the same time will make good public transportation possible. The three innermost of the proposed centres – Brooklyn, Newark and Jamaica – can tap the existing rail network through reverse commuting from the centre of the region; but the outlying centres will depend mainly on much improved bus transportation, which must include built in priority over private car traffic. Within each centre, good planning plus new mechanical aids (such as travellators) should guarantee much better movement than people now enjoy, with an emphasis on easy pedestrian routes. And, by grouping higher density housing around these new centres, there will be a good transportation alternative for those who do not want or cannot use the private car – the young, the old, the sick and the poor. But at the same time, planning must cope with the big expected increase in car use, by new expressways which would cater for as much as one third of all the region's vehicle miles travelled.

The draft Plan was under intensive discussion in the late 1960s and early 1970s. It demanded the co-operation of many different agents both private and public – city and county planning agencies, transportation agencies, state and perhaps Federal park authorities, private developers. Some parts indeed would require major changes in national policies – particularly the idea for relieving the financial burdens of the cities, which may be partly met by President Nixon's 1973 revenue sharing plan. But though the proposals may seem utopian for a private organisation lacking any powers, past evidence suggests that the Association may perform a remarkable catalytic function in coordinating the actions of different organisations for the mutual good of all. It may seem unusual to the citizenry of countries which have more highly developed formal regional planning machines, but the only final test will be whether it achieves its stated goals.

The region's future: the changed world of the 1970s

This was the outlook in the late 1960s. But then, within a very short time, a complete change occurred in the region's future prospects – and though part of this resulted from the recession of the mid-1970s which might soon be remedied, another more important part looked like being structural and perhaps permanent.

First, population growth in the region levelled off – an expression partly of a dramatic fall in birth rate (by 25 per cent in the years 1970–73 alone), partly of a new trend of migration out of the region. Average growth, which had exceeded 200,000 a year throughout the 1950s and 1960s, was down to a mere 23,000 between 1970 and 1973. As a result, future expectations of demographic growth had to be reduced: against a 1973 base of 19·8 million, from 30 million in the year 2000, as forecast in 1968, to a stable 27 million by the year 2020.

The internal mechanics of population distribution were significant too. By the early 1970s not merely the core of the region as defined by Regional Plan Association, but also the Inner Ring, were experiencing out-migration. Thus the new forecast, made in the mid-1970s, was that by 1990 the population of the core might have fallen by as much as one million; the Inner Ring might have suffered modest decline; while the Intermediate and Outer Rings might have increased by a million or more. Significantly, the biggest projected increases in the population were in the 25–34 age group, who were the major homebuilders and child rearers – and hence the prime candidates for further suburban sprawl. Coupled with a continuing process of division of the population into smaller households, this meant that future land demands might still be heavy: Regional Plan Association were predicting an increase in the total urbanised area from 2830 square miles (in 1970) to 3830 square miles in 1990.

Secondly, and associatedly, economic growth had drastically tapered off. Against an increase in employment of 2 million (30 per cent) during the period 1950–70, the period 1969–74 saw zero growth: a happening unprecedented since the great depression of the 1930s. Manufacturing, static during the 1960s, now suffered a massive loss: 255,000, or nearly 12 per cent, in the short period 1970–72 alone. The losses in employment were particularly marked in New York City, which recorded a fall of 194,000 in 1970–72 – mostly in manufacturing. By this time, the only potentially dynamic sector in the city was white-collar employment; but even there the early 1970s had seen an accelerating loss of corporate headquarters offices.

The reason, as George Sternlieb put it, was that New York had become an historic anomaly. It had provided a convenient location for immigrant entrepreneurs, and immigrant labour, in an era when strong cultural and institutional barriers restricted flows of capital and labour. But by the late twentieth century, the United States has an increasingly homogeneous labour force, a national capital market and uniformly good transportation and communication systems. In this world, New York City's traditional features – high densities of activity, congestion, difficult travel conditions, high wages, strong unionisation – are a positive disadvantage for many firms. Manufacturing, in contrast, is tending to locate in the environmentally superior areas of Florida or the far west, or alternatively in the formerly depressed rural areas of the old south. The last place to do effective business, it now increasingly appears, is in the older, bigger cities of the east – of which New York is the archetype.

One major emerging problem, common to other large world cities, is a mismatch between available jobs and the labour force. Though New York City offers a uniquely large and diverse labour market, it is increasingly dominated by the tertiary sector: 80 per cent of jobs are in finance, insurance, real estate, government and other services, and 60 per cent of all jobs are white-collar jobs. But the increasingly black and Puerto Rican population of the inner city – especially the male element – are unsuited for these jobs: only one third of blacks, and 27 per cent of Puerto Rican males, were in white-collar occupations in 1970, though around half their female counterparts were. So it is unsurprising that since the 1970–71 recession, New York City unemployment has exceeded the national rate.

In consequence the city has a huge – and increasing – problem of welfare dependency. Within a stable population of roughly 8 million, welfare recipients rose between 1960 and 1970 from 328,000 to 1,200,000, or from 4 to 15 per cent of the entire population. These welfare dependents tend heavily to belong to ethnic minority groups (around 80 per cent, against 30 per cent in the whole population), to be less educated than the average New Yorker, to have come to New York from outside (especially from the South or from the Caribbean), and to suffer from physical or mental illness; there are many multi-problem families. Ironically, then, a city that is increasingly dependent on high-skill, high-salary jobs can make less and less use of an increasing unskilled, poorly educated workforce.

The crisis of New York City

The fiscal crisis of New York City, which made world headlines during 1975, had one immediate cause: a massive loss of confidence in the city administration on the part of the major financial institutions that had previously been willing to lend money on the city's bond isues. But at root the crisis lay much deeper: in the evolving economy of the city, in the political response to a growing structural crisis, in the power held by different interest groups in the city.

At bottom was the decline in the city's economy. A loss of 400,000 jobs between 1969 and 1975, some 11 per cent of the total employment, meant a massive erosion of the tax base and a simultaneous increase in the city's welfare burdens. But simultaneously, through this entire period – though less rapidly than in the era of Lindsay's mayorship, from 1966 to 1973 – employment in the city's own labour force continued to grow: by 244 per cent overall in the decade 1966–76. In fact, by the mid 1970s the city was the second largest employer in the United States after the Federal government, with some 350,000 on its payroll.

There are many possible explanations; but they fall into two main schools. One, the conservative, holds that the villains were the city politicians – and behind them the city labour unions. The city had traditionally been a profligate spender: on the City university, on the public hospital system, on public housing and on transit subsidies. The taxes to pay for these services came for the most part from business; the services, for the most part, benefitted the really poor less than the average middle class voter. And it was these services, plus welfare, that showed the biggest increases in spending over the 1966–76 decade; basic services, like sanitation or police, grew much less. But the well established public service unions, such as the teachers, also benefitted hugely – especially through generous pension agreements, which led to a massive funding problem for the city.

The alternative explanation holds that the city has been wronged. When the comparison is fairly made, it is argued, New York is no more profligate in most services than comparable cities. It spends less on welfare per head, for instance, than Philadelphia or Baltimore. One reason for the city's crisis, according to this school, is that the city has an exceptional concentration of social problems such as drug addiction. Another is that, unlike cities in many states, the city has to provide more support for its services because the state provides less. The city has no county aid for courts or hospitals, no tax district for its schools. It must raise one-third of its total welfare budget itself, because it gets no benefit from the rich counties that ring it to the north and east. Since the government structure is unitary, the trouble-ridden components drag all the rest down. Such is the counter argument.

Whatever the true explanation, the evident fact is that the city embarked on a potentially very dangerous fiscal path. From the mid 1960s onwards, it issued short-term bonds to meet the increasing gap between income and expenditure. As these became due for payment, it was forced to roll them over: that is, to issue new bonds to pay the interest and principal on the old ones, and to meet the continuing expenditure gap. By 1976, it had $2·6 billion of such debts, while its current account deficit for the year was expected to be $726 million.

At this point, for whatever reason, the financial institutions lost confidence. In March 1975 the city found for the first time that its bond issues would not sell. The resulting crisis led in June 1975 to the formation of the Municipal Assistance Corporation – or, as it soon became known in tribute to a famous hamburger, the Big Mac. MAC was a State corporation pledged to borrow on behalf of the city, with a cover provided by state taxation and a promise to reform the city's fiscal practices. But the market remained nervous, and in September the State was forced to pass a Financial Emergency Act whereby $2·3 billion was raised to meet the city's immediate cash needs, with an emergency Financial Control Board to set the city's fiscal practices on a sound basis by mid 1978. Yet collapse still loomed, to be stilled only by a Federal act guaranteeing funds in December 1975.

Thus, temporarily, the city's crisis has abated. But the root causes are still present; and they interact. The likelihood is that the tax base will continue to erode as manufacturing – and even white-collar jobs – desert New York for other cities and regions. Yet this can only cause the burden of dependency to increase further; while inherited problems like the funding of the World Trade Center, or the deficits of the Long Island Rail Road, will not go away. Nor has the political sociology of the city altered: the great public service unions retain their power, and in a city so dependent on public services as New York the threat of a strike is not taken lightly. Many argue that the only answer is for the Federal government to intervene, by diverting investment from the southern and western states where so much of it has gone since 1945. Yet much of that Federal spending has been on defence, and it is difficult to see how in the short run it could readily be channelled into the city.

The history of New York City in the 1970s, some pessimists say, is the fate of many other world cities in the 1980s and 1990s. Earlier than other great metropolitan areas, they argue, New York has experienced the chill effects of major shifts in the geography of basic industry – shifts that can now also be seen beginning to affect the fortunes of London and Paris, Amsterdam and perhaps even Tokyo. Truly, also, New York has its unique features – not least the American tradition of forcing cities to stand on their own without central government aid, now somewhat dented by necessity. But the New York crisis certainly bears pondering by planners and politicians in other world cities. It might happen there too.

8 Tokyo

Of all the world cities, Tokyo is richest in paradoxes. In terms of population it is the largest city authority, and also the largest metropolitan area in the world; but its public services are structured for a city between one-fifth and one-half the present size. Its factories produce some of the most technologically sophisticated products in the world; yet, despite a rate of economic growth almost without parallel during the 1960s and 1970s, its wage levels and living standards are still noticeably below those of the other world cities (save Moscow) considered in this book, and they contrast sharply in turn with relative poverty in Japan's provincial agrarian regions, only a few hundred miles away. Its rate of population growth is by far the highest of any of the very big cities of the world; it has the biggest problems in accommodating the extra millions. It is a metropolis, where, in 1974, an elaborate network of expressways was in an advanced stage of construction, but where only 52 per cent of the city's 11 million people enjoyed main drainage. Of all world cities it is the one whose citizens have devised the most varied and original solutions to their problems; but also the one where almost all schemes have a habit of failing for lack of funds.

Tokyo's size, as with almost every other world city, presents a nice problem in definition. There is the *historic city*, or *ward area*, of Tokyo: enlarged many times, the city numbered 23 wards in 1970, with 8,840,942 people at the census of that year. There is the *administrative Tokyo*: the area of the Tokyo Metropolitan Government (TMG), which provides local government services for the old city, with its 23 wards, and the suburbs immediately around it. At the 1970 Census of Japan, it had a population of 11,408,071, having become the first city authority in the world with over ten million population. But outside this limit, rapid population growth has

219

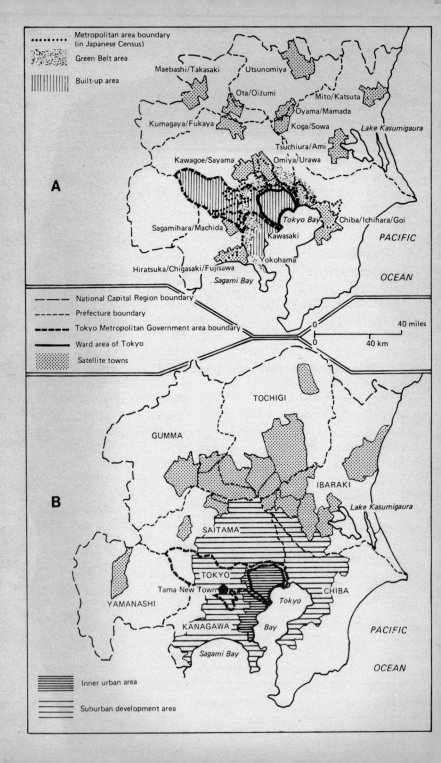

A

Metropolitan area boundary (in Japanese Census)

Green Belt area

Built-up area

Maebashi/Takasaki   Utsunomiya

Ota/Oizumi   Mito/Katsuta

Kumagaya/Fukaya   Oyama/Mamada

Koga/Sowa

Kawagoe/Sayama   Tsuchiura/Ami

Omiya/Urawa   *Lake Kasumigaura*

Tokyo Bay   Chiba/Ichihara/Goi

Sagamihara/Machida   *PACIFIC*

Kawasaki

Hiratsuka/Chigasaki/Fujisawa   Yokohama   *OCEAN*

Sagami Bay

National Capital Region boundary

Prefecture boundary

Tokyo Metropolitan Government area boundary

Ward area of Tokyo

Satellite towns

0   40 miles

0   40 km

B

TOCHIGI

GUMMA

IBARAKI

Lake Kasumigaura

SAITAMA

TOKYO

Tama New Town   CHIBA

Tokyo

YAMANASHI   *Bay*

KANAGAWA   *Sagami Bay*   *PACIFIC*

OCEAN

Inner urban area

Suburban development area

already created a *Tokyo agglomeration* – a continuous urban area having close functional links with central Tokyo. There are two ways of measuring this area. International Urban Research, using commuter flows as the basis, defined an area whose nearest equivalent, at the 1970 Census, contained 23,873,453 people. The Japanese Census itself, on a basis of 'densely-populated enumeration districts' (more than about 1,500 on each square mile) came out with a distinctly smaller population: 15,017,968, distributed in sharply radial fashion along the major railway lines, with some isolated concentrations up to 30 miles from Central Tokyo. Lastly, there is the *planners' Tokyo*: the area which it is necessary to consider as a whole, if a more viable structure is to be found for Tokyo in the future. The area defined in the National Capital Region Development Law of 1956 extends up to a radius of 60–75 miles from Tokyo station; it had a population of some 30 million in 1970 and no less than 33 million by 1975. These definitions of Tokyo are shown on map 8.1a and b.

Tokyo in history

Tokyo is no newcomer among the world's great cities though it achieved world city status quite late in its history. As long ago as 1785 it had a population of 1·4 million people, and was almost certainly the biggest city of the world in terms of population; London, its nearest west European competitor, had less than 900,000 at that time. Yet Tokyo, then known as Edo, could not claim to be a world city for the simple reason that the city was almost completely shut off from the world. Both the size and the isolation result from history. By Japanese, if not by world standards, Tokyo is a young city: the empire dates from about AD 300 and the ancient capital of Kyoto from 794, but the first fort on the site of Tokyo was established only in the twelfth century and the permanent fort of Edo – which became the nucleus of the later city – was built by the warrior Ota Dokan as

8.1 *The Tokyo region.* With the fastest absolute growth in any world city, Tokyo presents an acute problem of definition. The 'Ward Area' contained 8,840,942 people in 1970, but the area of the Tokyo Metropolitan Government was somewhat larger, with 11,408,071 people. Far larger was the National Capital Planning Region, with over 30 million people.
A The main planning divisions pre-1965: the green belt and satellites were closely modelled on Abercrombie's 1944 London Plan.
B Post-1965: The previous scheme having proved ineffectual, Tokyo planners distinguished a suburban development area and another more distant zone (unshaded on map) where development would be controlled.

late as 1456–7. Yet less than a century and a half later, Tokyo was the *de facto* seat of power in Japan. When the fort at Edo was built, power had already passed from the Imperial Court at Kyoto to warring lords and their bands of retainers. One such lord, Tokugawa Ieyasu, occupied Edo in 1590 and established a territorial governorship, or shogunate, there in 1603. In 1615 he rose in revolt against Toyotomi Hideyori, the son of Toyotomi Hideyoshi who had managed to achieve nominal national unity thirty years before, and defeated him. From 1615 onwards, then, Japan was unified peaceably under the Tokugawa régime; and the seat of that régime was Edo.

The Tokugawa régime effectively isolated Japan from the rest of the world for over three centuries. It established also a peculiar system of power which was directly responsible for the size of Edo's population. The individual lords, or *daimyo*, had to stay in Edo for part of the year, leaving hostages when they went to their own fief. Thus large numbers of retainers, the *samurai*, were quartered in Edo. As late as the mid-nineteenth century the *samurai*, then a superfluous and parasitic class, numbered two million people or 6·25 per cent of the Japanese population; but in Edo they made up 30–40 per cent. They created there a big luxury demand, which was satisfied by a complex economic organisation including merchants, craftsmen and a putting-out system using cheap agricultural labour. This system was well suited to rapid and supple adaptation to changes in demand; and it provided an extremely favourable structure for the rapid development of consumer-goods industries of a specifically metropolitan type, as soon as western technology could be applied. So the conventional view – that the Tokugawa period was economically backward and provided an unfavourable background for further development – could in this instance hardly be further from the truth.

After the collapse of the Tokugawa régime, indeed, the Japanese adopted western techniques with remarkable speed. The Tokugawa régime collapsed, the Emperors were restored (no longer at Kyoto but in the fort at Edo, which became the Imperial Palace of the renamed Tokyo), in 1868. Telegrams arrived in 1869, a postal service in 1871, a steam train in 1872, the gas lamp in 1874 and the electric lamp in 1878. Under the new Meiji régime, industry grew and with it population. Tokyo's own population had fallen in the latter days of the Tokugawa shogunate because of the gradual dispersion of the *samurai* class: it was 596,000 in 1873. But then it rose rapidly to 810,000 in 1878 and to 1,370,000 in 1889, at the birth of the new administrative city of Tokyo. By 1920 the population was 3,358,000; the disastrous earthquake and fire of 1923 did little to halt the city's progress, but rather helped to decentralise the city. Its population spread westwards, on to the higher land away from the bay, while industry developed especially southwards along the bay coast between Tokyo itself and the old but rapidly expanding port city of Yokohama. By 1942 the city population had reached 6,916,000 and the entire area of the prefecture (which embraced the city, together with outlying cities, counties and islands in Tokyo Bay, and which became the area of the new Tokyo Metropolitan Government in 1943), was up to 7,358,000. Wartime bombing reduced the population of the metropolitan government area to just over three million in 1945; the population did not exceed the pre-1945 record until 1953 when 7,448,562 was recorded. Yet in 1962 the metropolitan government became the first administrative city in the world with a population to pass the ten-million mark, and by 1970 the population was 11,408,000.

It is common to think of this extraordinary growth in population as being due to rapid natural increase. But that overlooks the fact that natural increase in Japan reached a maximum in the late 1920s and early 1930s, since when the reduction in the birth rate has been much steeper than the continued fall in the death rate. During the 1950s and 1960s natural increase in Japan as a whole fluctuated around 10–12 per thousand, comparable with the United States and little more than two-thirds the interwar rate. During the 1950s indeed no less than 70 per cent of the growth of the Tokyo population represented net migration, chiefly for jobs and for higher education. However, during the 1960s the rate of growth of the Tokyo Metropolitan Government area progressively declined; over 4 per cent a year in the late 1950s, it was down to 2·4 per cent a year in the early 1960s and only 1 per cent a year in the late 1960s, a rate which approximately represented natural increase. By this time, therefore, roughly as many people were leaving the Tokyo area as were migrating into it.

Tokyo's functions

It should not be imagined from this that Tokyo is losing its dynamism. What is happening is that Tokyo's growth is now extending well beyond the boundaries of the metropolitan government; here are the areas that are gaining rapidly by migration from Tokyo itself. Overall, the migration trend is still strongly towards the

Tokyo region – a fact that is chiefly to be explained in terms of a very rapid structural shift in the composition of the Japanese labour force. As almost everywhere else, agriculture employs a decreasing section of the population, though in the 1960s there was still too much under-employment and low productivity in agriculture, which was a principal cause of Japan's low per capita income. Table 13 shows percentages of employees in the three main sectors of the Japanese economy, quoted by Professor Kiuchi of Tokyo.

Table 13   Japan: employment structure

	1930	1960	1980 estimate
Primary (agriculture etc.)	49·4	32·9	15·8
Secondary (manufacturing and construction)	20·4	29·1	40·3
Tertiary (services)	30·2	38.0	43·9

The impact of these changes can be seen both in Tokyo's booming inner business districts and in the factory areas of the northern and southern suburbs. Services accounted for over 40 per cent of the Japanese labour force in the early 1970s; but in Tokyo they made up over 60 per cent, and they are sharply concentrated in or near the centre of the city. South of the Imperial Palace, the old Edo fortress, is the administrative quarter; east of it, near the central station, the Marunouchi area is the centre of Japanese financial life, with the headquarters offices of banks and big industrial corporations. Many of these firms moved here from Osaka after 1945, especially those concerned with foreign trade. Farther east again is the main retail district, including Tokyo's two chief shop windows, Ginza and Nihonbashi streets. And north of these again, in Asakusa, the wholesale quarter is concentrated.

But this is not the only cause of Tokyo's magnetism. To the north east of the core, on the low-lying flats along the numerous water-courses of the Sumida river, is a great factory zone with more than three quarters of a million workers in the late 1960s. To the south, along the bay shore towards Kawasaki and then again between Kawasaki and Yokohama, are further great industrial con-centrations. Here there is some division of function. Despite the deepening of the channel into Tokyo Bay in 1923, and the subsequent major development of the port of Tokyo, Yokohama remains Tokyo's outport; and most of the industries near it are logically the heavier types depending on bulky raw materials – refineries, primary metals, chemicals, cement. The inland areas of the north tend to concentrate on lighter and more complex products which are perhaps most typical of the evolution of the Japanese economy since 1945. The fastest-growing industries in Japan in the 1960s and 1970s were the science-based, consumer durable industries like cars, transistor radios, tape recorders, electronic calculators, and cameras. And in Japan, perhaps even more than in other countries these tend to be specifically metropolitan industries, which depend on the existence of big manufacturing complexes embracing large plants and a host of smaller suppliers of materials, components and specialised services; two thirds of Tokyo's labour force is still in small and medium-sized businesses.

Structural shifts in the economy, coupled with the continued existence of a depressed agrarian class in the rural provinces, explain much of the attraction of Japan's big cities but above all the two giants of Osaka and Tokyo. Average per capita income in Tokyo is nearly twice the national average and about three times the average of the poor agricultural communities of Southern Kyushu. Such large regional income disparities are unusual in a developed country and they are bound to lead to continuing labour flows into the metropolitan region. They help to explain Tokyo's overwhelming problems – the problems of over-rapid growth.

Growing pains

The rate of growth of the Tokyo agglomeration has hardly any parallel in the world in the period since the end of the Second World War. Between 1955 and 1960, population in the Tokyo Metropolitan Government area rose by an average of 329,000 a year; from then to 1965, by 237,000 a year, thence dropping to 108,000 a year between 1965 and 1970. Hardly any urban agglomeration could bear such a rate of growth without strain. But Tokyo's structure of public services happens to be singularly ill-adapted to deal with the problem.

A disproportionate part of the employment generated since 1945 is in the industrial zones but above all in the central business district. Yet ever since the 1923 earthquake Tokyo's population has been spreading into ever more distant suburbs, and above all on to the higher ground west of the centre. Between 1923 and Pearl Harbor the highest rates of growth were recorded in the outer wards of the city proper; since 1945 they have been in the areas outside the city, and even outside the area of the Tokyo Metropolitan Government. True, the Japanese have long kept a tradition of close in-city living – the Toshima ward in north-west Tokyo recorded 27,243 to the square kilometre or 70,559 to the square mile in 1970 – but the central wards have been losing population as new offices and shops have displaced homes, and while the Tokyo ward area suffered a slight population loss during 1965–70, suburbs have sprawled ever farther from the centre. The process has been generated by rising land prices at the centre, by the traditional Japanese preference for the single-family house, and by the anti-earthquake building regulations, in force until recently, which limited multi-storey dwellings to 31 metres or 102 feet.

The great growth in population, but above all its outward spread, has been responsible for three overwhelming problems in the Tokyo of the 1960s and 1970s. They concern housing; basic public services like water and sewage; and transport.

Housing. During the Second World War 768,000 dwellings, or 56 per cent of Tokyo's housing stock, were destroyed, leaving 51 per cent of the population homeless. This tremendous problem had been met by 1960, though even then too many people were still living in temporary accommodation – boats, old railway trains, abandoned factories – which they had occupied after the war. Between 1945 and 1954 an estimated 970,000 homes were built (88,000 a year); from 1955 to 1967 the total rose to 1,900,000 (158,000 a year, an average which includes rebuilt housing). These are impressive totals. But less than a quarter of the new dwellings have been built by public bodies, like the Metropolitan Government Bureau or the Metropolitan Housing Supply Corporation, for rent. (And public housing made up only 10 per cent of the total in Tokyo in 1968.) These public dwellings are small and by western standards some of them lack essential facilities like bathrooms. But they are relatively cheap, and the demand for them far exceeds the supply. Another public agency, the Japan Housing Corporation, builds bigger dwellings, usually flats; since it must break even on each project it charges higher rents, but its flats too are heavily in demand. Paradoxically, therefore, more public housing is provided for middle income than for low income groups. Private luxury apartments are built in big numbers near the city centre but their rents are more than the average family's monthly income. So the great majority of families must look to private housing in the suburbs. Some try to obtain public help through a loan for house buying: a public body, the Japan Housing Finance Corporation, will advance 80 per cent of the standard cost both of land and of construction. (The standard cost is, however, lower than the real cost.) But this means a large problem of finding land, and even so there is again severe competition, resolved in the last resort (as with the publicly rented housing) by a lottery. Land is expensive because it is scarce; farmers on the edge of the city are determined to hold on to it until the last possible moment so as to realise the best price for it, and as compared with prewar days land prices had risen 1,600 times up to 1967. (The general wholesale price increase was only about one quarter as great.) From 1955–65 alone the increase was ten-fold, and Professor Shibata has estimated that land prices in Tokyo may be as much as ten times as high as in New York or London. In 1970 it was calculated that to buy a $150\,m^2$ plot within commuting distance would take the average Tokyo worker $6\frac{1}{2}$ years, against 290 days in France, 174 days in Germany or 45 days in the United States. Interestingly, this indicates that weak planning controls, which make building land quite freely available, do not necessarily reduce the rate of inflation on that land.

Thus there is a continuing housing crisis. In 1968 45 per cent of Tokyo's families were living in tenement buildings, often with shared toilet and kitchen; typically, a tenement family would have only $10\,m^2$ (107 square feet), one-tenth its European equivalent and two-fifths the very modest official norms of the Metropolitan Government. Further, since most tenements are wooden, they are a serious fire and earthquake hazard. And typically, a single privately rented room may cost as much as a whole flat from a public corporation. Average housing rentals per square metre in 1967 were nearly twice those in Osaka, Japan's second city; they had increased sixfold between 1955 and 1965, while incomes only doubled.

There are no easy remedies. In a 1968 survey, 834,000 households (28·1 per cent of the total) were classified as living in sub-standard accommodation, while another 1,017,000 (34·2 per cent) considered themselves inadequately housed. (There was a 17·6 per cent overlap between these two groups.) The main complaint was lack of space. According to a 1966 survey, more than 50 per cent of the lowest income group of manual workers required rehousing. The Tokyo Metropolitan Government's five year housing plan, announced in 1967, aimed at building more than 10,000 units a year. But this is miniscule in relation to needs, and its achievement will depend on funds which may be swallowed up by the ever-rising cost of land. Achievement will depend on funds – the traditional stumbling block in all schemes for the improvement of Tokyo over a long period.

Basic services. Coupled with the housing shortage is a dire deficiency in basic public services. In 1967, 10 per cent of the population of the Ward Area did not enjoy a piped water supply, and had to use wells. Even in some of the areas of piped supply, water was only available for two hours a day in the summer peak period. And there are local disparities; in the Nerima Ward for instance only 26 per cent of the population was connected. Outside the Ward Area the position was worse: only 64 per cent had piped water supply. Per capita water consumption is still well below American levels, but it is increasing rapidly with more and more bathrooms and washing machines; and by 1980 maximum daily consumption is expected to be double that of 1962. An acute water shortage in the early 1960s was overcome by 1970 through the construction of dams on the river Tone and Arakawa; this increased the supply capacity by nearly one-third, but it was estimated that between 1970 and 1985 demand would further increase by two-thirds. There is an obvious need to allow the Tokyo Metropolitan Government to supply water outside the Ward Area, which is not the case at present.

Even more alarming is the deficiency of the sewage system. Within the Ward Area proper, in 1974, 48 per cent of the population still had no sewerage, and had to depend on the collection of excreta by gangs of nightmen; in 1967 only 35·5 per cent had the use of flush toilets. In 1950, as a temporary measure, it was arranged that a fleet of contractors' boats should dump waste into the Pacific Ocean; and in 1962 the ironically named 'Honey Fleet' was still disposing of 44 per cent of the total collection of night soil in this way. This was costly both in labour and in equipment, and it increased the already serious traffic congestion; it was abolished only in the late 1960s. The plan was to extend 100 per cent sewage to the Ward Area by 1980: in Tama new town, where only 14·5 per cent were served in 1974, the target was 1985. Similarly, 46 per cent of Tokyo's house garbage was being dumped into Tokyo Bay, for reclamation purposes, in the mid-1970s; but if this policy continues there will soon be major problems for fishing and for shipping fleets, and the earlier plan – to incinerate 100 per cent by the end of 1970 – was badly delayed.

By the 1970s the population of the Ward Area was almost static, while that of the surrounding ring was rapidly increasing. Factory employment, too, was dispersing; but headquarters office employment was still increasing in Tokyo. Commuter traffic has been rising at an average of 5 per cent per annum, and by 1970 Tokyo registered one of the biggest commuter movements in the world: the central area (conventionally defined as the three wards of Chiyoda, Chuo and Minato) was taking in 1,694,000 people daily, of whom well over half-a-million came from outside the 23-Ward Area. Hence the forecast in the mid-1970s was that by 1985 commuters to central Tokyo might nearly double, to 2,530,000, about half of whom would travel relatively long distances from outside the Ward Area. Already, by 1970, within a 40-kilometre (25-mile) zone from the centre, 40 per cent or more of the workers commuted to Tokyo. Total in-commuting to the Ward Area, 1·8 million in 1970, is expected to rise to 2·8 million by 1985. Yet this expansion of traffic has been accompanied by almost no expansion in physical facilities, and it is estimated that the transport system is designed for a maximum population of five million people. Except for a few subway extensions since 1945, virtually the whole of the system dates from the period between 1920 and 1940. And its geography is curiously ill-related to the commuting pattern. By a government decision of 1935 (impelled by the need to co-ordinate the rail system during the war with China), the area within the so-called Yamate loop line (operated by the National Railway System) was monopolised for the Tokyo Metropolitan Traffic Bureau. But a very large proportion of the commuters travel from the western suburbs by the so-called private railways, which were built in the 1920s and 1930s, and which have to terminate at stations on the Yamate loop line – three to four miles from the central business district (map 8.2). This in turn throws an enormous strain on the National Railways, which carry many of the passengers into the centre, as well as on to the underground railway, bus and streetcar systems. The National Railways alone carried 6·6 million passengers daily in Tokyo in 1961, and the total was rising by 350,000 a year. Their Chuo line is the only radial line from the western suburbs which connects directly with the central business district; in 1972, during a typical morning rush hour it recorded its passenger load was 260 per cent of capacity. This was a record; but many lines recorded double their capacity or more.

Despite the celebrated army of 700 student pushers, therefore,

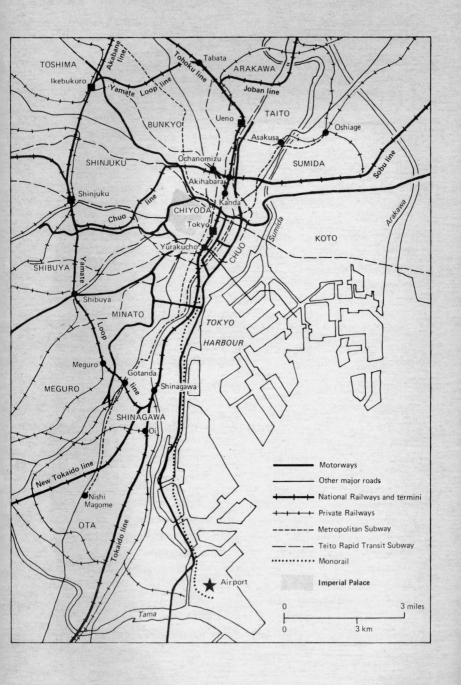

TOSHIMA

Ikebukuro

Akabane line

Tabata

Tohoku line

ARAKAWA

Yamate Loop line

Joban line

BUNKYO

Ueno

TAITO

Oshiage

Asakusa

SUMIDA

Ochanomizu

SHINJUKU

line

Akihabara

Sobu line

Shinjuku

Kanda

Chuo

CHIYODA

Arakawa

Tokyo

Yurakucho

KOTO

Sumida

CHUO

SHIBUYA

Yamate

MINATO

TOKYO

Shibuya

HARBOUR

Loop

Meguro

Gotanda

line

Shinagawa

MEGURO

SHINAGAWA

Oi

New Tokaido line

Nishi
Magome

OTA

Tokaido line

★ Airport

	Motorways
	Other major roads
	National Railways and termini
	Private Railways
	Metropolitan Subway
	Teito Rapid Transit Subway
	Monorail
	Imperial Palace

Tama

0   3 miles

0   3 km

Tokyo's problem gets steadily worse. The short-term answer is simply more capacity; and out of necessity, this is being provided. A plan for eleven new subway lines, totalling 178 miles was being energetically executed by 1974: eight lines totalling 168 kilometres (102 miles) were open. Critics, however, complained that during the 1960s, roads had a disproportionately large share of the total construction budget (map 8.3). The medium-term answer is to integrate the different parts of the system under one authority, on the London model, as was recommended by the Metropolitan Transportation Advisory Council, appointed by the Governor of the Tokyo Metropolitan Government in 1960. This would permit more effective use of investment funds and would put fares on the same basis everywhere. But the long-term and finally the only effective answer is not the reform of the transportation system alone, but the reshaping of the pattern of economic activities and land uses which is responsible for the present impasse.

Still, a small proportion of Tokyo's commuters travel by private car, for registered motor vehicles totalled only 2·6 million in December 1973: half these, just over 1·5 million, were private cars, giving only one for every 6·5 inhabitants. But the total stock of vehicles has been increasing by 5–7 per cent a year; and Tokyo's traffic snarl-up is in any case already one of the worst in the world. For street space in the Tokyo Ward Area is only 12·7 per cent and, in the entire TMG area, only 6·3 per cent of the total area, compared with 23 per cent in London, 26 per cent in Paris and Berlin, 35 per cent in New York and 43 per cent in Washington. Again, the immediate response of the Metropolitan Government has been investment in new facilities – this time of a spectacular order. Remembering the scenes of chaos which accompanied the Asian Games of 1956, when some spectators failed to reach the stadium all day, the authorities determined on the construction of 44 miles of four-lane metropolitan expressways on eight main routes, to be completed in time for the Olympic Games in October 1964. Though not all of the network was completed in time for the games, by the end of 1974 97 kilometres (60

8.2 *Tokyo: transport problems and plans.* Tokyo commuters suffer acute problems of access to their congested central area. By a 1935 government decision the private railways, which serve the fast-growing western suburbs, stop short of the central area, and passengers must transfer to the State-operated Yamate loop line. The central subway network is now being energetically extended. Tokyo's narrow, traditional street pattern is being relieved by a major programme of expressway construction.

miles) had been opened, out of an extended plan for 171 kilometres (106 miles); execution has been held up because of difficulties over compensation, expropriation, astronomical land costs (up to 3,500,000 Yen or £3,460 for 3·3 square metres or 35·5 square feet in the city centre) and difficulties of rehousing the inhabitants of the 59,000 dwellings to be displaced. These expressways have a modest design speed of 37 miles per hour, with many access ramps; built by a special Metropolitan Expressway Corporation set up by the Metropolitian Government, they are distinct from the full-scale inter-urban motorways in the suburban fringe areas. Meanwhile, the city traffic department wages a running war against drivers of heavy lorries and tourist buses, which jam the city's narrow streets, and against owner-drivers who leave their cars parked in the streets day and night. Regulations insist that new offices and hotels are accompanied by private parking lots, and that private car owners possess garages as a condition of their licences. This last regulation in particular had provoked bitter resentment.

Regional policies: capital and nation

But massive investment alone may merely encourage further growth, so generating a vicious circle. And the costs are huge: the Ten-Year Plan of the Tokyo Metropolitan Government, published in 1963, contemplated an investment of 3,073,000 million Yen (£3,040 million) in improving the infrastructure of the city. The Japanese almost certainly suffer from the most acute problem of metropolitan overgrowth in the world, and since the mid-1950s they have been evolving positive regional policies to try to counteract its worst effects.

First, they have devised policies to promote regional growth in the less favoured regions of the country. These measures are embodied in the Law of Promoting Industries in Under-Developed Regions, of 1961, and the Law of Promoting Construction of New Industrial Cities, of 1962. The latter measure is especially interesting because it seeks to develop certain areas in the provinces as major regional cities, so that they may act as effective counter-magnets to Tokyo. Suitable sites are to be proposed by prefectoral governors in the regions and agreed by the central government. Plans will then be drawn up by provincial governments in consultation with advisory councils. The aim is an ambitious one: it is to develop cities of one million people and more, and with a full range of urban services. Only cities of this order, the Japanese think, can counter the attractions of giants like Tokyo or Osaka.

Secondly, though, the fact has to be faced that many of the tertiary functions (in particular) will continue to grow in Tokyo; so it is critically necessary to provide a new structure for the internal development of the metropolitan region, in order to avoid further pressure on the already hopelessly congested core. The National Capital Region Development Law of 1956 aimed to provide such a structure. It applied to the wide planning region within 60 to 75 miles of central Tokyo, including the whole of the Tokyo Metropolitan Government, three whole prefectures and parts of four other prefectures; and it was intended that all these authorities would co-operate in the work of a National Capital Region Development Commission, which would prepare a plan of construction pro-grammes to be carried through by the Metropolitan Government and the individual prefectures. In practice, however, the Commission proved a weak body with virtually no powers or financial resources of its own.

The basic principles of development under the original 1956 law were based on Sir Patrick Abercrombie's plan for Greater London in 1944. First the plan delineated a built-up area extending about 10 miles in any direction from Tokyo Central Station, and incorporating all the 23 wards plus the cities of Yokohama, Kawasaki and Kawaguchi. Here further outward urban sprawl should be prevented. To this end a second zone – the 7-mile-wide green belt zone – was intended to encircle the development area: but in fact planning powers proved inadequate to hold this belt against pressures for development. A considerable potential population growth would have to be accommodated elsewhere, in the peripheral zone between 17 and 45 miles from central Tokyo; here the plan proposed satellite towns to absorb decentralised population and employment (map 8.1a). The Law for Town Development in the National Capital Region (1958) provided a specific method for developing the satellites. The central government would provide funds, subsidies for local authorities and technical assistance; individual government departments might also help local authorities and the Japan Housing Corporation; and the government would advance funds to developers if they were recognised by the National Capital Region Development Corporation. By 1967 a number of these satellites had been designated; though originally termed new towns, they did not

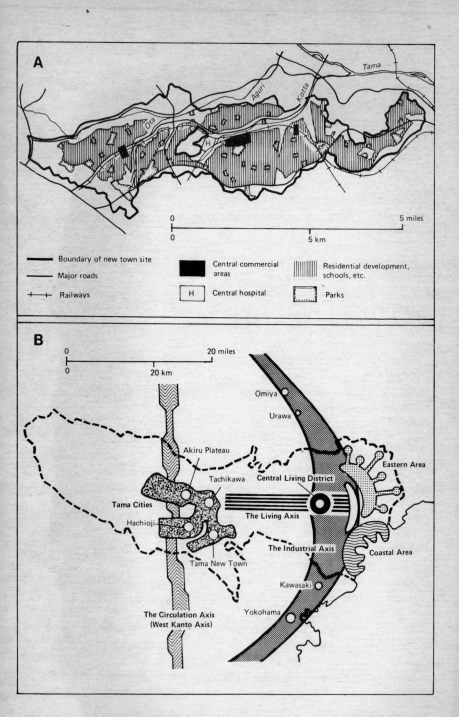

A

Tama

Aguri

Kotta

Ota

H

0   5 miles
0   5 km

— Boundary of new town site
— Major roads
+—+ Railways

■ Central commercial areas
☐ H Central hospital

⦀ Residential development, schools, etc.
⬚ Parks

B

0   20 miles
0   20 km

Omiya
Urawa

Akiru Plateau
Tachikawa

Central Living District

Tama Cities

Eastern Area

Hachioji

The Living Axis

The Industrial Axis

Tama New Town

Coastal Area

Kawasaki

The Circulation Axis
(West Kanto Axis)

Yokohama

represent self-contained communities as the British model, and one of the largest – the so-called new town of Tama – was in fact a giant commuter development designed for 400,000, 18–25 miles west of the city centre and built by a number of different agencies including the Tokyo Metropolitan Government, the Japan Housing Corporation and four different local authorities (map 8.3a).

The original plan worked on the basis of a 1975 population, for the entire region, of 26,600,000 (against 19,800,000 in 1955). But the 1960 Census showed that the population was increasing even faster than had been expected, and the figures had to be revised. Population was then expected to rise from 22,520,000 (in 1960) to 28,200,000 (in 1975), to be distributed: in the inner built-up area, 12,250,000, in the outer area 15,950,000. (Without planning, the inner area might sprawl so as to contain 16 million of the total.) By 1963, 15 satellites had been designated, and they were expected eventually to number 30. They had 1975 final target populations ranging from 150,000 to 670,000; the additional population for each of them, on average, was about 100,000.

The National Capital Region Plan was a positive plan for regional decentralisation; it could not be expected to work without some fairly tough negative controls at the centre. So the Law Restricting Industrial and Educational Establishments in the Built-up Area within the National Capital Region (1959), an adjunct to the regional plan, restricted major factory, university and college building projects within the 23-ward area plus the neighbouring cities of Musashino and Mitaka. But even after this law, by the mid-60s 80,000 new jobs had been created on average each year in small plants and in extensions of existing plants, and the job of providing a new structure for the built-up area itself was equally urgent. Within this area, the Metropolitan Government sought to channel investment funds into the development of office and retail sub-centres away from the existing central area, especially along the line of the Yamate loop railway which is the destination of so many commuters from Tokyo's western suburbs. The most dramatic project so far is the development

8.3 **A** *Tama New Town.* Designed for 400,000 people, this 8-mile long town 18–25 miles west of Tokyo will form the nucleus of a polycentric urban complex.
B *Bi-polar Tokyo.* The Tama complex will form the western end of an east-west 'living axis' connected to the centre of the region by good transport links: thus it is hoped to develop it as a counter-magnet to Tokyo proper, with a special stress on higher education, research and culture.

of the Shinjuku sub-centre next to the important railway station on the Yamate loop, three miles due west of the Imperial Palace. Here, removal of the Yodobashi water filtration plant freed 240 acres for development as a business centre; the whole project was completed in the early 1970s, creating a major island of CBD activities – offices, shops, and entertainment – separate from the historic Ginza – Marunouchi core.

By 1965 it was clear that the main lines of the original Tokyo regional plan – particularly the preservation of the green belt – had no hope of realisation; the powers to achieve it were simply lacking. Population increase and new development were very marked in the green belt ring; it added over 2 million to its population between 1955 and 1965. Therefore in 1965 a revision of the National Capital Region Development Law (which extended the boundaries of the National Capital Region) recognised a *fait accompli*; it abandoned the green belt and substituted a new suburban development area extending beyond 30 miles from the centre. Within this zone, population growth would be encouraged at suitable points; these would include most of the former satellite towns (the term itself was eliminated) which would be fewer in number, but larger than in the original plan. The new suburban growth areas would be physically contiguous with the existing urban area, but an effort would be made to preserve open space between them; in this respect the 1965 revised plan somewhat resembles the corridor or axial plan for Washington, or the even earlier finger plan for Copenhagen, in which lines of urban development are separated by sectors of open land (map 8.1b). Then, in 1968, a revision of the basic City Planning Law gave further substance to the concept by distinguishing urban promotion areas (with provision of infrastructure) and urban control areas where there would be no development in principle. But significantly in the Tokyo case, these were to be at the far periphery where there was least pressure for development; here, as not in the past, Tokyo planners seemed to be accepting the inevitable.

These are official, legal responses to the immediate problem of controlling growth. But Tokyo probably has a greater wealth of original and unconventional expert ideas for its future development than any other major world city. They reflect the extraordinary technical ingenuity that is typically Japanese, allied to a passionate interest in the problems of metropolitan growth. One set of solutions is based on a major extension of Tokyo eastwards into the bay. The technical means range from reclamation through the sinking of piers to create a 'Venice of the East', and the construction of a series of bridges, to a city built on rafts. Another school sees the solution in building upwards. With an average building height in the 23-ward area of only 1·35 storeys, Tokyo must be the lowest-rise major city of the world, and during the 1960s the Ministry of Construction lifted the 102-feet height limit imposed after the 1923 earthquake. Yet another idea is the development of a Japanese Brasilia 90 miles from Tokyo, built on 116 square miles of state-owned land at the foot of Mount Fuji. A super-highway would connect the two centres within one hour and 180,000 civil servants and their families would be decentralised from Tokyo. This last scheme neatly accords with official policy, for in 1961 the government announced a plan to move 78 government offices and institutions out of the capital; and they estimated that the total numbers affected, directly and indirectly, would also be 180,000. Interestingly, though, the proposed move has met with a great deal of rooted opposition. Despite the problems of overgrowth currently facing Tokyo, it appears that some of its citizens prefer it with all its faults.

More likely – because eminently practicable – is a fairly modest proposal by the Tokyo Metropolitan Government: to create sufficient new jobs in the Tama New Town area, particularly in the public sector through new universities and cultural institutions, so as progressively to give the whole region a bi-polar structure. At first this will be fairly limited: only 80,000 out of 200,000 Tama workers are expected to find jobs in the new town area itself. But, coupled with the development of strong two-way transportation links, the proposal could create a new axis along a roughly east–west line, some twenty miles in length between the present centre, via the Shinjuku sub-centre, to Tama (map 8.3b).

Tokyo government: A growing fiscal crisis

By 1976, Tokyo was fast joining New York as a world city in crisis. Throughout the boom years of the 1960s and early 1970s, economic buoyancy had produced a steady and substantial growth in tax yields, which the Tokyo Metropolitan Government needed to support an ambitious programme of improvements; in 1975 alone, this increase was 14·5 per cent. But for the fiscal year 1970, it was cut back to 8·7 per cent: fairly spectacular by western standards, but producing an expected deficit of 100,000 million Yen.

Officials were agreed that the remedy lay in two directions. First, there had to be administrative streamlining, which would concentrate the city's efforts on the most essential programmes: the growth in the city's workforce, which had proceeded inexorably in the early 1970s, had to cease and even be reversed; and the housing programme would need to be concentrated on essentials, especially homes for low income groups. Secondly, though, no amount of pruning would suffice unless the city found new revenues to maintain its essential programmes. The present revenues, derived from a combination of income, corporate and residence taxes, might be supplemented in various ways: new business taxes, real estate tax, petrol sales tax, an end to present tax concessions (for instance, to large businesses), extra profit taxes. The city might acquire greater freedom to issue bonds – though that might run the risk of the New York experience. There might be greater central government subsidy – for school construction, and for salaries of police or teachers. And tax assessments might be recast, to give a greater share of revenues for the cities. Above all, therefore, Tokyo needed greater fiscal autonomy. And associated with this, it needed greater powers to tax and acquire land. Without these extra financial powers, the city simply could not maintain its pressing programmes to bring greater order and dignity to the everyday lives of its citizens.

The Tokyo experience

This chapter ends as it began, with paradoxes. Tokyo indicates that great economic dynamism, which attacts population to a major urban area at an unprecedented rate, may create social problems with which the administrative machine cannot cope, leading to a situation of near-breakdown in essential public services. It shows too that in such an economically buoyant society, considerations of land use planning are likely to take a bad second place in competition with the overwhelming desire to exploit every economic opportunity; put at its bluntest, most Japanese decision-takers – and perhaps most Japanese people – have little time for planning at present. Lastly, and most tellingly, it shows that a society in a state of relative laissez-faire, while undoubtedly imposes considerable social costs on its citizens, does not necessarily bring compensating benefits. It is paradoxical indeed that Tokyo, with an ineffectual planning machine powerless in practice to stop uncontrolled development, suffers a rate of inflation of land prices in excess of London with its tight control of land use. Thus, despite freedom to spread, the citizens of Tokyo remain considerably more crowded, and more short of house-room, than their equivalents either in Western Europe or North America. The relationship between planning controls, urban form and life styles is thus a complex one. And lastly, Tokyo's experience shows that when world recession strikes, the great city in a previously buoyant economy may be stricken most grievously of all; its programmes, based on high expectations of growth, may face unprecedented crisis. Tokyo's recent story, in many ways, is a chastening one for the planners of other world cities.

9 The future metropolis

We have looked at the development of seven great urban regions in the recent past and up to the present time. We have seen that in the century and a half since the industrial revolution, almost without exception all these metropolitan centres have shown continuous population growth, both absolutely and in relation to the countries of which they form a part. We have found this to be true in countries large and small, densely and sparsely populated, capitalist and communist; countries dedicated to laissez-faire, and countries wedded to the idea that planning may control growth. We have looked at varied attempts to limit the growth of metropolitan cities and have found no case where these attempts have met with any sure success. We have observed that in every city this growth brings problems; but that those problems may vary in intensity, according especially to the internal disposition of functions and land uses within the metropolitan region. We turn last to the future. May the trends of the last century and a half be safely projected forward for half a century more? If so, what will be the result? If not, what modifications or changes are foreseen, and how certain will their action be?

In truth many important trends have operated in the growth of cities since 1800. And save perhaps for the fact of overall growth itself, few if any have operated continuously at the same pace, or even in the same direction. In this final chapter, one critical central question is whether this overall trend to growth will continue and, if so, in what form. But we look also, as guidelines to the future, at other trends which in the past have shown important changes over time: trends in the internal organisation of metropolitan cities. One concerns the extent and form of the residential suburbs; the other, the future role of the central business district and its relationship to the

240

rest of the metropolitan economy. In looking at these trends, it will be useful first to examine them from the standpoint of the mid-1960s, when the first edition of this book appeared; and then from the changed perceptions of the mid-1970s.

The 1960s view: continued suburban spread

A first certainty is that if the world cities grow, their suburbs will spread. We may say this in confidence because there is no counter-evidence. In every major modern city for which we have precise statistical data, the frontier of building is being pushed outwards; the newer suburbs at the fringe show more rapid growth than the more densely populated inner districts. This has been true ever since the development of modern urban transportation techniques. First, after 1870 the streetcar and the railway allowed extensive ribbon development along the lines of the main radial arteries; later, after 1920 the motor bus and the private motor-car allowed the spaces between these arteries to fill in also, forming a more or less homogeneous urban spread with minor differences in type of housing and density of population. This, with local modifications, is the pattern of London, New York and Tokyo. It is even true of Paris and of Moscow, though with the important difference that much of the suburban development has taken place in a multi-storey form and at higher densities than in cities subject to the Anglo-Saxon tradition of individual housing.

Therefore the only question is whether growth will continue. In the mid-1960s, this seemed certain; by the mid-1970s the evidence was more contradictory. If it continues, then evidence from the past shows that in guiding residential growth, the planner's range of possibilities is limited. He can to some extent determine the residential densities, the size and distribution of centres for shopping, services and office employment, the disposition of open space. He can permit almost uniform low-density development with a scatter of service and employment nodes, and of small and medium-sized public and private open spaces, as Frank Lloyd Wright suggested in his plan for Broadacre City and as is now happening over much of the metropolitan area of Los Angeles. He can encourage growth along the main radial transportation lines so as to provide high-speed access from the centre, with green wedges in the less accessible areas between those lines, so forming a star-shaped pattern such as is proposed for Copenhagen and for the extensions of the Dutch

Randstad. He can ring the existing suburbs by a green belt and concentrate all subsequent development in a number of separate satellite centres of limited size and with separate services, as has been done in London and in Moscow. He can try to limit the demands which suburban development makes on land by building suburbs at higher densities, involving the use of multi-storey blocks, as in Moscow and Paris.

But in all this he is likely to have only the vaguest idea of the real advantages and disadvantages of his preferred scheme. From the United States Kevin Lynch has tried at least to set out the chief heads of the balance sheet. Uniform low density has more advantages than many European planners might think: it encourages flexibility, it can provide a choice of housing, it allows local participation, it reduces congestion and this increases accessibility by car. But it is expensive, it involves long distances in travel, and it does not readily provide for accidental contact between people and people or people and things, for political identity, or for a visually satsifying environment. Further, it may actually reduce accessibility for non-car-owners because it makes maintenance of a good public transportation system difficult, if not impossible. The satellite concept retains many of these advantages but adds spontaneous communication (via the service centres), local participation on a wider scale, and better visual image. However, flexibility may be lost, while time-distance especially to the centre of the metropolitan region, remains high. The urban star arrangement gives fast radial movement and the possibility of a wide range of housing, as well as good visual image; but there are difficulties of circumferential movement, of potential congestion at the centre and along the radials, and of increasing time-costs as the pattern develops away from the centre. High-density development gives good spontaneous communication, high accessibility and low time-distances, good visual image and strong community sense; it would probably have low running costs. But it would be relatively uncomfortable, there would be a poor individual range of housing types, individual participation might be more difficult (because of the size of the metropolitan mass), and initial costs might be very high. And as Lynch points out, it would be a contrary tradition. In countries with a free and varied housing market, like the United States, evidence shows that the great majority of the metropolitan population, provided that they can exercise choice, will opt for a single-family dwelling at a medium or even a low density.

The more one looks at the problem, in fact, the more one is driven to the conclusion that the form of the residential areas is really a secondary problem, as soon as one has made fairly basic decisions about the type of housing which is to predominate; and in most societies, this is a decision depending very largely on the general social *mores*, and only to a minor extent on the planner's preference. What is much more fundamentally important is the distribution of employment; for that will determine the journey to work and will also more generally dominate the generation of traffic during the working week. Above all, one question is critical. Will the tendency continue for employment to concentrate in relatively small central business districts? In the biggest metropolitan centres, it is usual to find between one-quarter and one-third of total employment of the whole urban agglomeration concentrated within a space of ten square miles or less, right at the centre. And in almost every metropolis, the growth in this employment at least keeps pace with growth in the rest of the urban agglomeration. In absolute terms, it presents an ever-growing problem: probably the most serious which the modern city faces.

The future of the central area

In the older European or Asiatic city the central business area often shows amazing continuity over time. The centre of London, or Paris, or Cologne is where the Romans put it two thousand years ago; that of Tokyo where a warrior established his fort in the fifteenth century. Even the site of Manhattan was picked out by the first Dutch arrivals in the early seventeenth century. Yet though the geographical form remains the same, the economic reality has often showed large changes, even within recent decades.

Up to 1850 or even later, though precise statistical evidence is often lacking, much of the growth of metropolitan cities seems to have been occasioned by an increasing concentration of the *goods-handling* activities within the central areas. Here raw materials and finished goods were transhipped, traded and stored; here a variety of raw materials, often imported, was worked up into finished goods. The typical activities were commodity trading, both wholesale and retail, and a variety of industries ranging from the bulk processing of imported necessities like flour or sugar, to the handicraft production of luxuries for the rich. Only belatedly, after about 1650, had these physical functions produced forms of service industry which were not directly concerned with goods handling: activities like banking, insurance and dealings in business stocks and shares. In this period up to 1850, cities grew most rapidly where goods were readily traded, around seaports or river ports, or at natural junctions of the new railway routes of the nineteenth century. But as seen in chapter 1, after 1850 a rapid change came over the centres of the metropolitan cities: the traditional activities were joined, and then even sometimes displaced, by new types of activity which were characteristically carried on in offices. This was no sudden once-for-all process; it has gone on happening ever since, and it threatens to be a major feature of the development of the great metropolitan centres in the immediate future. Indeed, the process may be speeding up; the 1960s and 1970s have seen a radical reconstruction of factory industry in most advanced industrial countries, leading first to great advances in productivity that actually reduced total manufacturing employment and, second, to a movement of that employment to suburban and smaller city sites.

Yet beyond this, the exact form of the change is exceedingly difficult to predict, because of the speed of change and the inadequacy of our understanding. The economist and the economic geographer can explain very precisely why, in the twentieth century, the iron and steel industry has been shifting towards tidewater locations, or traditional metropolitan manufactures like clothing and printing have deserted London and New York for smaller provincial towns in the deep countryside. But they are far from being able to explain precisely why advertising agencies gravitate towards Manhattan or the West End. Yet the general principle is evident enough. At the very centre of the structure of the central business district of each world city there is found a relatively small nucleus of highly skilled professionals. All these people, in one way and another, live by creating, processing or exchanging ideas. The stockbroker, considering the fortunes of a hundred companies in a dozen countries; the company lawyer, pondering a difficult piece of patent law; the consultant, considering whether to recommend an operation; the university professor, arguing about urban growth in a seminar; the government servant, discussing whether to approve new investment in schools or roads or power stations; the editorial director of the publishing house, taking advice on a manuscript; the newspaper features editor, looking for a specialist to write on the latest trouble-spot in Africa; the television producer, discussing a script on the housing problem with a journalist and a university researcher; the advertising copywriter, talking about a campaign with the accounts executive and then with a number of technical specialists; the freelance photographer, taking varied assignments from half a dozen photographic editors; all these people live only on their ideas, on transmitting those ideas readily and economically to others and on receiving their ideas in exchange.

The central business district therefore can be seen as a highly specialised machine for producing, processing and trading specialised *intelligence*. And of all commodities, intelligence has the highest costs of transportation. As the American economist Robert Murray Haig pointed out as long ago as 1926 in his classic study of the metropolis, this is why activities depending on transmission of information are compelled, but are also willing, to pay the highest urban rents for the most accessible central sites, displacing other activities from the city centres as they do so.

The process is a continuing one; for the ideas industries are growing many times faster than industry as a whole. As late as 1850, they included only a very small number of traditional professions like banking, medicine or law. But as increasing mechanisation and then automation have reduced the physical agony of growing wheat and turning it into bread, of picking cotton and processing it into shirts, so new types of economic activity have come into prominence. The road to economic advance no longer lies in concentration on the brute processes of physical production, but rather in increased attention to research, to education, to better understanding of the organisation of the production and the sales processes. And even the nature of brute production changes. The market for bread or shirts expands less rapidly than the market for fashion magazines or television programmes; bread and shirts, in any case, can be produced more and more efficiently with fewer workers, while the production of ideas is impossible to automate; an ever-growing proportion of physical production represents processed ideas. Given this, as Haig said, the question is changed from 'Why live in the city?' to 'Why not live in the city?'

It should be possible to give precise expression to these trends; and Richard L. Meier has tried to do so. He has estimated that the transmission of pieces of information has been rising, in recent years in advanced countries, at between 3 per cent and 6 per cent per year. But this transmission rate is much higher in the great cities than elsewhere: Meier calculates that in New York, London or San

Francisco the average citizen may receive 100 million bits of meaningful information a year, that is about 100 times the average of even major cities in developing countries like Addis Ababa, Jakarta or Teheran, and their rate is in turn ten times that of market towns. There is clearly a real possibility that in a world increasingly concerned with the transmission and receipt of information, very few centres will be able to compete. The economic life of the world will be concentrated into a few major information centres.

This may be averted. In recent years revolutionary advances have been made in person-to-person communication and in the storage and processing of data. Melvin Webber has argued that these techniques allow urban standards of information to extend across whole countries, and that the whole of the United States (for instance) now has an 'urban culture', that is a high-information culture. He argues further that improvements in urban transportation allow the diffusion of face-to-face contacts over very widely scattered urban areas. Thus in Los Angeles, though the pattern of activities is very dispersed and the city centre is much less strongly developed than in other American cities of similar importance, he guesses that an establishment on Wiltshire Boulevard has as many linked establishments within any given time-distance as has a similar establishment in Rockefeller Center in New York. Given the likely development of electronic control of automobile traffic, permitting bumper-to-bumper flows along freeways at 150 miles per hour, Webber argues that the Los Angeles pattern could show further decentralisation. There could be a very widespread urban sprawl with almost complete diffusion (or at most weak local concentration) of economic activities and homes, all interconnected by universal high-speed private transportation.

This type of development may be true for a city that can be structured from the first in terms of universal motor-car transportation, so that Los Angeles may provide the model for fast-growing cities in developing countries – in Latin America for instance. But some qualifications need to be made. In the first place full electronic control on the freeways is some way off, and meanwhile rush-hour jams put severe limitations on the mobility of the Angeleno. It remains doubtful whether the worker on Wiltshire Boulevard could make the same boast as the New York businessman described by Haig in 1926: that from his Times Square skyscraper, he could reach anyone of importance in the business world within fifteen minutes.

But secondly, most world cities are prisoners of history. Their physical structures are highly centralised, based as they are on well-developed radial public transportation, which gives maximum accessibility at the centre and much poorer accessibility elsewhere; while the established pattern of land uses and land values makes major change difficult. In such cities, advances in the technology of person-to-person communications have had little effect on the centralisation of the ideas industries. Rather, earlier advances like the penny post and the telephone appear to have increased the hold of the central business district. Meier suggests an explanation: technology merely speeds up and so increases the number and range of preliminary contacts, so multiplying the number of possible person-to-person encounters where critical decisions are made. As Aaron Fleischer had put it in an analysis of the limitations of communication by television, a mechanical device 'may not be adequate for transactions that would terminate in a handshake – or a fist fight. Clearly, it would not suffice for encounters that culminate in an embrace.'

Recent research on office communications – by Cowan, Goddard and Reid in Britain, and by Thorngren in Sweden – suggests that office work can be usefully split into categories. At one extreme, there are highly speculative exchanges of intelligence or ideas of an under-standardised type. They require face-to-face contact in meetings which may be set up a long time in advance – conferences for instance. At the other extreme are routine control processes. They can often be executed by telecommunications without any pre-arrangement. Intermediate between these extremes are a range of planning processes involving a mixture of face-to-face contact and telecommunications. Clearly, the more telecommunications can be substituted, the greater the possibility of decentralisation from large business centres. But many organisations and even many individuals are involved in a mixture of functions – making it difficult for small organisations to move out. In so far as the need for face-to-face contacts remains, complete decentralisation – as in the science fiction vision of everyone working at home – seems unlikely. Further, Reid stresses, better and cheaper electronics may encourage more face-to-face contact and business travel, as the telephone gave a stimulus to the letter post.

The overall likelihood therefore is that the ideas industries will continue to grow in the metropolitan centres. They will displace other activities, long associated with the centres: many types of manufacturing, wholesaling and warehousing, the more generalised and popular types of retail shopping, and those types of office activity which involve the assemblage, processing and storage of data, and even the taking of routine decisions on that data. Such routine activities will increasingly be performed by electronic machinery with the help of a small staff of skilled programmers and computer operators. Though electronic storage should lead to dramatic savings in space, it is likely that wherever the routine activities can be economically split off from the decision-taking processes they will be displaced from the high-rent central sites into the suburbs near to their labour force – or even to smaller rural centres. (Thus, in the United States, manufacturing employment has grown most rapidly in the towns of the rural south). Finally, it is even possible that some of the ideas industries themselves – those with less well-developed linkages, such as higher education, some types of research, and parts of the government machine – might also be displaced from the centre, provided that the planner is willing to take resolute and even unpopular action.

Towards a new metropolitan structure

It is possible to go beyond this? Perhaps, but it will require a more accurate understanding of the way the metropolitan economy works, and also a greater capacity for imaginative action, than most urban planners now apparently possess. We have seen that in Europe the polycentric metropolitan regions, like the Dutch Randstad or the German Rhine–Ruhr region, apparently work with no less efficiency than single-centred giant cities like Paris or London; and that they suffer much less severe problems of traffic congestion or long commuter journeys. They achieve success by concentrating specialised types of activity, or systems of urban linkage, into partly specialised centres. In a different way it is claimed that Los Angeles and other cities of the western United States achieve equal success by pure dispersion of activities and by a transportation system which makes for equal accessibility over the whole of the metropolitan area. These patterns have been produced by history. But it might be possible to move existing centralised cities some little way in the direction of one or other of these models by conscious action. From the United States, both Kevin Lynch and Melvin Webber have suggested ways in which this might be done.

Lynch has suggested a variant of the dispersed pattern. The transportation system, however, would not be random but based on a triangular grid, coarser at the edges of the urban area, finer in the interior (map 9.1). Densities would vary, with intensive peaks at the junctions of the circulation system and with high concentrations along the main transportation lines, but with wide regions of low density inside the grid. Belts and tongues of open land would form another type of grid, penetrating this network. Within the system there would be a hierarchy of central concentrations: the larger the centre, the more specialised the activities. Lynch argues that planners could guide existing metropolitan centres into this polyform type of development by encouraging further growth; by constructing a triangular transportation grid, to give maximum accessibility throughout the area; by encouraging the present central area to specialise and develop into a loose cluster, while allowing rival centres to develop elsewhere within the network. Apart from the higher densities in the centres and along the major channels, zoning of land uses and densities would be used sparingly. The result would be a much freer form of metropolitan development than most planners – especially European ones – would now countenance; having provided guidelines, the planner would leave natural economic and social forces to determine the pattern of development. In fact, the existing urban structure of Los Angeles (map 9.2) – a metropolitan area that has grown freely, without much conscious planning control – closely resembles the Lynch model.

Webber has taken this line of thinking one stage further. In his view, traditional urban planning has suffered from an obsession with spatial form and structure; and most of the forms that have been suggested are no longer viable. Instead, he has argued that we should accept the idea that 'the optimum settlement and land use patterns are likely to be as pluralistic as society itself'. Having determined the right social organisation, the spatial organisation will logically follow; and we will find it very complex indeed. The land use pattern will be highly diversified. There will still be concentrations in centres and sub-centres, because transportation costs will never be reduced to zero, and because external economies will still result from clustering of similar and even unlike establishments. But there will also be a need for many scattered developments for a great variety of establishments which do not need such contacts, in a great variety of land-use complexes and density patterns.

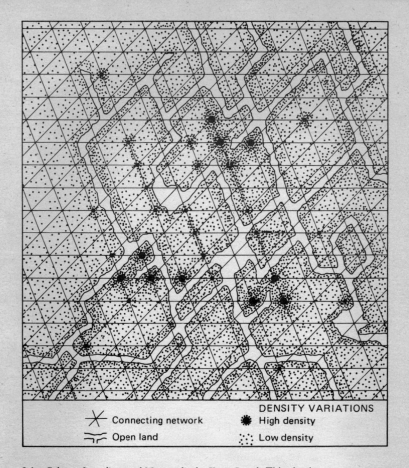

DENSITY VARIATIONS

✳ Connecting network · High density

︾ Open land ⠘ Low density

9.1 *Scheme for a dispersed Metropolis, by Kevin Lynch*. This plan is
based on a triangular transportation grid. Densities rise very high at
intersections and are high along transport lines, but there are wide low-
density regions within the triangles. Belts and tongues of open land
form another intersecting pattern. This is really a polycentric plan with
a hierarchy of central concentrations: the biggest centres have the most
specialised activities.

The ideas of Lynch and Webber were closely related. They
represented the central new contribution to planning theory of the
1960s. At that time, they represented a sharp break from most
traditional planning thought in that they tried to go back to the actual
processes which operate in the metropolis, ask how they could be
made to work as efficiently as possible, and only then built the spatial
structure around these workings. They were necessarily tentative in

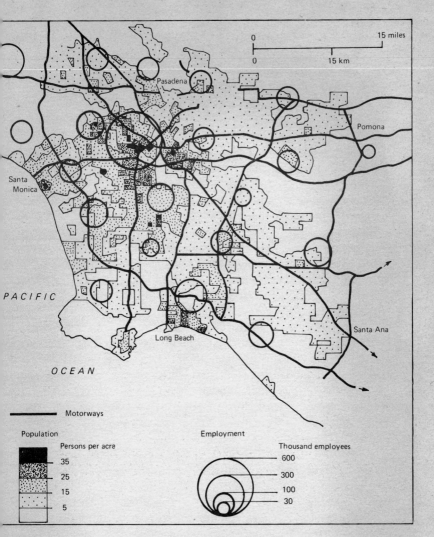

	0			15 miles
	0		15 km	

Pasadena

Pomona

Santa
Monica

PACIFIC

Santa Ana

OCEAN

Long Beach

——— Motorways

Population

Persons per acre

- 35
- 25
- 15
- 5

Employment

Thousand employees

- 600
- 300
- 100
- 30

9.2 *Los Angeles*. The southern California metropolis, with a
population of close on 10 million in 1970, is the archetype of the loose,
dispersed, polycentric world city – though it arose spontaneously, not
by plan. Some commentators in the 1970s were arguing that it could
not survive in an energy-hungry age.

that they were based on no precise knowledge of the optimum
operation of the urban processes. Until very recently almost all
thinking about the organisation of cities, like the classic 'concentric'
theory of Burgess or the 'sector' theory of Hoyt, has been essentially
descriptive, not based on analysis of processes at all. In the mid-1960s

there was great interest in economic models which showed the optimum mode of development of an urban region, given certain criteria. Such a model allowed one to consider the optimum location of production in relation to transportation costs, given certain limitations in the form of the existing distribution of population and resources at the start of the planning period. It is clear that there are very great problems in applying this type of inter-regional analysis to the internal development of a metropolitan region. The data may be deficient; the time scales are often shorter and more varied, the freedom to change land use may be greater. And above all, the importance of economies and diseconomies of scale may lead to situations which are not amenable to the relatively simple techniques of linear analysis. In the late 1960s and early 1970s great progress was made in the development of urban models in the course of the planning studies which have been made for many American and European metropolitan areas. But they proved more useful in predicting the future spread of homes and local services than in giving to the planner an optimal distribution of basic industry; and they did not remove the need for judgement in evaluating different possibilities of urban development. The dream of the 1960s – a linear programming model that would not merely predict, but would also evaluate the optimal location of all activities in the metropolis – has so far proved elusive; and by the late 1970s, few planners would have much hope of soon finding such a planners' holy grail.

The changed world of the 1970s

In almost every respect, by the mid-1970s the world of the urban planner seemed quite different, even opposite, from that of the mid-1960s when the first edition of this book appeared. The question must be how far this transformation is objectively real, how far it is a changed perception on the part of planners and others who interpret the urban world.

The first change is in the fact of growth and in attitudes towards it. In the mid-1960s, growth was seen as inevitable, almost automatic and in many respects highly desirable. Most forecasts assumed rising populations and constantly increasing Gross National Product. But by the 1970s, birth rates were plummeting to their lowest-ever levels, and the world was gripped in the worst recession since the 1930s. (How far these two events were connected, through contracting expectations of future market growth, few economists seemed to be ready to say). One particular feature, in all this, was the continuing radical contraction of manufacturing employment opportunities, as rationalisation of production was joined by competition from third world countries in a world market that had ceased to grow. Some indeed were speculating whether, in the long run, most kinds of manufacturing had a future in advanced industrial countries; there, perhaps, the post-industrial era had dawned. In any event, manufacturing in the great metropolitan cities everywhere seemed to be in rapid decline.

In any event, economic experts increasingly doubted whether continued growth was possible or desirable. They pointed to the energy crisis of the early 1970s as harbinger of more serious, and permanent, shortages to come. Finite energy supplies, plus the risk of global ecological disaster, would compel a low- or no-growth policy in the advanced industrial nations before the end of the twentieth century – so these experts argued. In particular, it would prove impossible to maintain, let alone develop, the high-mobility lifestyle characteristic of North American and west European metropolitan areas in the 1960s and early 1970s. Instead, events would compel a return to the higher densities, and the close intermixture of homes and jobs, characteristic of cities in an earlier age.

The third change, again associated closely with the last, is that the main concerns of planners have shifted. In the mid-60s, the emphasis was on planning as an engine of greater efficiency and convenience, helping economic growth to produce a fairly homogeneous consumer lifestyle which would meet the demands of the great majority. It seemed, in this, that planning could be based on consensus: the good of one was indeed the good of all – or at least of most people. In the changed world of the mid-1970s, planning is seen as far more concerned with questions of distributional equity: as a process that produces winners and losers. Too often, radical planners argue, planning has favoured the haves at the expense of the have-nots: the affluent majority (or even minority) at the expense of less advantaged groups. In particular, the decentralised high-mobility lifestyle of the 1960s was bought at the expense of lower mobility for those outside the system, as rising car ownership brought poorer public transport and longer distances to work, to shop, to school, to recreation opportunities. Even in affluent California, it was noted, thirty per cent of adults had no immediate everyday access to a car; in less affluent inner London, the proportion rose as high as three-quarters.

Lastly, and again associatedly, growth and expansion of the entire metropolitan area could no longer be seen as an entirely painless process. In the era of growth of the 1960s, suburban decentralisation could be pictured as necessary and even desirable to relieve pressure – of new economic activities and new in-migrants – in the heart of the city. In the stagnant or declining world of the 1970s, this is by no means so self-evident. The inner city is seen to be decaying both

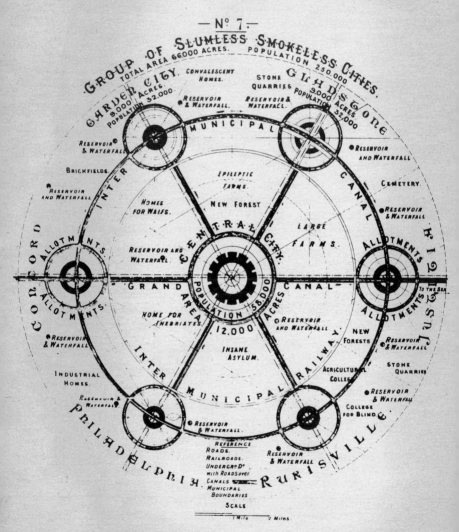

economically and demographically. The new tertiary industries are no longer increasing fast enough at the centre to counter the rapid decline of traditional manufacturing industry all around; and even some of the tertiaries, including headquarters' offices, are deserting the metropolis for smaller cities where rents are lower and labour easier to find. Thus the decentralising city is leaving an economic hole in the centre. And people, too, are continuing to leave the central city, in search of suburban or small-town homes and lifestyles. Further, the departing citizens are often the more skilled, the better educated, the more affluent; those who stay behind, or those who take their place, are too often the unskilled and under-educated and less affluent, whose capacities do not match the economic demands of the tertiary urban economy. Consequently, as the New York story most dramatically shows, the central city faces fiscal crisis as its tax base falls and its welfare burdens rise.

These are new problems for the world cities; yet some doubt whether they are truly urban problems at all. Rather, they are urban expressions of wider, deeper changes in the economy and society of the advanced industrial nations. The decline of manufacturing employment and its removal to low-cost small-town and rural locations; the mismatch between the high-skill tertiary metropolitan economy and the unskilled labour force; the problems of multiple deprivation and welfare dependency; the demographic stagnation of the advanced industrial countries; the pending energy crisis; all these are general, even global problems for national and even international action, which are beyond the capacities of even the most capable city politicians and officials to solve.

Nevertheless, some answers may be found at the level of metropolitan planning. And indeed they may even be traditional answers. Thus we are faced with one set of paradoxes: that in the worst recession since the 1930s, following a series of energy crises, people continue *en masse* to desert the cities for the suburbs, and to abandon public transport for the private car. There is a conflict, it seems, between the long-term perceptions of the planners and other urban analysts, and the immediate desires and aspirations of ordinary people. Yet perhaps it is possible to square the planning

9.3 *Social City*. Ebenezer Howard's master plan for a polycentric garden city complex, produced in 1898 before the motorcar became a factor in urban form. It proves remarkably adaptable both to high-mobility and low-mobility conditions.

circle – by returning to the basic concepts of that pioneer of planning theory, Ebenezer Howard. Writing in 1898, without realisation of the change the motor car would bring to urban form, Howard set forth the notion of Social City: a planned cluster of small cities, each with a mere 30,000 people, that would grow naturally as population increased, to any size that might be needed (map 9.3). Within each small garden city, any inhabitant would find within walking distance a certain range of jobs and services; if he needed a wider range, then he could travel easily and rapidly to other towns in the cluster, or to a larger central city. To this end, Howard suggested that we would today call a rapid transit system, connecting each of the towns in the cluster. Something like this is what the Germans now propose for their Ruhrgebiet, or the Dutch for their Randstad. It is a form that hedges bets for the future: it permits personal mobility so long as that is easily and cheaply available, but provides facilities close at hand should it become scarce. In many ways, Howard's great intuitive notion may be more appropriate for the last quarter of the twentieth century than it was when he wrote at the end of the nineteenth.

Again, we face a classic conflict between the loss of economic activities and people to the suburbs – or exurbs – and the resulting crisis of the central city. Yet it should be possible to resolve this – as Lewis Mumford and others were already arguing in the 1930s – by regional planning and regional government. In other words, interrelated movements and interrelated problems need to be handled within the same unit of administration. Admittedly, that solution will not seem immediately advantageous or desirable to the inhabitants of the more affluent suburban and exurban communities; they may not see the point of sharing in the problems of the central city, which many of them have fled. But the alternative – as American and European experience now clearly shows – must be more and more interference and redistribution from the distant centre, as government desperately tries to hold the balance between suburban apathy and urban crisis. In the not-so-long run, no government in an advanced industrial country can face a real threat of collapse of a London, a Paris, a New York: the result would be a loss of confidence in the entire market system, and national economic collapse. The central city may be destined slowly to decline, but it must be permitted to do so gracefully.

Bibliography

1 The metropolitan explosion

On population growth, the viewpoint of experts in the 1930s is set out in Alexander Carr-Saunders, *World Population: Past Growth and Present Trends*, Oxford, 1936. A good modern textbook on population is William Petersen, *Population*, New York, 1961. Shorter texts on population geography include John I. Clarke, *Population Geography*, Oxford, 1968; M.G.A. Wilson, *Population Geography*, Melbourne, 1968, and Wilbur Zelinsky, *A Prologue to Population Geography*, Englewood Cliffs, New Jersey, 1966. Important works by French demographers, which analyse world patterns of population growth, are Alfred Sauvy, *Fertility and Survival*, London, 1961; Sauvy, *General Theory of Population*, London, 1969; Pierre George, *Questions de géographie de la Population*, Institut national d'études démographiques, Cahier No. 34, Paris, 1959; and Germaine Veyret-Verner, *Population: Mouvements, Structures, Répartition*, Paris, 1959.

Adna Ferrin Weber's *The Growth of Cities in the Nineteenth Century* has been republished as one of Cornell Reprints in Urban Studies, Ithaca, 1963. Comparative figures of populations or urban areas are found in United Nations (Statistical Office of the Department of Economic and Social Affairs), *Demographic Yearbook*, 12, New York, 1960. Definitions of international metropolitan areas, with their 1955 estimated populations, are in International Urban Research (Director, Kingsley Davis), *The World's Metropolitan Areas*, Berkeley and Los Angeles, 1959. On this basis, the growth of metropolitan areas has been analysed by Jack F. Gibbs and Leo F. Schnore in 'Metropolitan Growth: An International Study', *The American Journal of Sociology*, 66, 160–70, Chicago, 1960. Updated analyses are Kingsley Davis, *World Urbanization 1950–1970*, Vol. 1 *Basic Data for Cities, Countries and Regions*, Berkeley, 1969, and Richard L. Forstall and Victor Jones, 'Selected Demographic, Economic and Governmental Aspects of the World's Major Metropolitan Areas', in Simon Miles (ed.) *Metropolitan Problems*, Toronto, 1970.

On the palaeotechnic and neotechnic eras, Patrick Geddes, *Cities in Evolution*, London, 1915; Lewis Mumford, *Technics and Civilization*, New

York and London, 1932, and *The Culture of Cities*, New York and London, 1938; Jean-François Gravier, *Paris et le désert français*, Paris, 1947, 1958, *Mise en valeur de la France*, Paris, 1948.

On the changes in economic organisation during the nineteenth century, important sources are: J.A.Hobson, *The Evolution of Modern Capitalism*, London, 1894, 1926; Thorstein Veblen, *The Theory of Business Enterprise*, New York, 1904; Werner Sombart, *Der moderne Kapitalismus*, München, Leipzig, 1916–27, Band 3; T.C.Cochran and W.Miller, *The Age of Enterprise: A Social History of Industrial America*, New York, 1942. R.M.Haig's analysis is 'Toward an Understanding of the Metropolis', *Quarterly Journal of Economics*, 40, 179–208, 402–34, Cambridge, Mass., 1925.

Good general comparative introductions to urban problems include: William A.Robson and D.E.Regan, *Great Cities of the World*, London, 1972; Brian J.L.Berry, *The Human Consequences of Urbanization*, London, 1973; Lloyd Rodwin, *Nations and Cities*, Boston, 1970; L.S.Bourne, *Urban Systems: Strategies for Regulation*, Oxford, 1975; and H.Wentworth Eldredge, *Taming Megalopolis*, 2 Vols., New York, 1967.

2 London

The physical development of London is described in J.T.Coppock and Hugh Prince (edd.), *Greater London*, London, 1964, especially chapters 3–6 inclusive. S.E.Rasmussen, *London the Unique City*, London, 1934, 1937, Harmondsworth, 1960, first distinguished the unique form of London's development. Peter Hall, *London 2000*, London, 1963, examines the planning problems of London in detail and argues that further growth is inevitable. Useful recent guides to London planning include Peter Hall, *Urban and Regional Planning*, Harmondsworth, 1975, Chapter 7, and John M.Hall, *London: Metropolis and Region*, Oxford, 1976. *The South East Study 1961–1981*, London, Stationary Office, 1964, outlined the government's suggested strategy for the whole region including London on the basis of continued growth. The *Greater London Development Plan* (GLDP) consists essentially of the *Statement*, the *Report of Studies*, and *Movement in London*, all London 1969, plus many supplementary reports. *Tomorrow's London*, London 1970, is a popular official exposition. *London under Stress*, London 1970, and *Region in Crisis: An independent view of the GLDP*, London, 1971, are independent analyses by the Town and Country Planning Association; Judy Hillman (ed.) *Planning for London*, London 1971, offers further independent views. The *Greater London Development Plan Report of the Panel of Inquiry*, London 1973, gives a definitive verdict on the plan. Greater London Council, *Modified Greater London Development Plan*, London, 1975, is the end-result.

The *Strategic Plan for the South East*, London, 1970, is accompanied by five supplementary reports, London, 1971, with detailed statistical analyses. It is updated by *Strategy for the South East: 1976 Review*, London, Stationery Office, 1976.

On office decentralisation, see P.Cowan, *The Office: A Facet of Urban Growth*, London, 1969, and the review by R.K.Hall, 'The Movement of Offices from Central London', *Regional Studies*, 6, 385–392, 1972. For factory decentralisation, cf. D.E.Keeble and D.P.Hauser, 'Spatial Analysis of Manufacturing Growth in South-East England, 1960–1967', *Regional Studies*, 5, 229–262, 1971, and 6, 11–36, 1972. D.E.C.Eversley, 'Rising Costs and Static Incomes: some Economic Consequences of Regional Planning in London', *Urban Studies*, 9, 347–369, 1972, is a challenging analysis of some of the consequences; G.Lomas, *The Inner City*, London, 1975, and Department of the Environment, *Inner City Studies: Liverpool, Birmingham and Lambeth*, London, Stationery Office, 1977, take the analysis further.

The most comprehensive review of London's social planning problems is D.Donnison and D.Eversley (ed.) *London: Urban Patterns, Problems, and Policies*, London, 1973.

3 Paris

The best introductions to an understanding of Paris are historical and geographical. Pierre Lavedan's *Histoire de Paris* (new edition, Paris, 1960) deserves to become a classic. For the recent period it can usefully be supplemented by the same author's *Histoire de l'Urbanisme: Époque Contemporaine*, Paris, 1952, and D.H.Pinkney's *Napoleon III and the Rebuilding of Paris*, Princeton, 1958. The standard introduction in geography is Pierre George and Pierre Randet's *La Région parisienne*, Paris, 1959; for the morphology of Paris, see also the early introductory chapters of P.-H. Chombart de Lauwe (and others), *Paris et l'Agglomération Parisienne*, 2 vols., Paris, 1952. An important set of essays on economic and social topics is *Paris 1960* (Edité à l'occasion du centenaire de la Société de Statistique de Paris), Paris, 1961. Good recent British texts are: I.B.Thompson, *The Paris Basin*, Oxford, 1973, and Hugh Clout, *The Geography of Postwar France*, Oxford, 1972.

Two useful general accounts of French planning are Niles M.Hansen, *French Regional Planning*, Edinburgh, 1968, and Lloyd Rodwin, *Nations and Cities*, Boston, 1970, chapter 6.

J.-F.Gravier's *Paris et le désert français* was first published in Paris in 1947; a fully-revised edition was issued in Paris in 1958. The Paris Regional Plan, *Plan d'Aménagement et d'Organisation Générale de la Région Parisienne*, was published by the Ministère de la Construction in 1960. An important analysis and criticism of the PADOG plan is contained in G.Pilliet, *L'Avenir de Paris*, Paris, 1961. The 'Livre Blanc' on the future of the Paris region is called *Avant-Projet de Programme Duodécennal pour la Région de Paris*; it was issued by the Premier Ministre: Délégation Générale au District de la Région de Paris, and published by the Imprimerie Municipale, Hôtel de Ville, Paris, in 1963. The revised 1965 plan, *Schéma Directeur d'Aménagement et d'Urbanisme de la Région Parisienne*, Paris, 1965, is a very important document.

The series published by the Institut d'Aménagement de la Region Parisienne, *Cahiers de l'Aménagement de la Région Parisienne*, contains many useful analyses, e.g. No. 6, 1966, on housing, No. 16, 1969, on seven years' progress in the region, No. 21, 1970, on new urban developments, No. 26, 1972 and No. 28, 1972, on transport, and No. 32, 1973, on offices. These may be supplemented by *Aspects Statistiques de la Région Parisienne* (published by the INSEE Paris division); No. 10, 1972, contains a useful analysis by Nicole Guignon on commuting patterns in 1968.

Much data from the 1962 Census, not yet completely outdated, is mapped in the monumental *Atlas de la Région Parisienne*, Paris, 1967.

Also useful is a series by geographers on Paris, published in the official *La Documentation Française*: Merlin on transport (Nos. 3517–18, 1968), Bastié on industry (Nos. 3690–1, 1970) and Beaujeu-Garnier on the future (Nos. 4142–3, 1974).

4 Randstad Holland

The early history of the Randstad cities is well written up in the introduction to Baedeker's *Benelux*, Stuttgart, 1958, both in the introduction by Th. Kraus and in the notes on cities; by H. van Werveke, 'The Rise of the Towns', in *Cambridge Economic History of Europe*, vol. III, chapter 1, Cambridge, 1963; and in the Supplementary Notes (*Toelichting*) to the report *De ontwikkeling van het westen des lands* (see below). Two books of especial interest and importance are by Gerald L. Burke, *The Making of Dutch Towns*, London, 1956, and *Greenheart Metropolis*, London, 1966. G. R. P. Lawrence, *Randstad Holland*, Oxford, 1973, is a useful introduction.

On the historical development of the three major cities, their economic and social structure and postwar planning problems, reference should be made to Pierre George, 'La Haye–Rotterdam–Amsterdam', *Comité des Travaux Historiques et Scientifiques, Bulletin de la Section de Géographie*, 73, 45–142, Paris, 1960.

The official reports on the regional planning problems of the Netherlands are published by the Government Physical Planning Service (*Rijksdienst voor het nationale plan*) in The Hague. The first important official report to deal with the prolem was *De verspreiding van de Bevolking in Nederland* (with English summary and maps), Publication No. 3 of the *Rijksdienst*, 1949. *Het Westen en overig Nederland*, Publication No. 11 of the *Rijksdienst*, 1956, was a policy report on the broad regional problem which suggested that the net migration between the west and the remainder of the country should be reduced to zero. The most important detailed report on the future of the west is *De ontwikkeling van het westen des lands*, in two volumes (1. *rapport*; 2. *toelichting*), 1958. This laid down the basic principles for planning the Randstad. Its themes were taken up and developed in the *Nota inzake de ruimtelijke ordening in Nederland*, 1960, which has been translated in full into German (*Der Regierungsbericht über die Raumordnung in den Niederlanden*, Materialien zur Landesplanung V, Institut für Raumforschung, Bad Godesberg, 1961), and in a condensed form into English (*Report on Physical Planning in the Netherlands*) and French. The *Second Report on Physical Planning in the Netherlands*, The Hague, 1966, was a condensed English language version in 2 volumes: I. Main outline of *National Physical Planning Policies* and II. *Future Pattern of Development*. The *Third Report* appeared in two parts, both summarised in English: the *Orientation Report* (Orienteringsnota), The Hague, 1973, and the *Report On Urbanisation* (Verstedelikkingsnota), The Hague, 1976.

For current developments, the annual report (*Jaarverstag*) of the Government Physical Planning Service is invaluable. It can be supplemented for English readers by the special issue of the *Tijdschrift voor economische en sociale geografie*, 51, No. 7, Rotterdam, 1960, on the contemporary Netherlands, with articles by J. Winsemius on 'Randstad Holland' (188–99), by Ch. A. P. Takes and A. J. Venstra on 'Zuyder Zee reclamation' (162–7), and by Suzanne E. Steigenga-Kouwe on 'The Delta Plan' (167–75), Another important article in English in the *Tijdschrift*, on industrial development, is by W. L. Lakerveld, 'The Netherlands' struggle in an industrialising world', *TESG*, 53, 113–119, 1962. A further special issue of the *Tijdschrift*, published in 1972, contains a series of articles on contemporary planning problems in Randstad and Polders, especially W. Steigenga, 'Randstad Holland: Concept in Evolution', *TESG*, 63, 149–161, 1972, and A. K. Constandse, 'The IJsselmeerpolders, an old project with new functions', *ibid.*, 200–210.

5 Rhine–Ruhr

The Rhine–Ruhr agglomeration was defined by Gerhard Isenberg in his work on the urban agglomerations of the Federal Republic, *Die Ballungsgebiete in der Bundersrepublik*, Institut für Raumforschung, Vorträge, 6, Bad Godesberg, 1957. Subsequently, cf. K. Schliebe and Hans-Dieter Teske 'Verdichtungsräume: eine Gebiets-Kategorie der Raumordnung', *Geographische Rundschau*, 22, 347–352, Braunschweig, 1970, and *ibid.*, 'Verdichtungsräume in West- und Mitteldeutschland', *Raumforschung und Raumordnung*, 27, 147–156, Cologne, 1969.

Important books on the historical development and present form of the region and some of its chief cities include: Hans Spethmann, *Das Ruhrgebiet*, 3 vols., Berlin, 1933–8; Baedeker's *Ruhrgebiet*, Freiburg, 1959; N. J. G. Pounds, *The Ruhr*, London, 1952; P. Wiel, *Das Ruhrgebiet in*

Vergangenheit und Gegenwart, Essen, 1963; H.Spethmann, 'Die Ruhrstadt', and Th.Kraus, 'Köln', *Die Erde*, 6, 61–5 and 96–111, Berlin, 1954; D.Weis, *Die Grosstadt Essen*, Bonner Geographische Abhandlungen, 7, Bonn, 1951; I.Vogel, *Bottrop: Eine Bergbaustadt in der Emscherzone des Ruhrgebiets*, Forschungen zur deutschen Landeskunde, 114, Remagen, 1959, and K.Kayser and Th.Kraus (edd.), *Köln und die Rheinlande*, Wiesbaden, 1961. For detailed analysis of changes in land use in the Ruhr, see the research paper by F.Meier, *Die Änderung der Bodennutzung und des Grundeigentums im Ruhrgebiet von 1820 bis 1955*, Forschungen zur deutschen Landeskunde, 131, Bad Godesberg, 1961.

The most important sources for regional planning in the Ruhr are the development plan, *Siedlungsverband Ruhrkohlenbezirk; Gebietsentwicklungsplan*, Essen, 1966, and the official Atlas, *Siedlungsverband Ruhrkohlenbezirk, Regionalplanung*, Essen, 1961. The *Gebietsentwicklungsplan* is No. 5 of the *Schriftenreihe* of the Siedlungsverband Ruhrkohlenbezirk (SVR) which contains many other useful volumes, especially: No. 11 *Generalverkehrsplan Ruhrgebiet*, 1968, No. 28, *Siedlungsschwerpunkte im Ruhrgebiet*, 1968; No. 29, *SVR 1920–1970*, 1970; No. 30, *Sanierung in Regionalen Grünflachen des Ruhrgebiets*, 1970; No. 33, *SVR Bericht 1965–1969*, 1970, and No. 37, *Siedlungsschwerpunkte im Ruhrgebiet – Untersucken zum Schnellbahn-system*, 1970. For a useful review article, see S.Froriep, 'Der Siedlungsverband Ruhrkohlenbezirk – sein Werden und Wirken 1920–1970', *Raumforschung und Raumordnung*, 28, 51–61, Cologne, 1970. The SVR publication *The Ruhr: Plans, Programs, Projects*, Essen, 1972, is a very useful popular review (also available in German and French).

For the Rhine portion of the Rhine–Ruhr region, see the annual reports of the *Landesplanungsgemeinschaft Rheinland*, especially the paper by Gerhard Isenberg, *Rheinische Stadtlandschaft: Struktur und Entwicklung*, Düsseldorf, 1962.

The economic problems and future of the Ruhr coalfield are treated in the official report by the *Land* government of Nordrhein–Westfalen: *Grundlagen zur Strukturverbesserung der Steinkohlenbergbaugebiete in Nordrhein–Westfalen*, vol. 1. *Ruhrgebiet*, Schriftenreihe des Ministers für Landesplanung, Wohnungsbau und öffentliche Arbeiten des Landes Nordrhein–Westfalen, 19, Düsseldorf, 1964, and in the *Entwicklungsprogramm Ruhr 1970–1973*, issued by the Ministerium für Wirtschaft, Mittelstand und Verkehr des Landes Nordrhein-Westfalen, Düsseldorf, 1970.

For traffic planning, see *Auswertungsbericht der Sachverständigen Kommission zum Generalverkehrsplan Nordrhein-Westfalen*, Düsseldorf, 1968.

The periodical *Informationen* contains regular news notes and longer analyses of developments in planning within the Rhine–Ruhr area and the

Federal Republic generally. J.A.Hellen, *North Rhine Westphalia*, Oxford, 1974, is a useful general introduction.

6 Moscow

Useful books and articles on Soviet city planning, by British and American authors, include: Maurice F.Parkins, *City Planning in Soviet Russia, with an interpretative bibliography*, Chicago, 1953, and 'Housing behind the Iron Curtain', *Journal of Housing*, 16, 126–30 and 136, Chicago, 1959; H.Myles Wright, 'A visit to Russia', *Town Planning Review*, 29, 162–78, Liverpool, 1958; R.J.Osborn and T.A.Reiner, 'Soviet City Planning: Current Issues and Future Perspectives', *Journal of the American Institute of Planners*, 28, 239–50, Baltimore, 1962; B.Michael Frolic, 'The Soviet City', *Town Planning Review*, 34, 285–306, with a full bibliography, Liverpool, 1963–4. F.E.Ian Hamilton, *The Moscow City Region*, Oxford, 1976, and G.Lappo, A.Chikishev and A.Bekker, *Moscow, Capital of the Soviet Union: a Short Geographical Survey*, Moscow, 1976. Many important Soviet academic articles about cities and regional development appear in translation. Particularly important is *Soviet Geography* (*SG*), published ten times a year in New York, with the following translations from the volume *Goroda-Sputniki*, V.G.Davidovich and B.S.Khorev (edd.), Moscow, 1961: V.G.Davidovich, 'Satellite Cities and Towns of the U.S.S.R.', *SG*, 3, No. 3, 3–35, 1962; and G.Ye.Mishchenko, 'Satellite cities and towns of Moscow', *ibid.*, 35–43. The periodical also contains useful news notes on recent events in the Soviet Union, notably: 'Preliminary results of the 1970 Soviet Census', *SG*, 11, No. 7, 580–595, 1970, and 'Population of Moscow City and Moscow Oblast in 1970 Census', *SG*, 12, No. 7, 453–457, 1971.

Soviet articles on the population geography of the USSR include: O.A.Konstantinov, 'Some conclusions about the geography of cities and the urban population of the USSR based on the results of the 1959 Census', *SG*, 1, No. 7, 59–74, 1960, and V.N.Starovsky, 'On methods of predicting the growth of the population of the Soviet Union', *Current Digest of the Soviet Press*, 12, No. 14, 9–11 and 39, Washington, 1960.

The most useful source of all for current Soviet planning is the *Current Digest of the Soviet Press*, Washington (weekly), which reprints important articles from *Pravda* and *Izvestia* verbatim or in summary, as well as articles of general economic interest from academic journals. Much of the information in this chapter has come from this source. Two sources of special value for Soviet planning are the collections of translations from Soviet authorities published in *Récherches Internationales à la Lumière du Marxisme*, vols. 20–21, 208–29, Paris, 1960, including an article on Kryukovo by G.Dukelski, 'Les premières microrayons de la première Ville satellite', pages 237–45; and in the *Soviet Review*, vol. 2, No. 4, New York, 1961, with an article by A.Zhuravlyev and M.B.Fyedorov, 'The Micro-

District and new living Conditions', pages 37–40. S. Strumilin's description of Soviet society under full communism, 'Family and Community in the Society of the Future', is translated in *Soviet Review*, 2, No. 2, 3–29, 1961. An exceptionally useful review of Soviet thinking on new towns, especially around Moscow, is *Urbanisme et Villes Nouvelles en Union Sovietique*, Cahiers de l'IAURP, 38, 1975.

7 New York

No chapter on the New York region could fail to draw heavily upon the publications of the Regional Plan Association of New York. An essential basis for all study of the contemporary New York region is the *New York Metropolitan Region Study* (Raymond Vernon, director), carried out for the Regional Plan Association by the Graduate School of Public Administration, Harvard University, between 1956 and 1961. It is published in nine volumes, all published in Cambridge, Mass.: *Anatomy of a Metropolis*, 1959, by Edgar Hoover and Raymond Vernon; *Made in New York*, 1959, by Roy B. Helfgott, W. Eric Gustafson, and James M. Hund; *The Newcomers*, 1959, by Oscar Handlin; *Wages in the Metropolis*, 1960, by Martin Segal; *Money Metropolis*, 1960, by Sidney M. Robbins and Nestor E. Terleckyj, with the collaboration of Ira O. Scott, Jr.; *Freight and the Metropolis*, 1960, by Benjamin Chinitz; *One-Tenth of a Nation*, 1960, by Robert M. Lichtenberg, with supplements by Edgar M. Hoover and Louise P. Lerday; *1,400 Governments*, 1961, by Robert C. Wood, with Vladimir V. Almendinger; and *Metropolis 1985*, 1960, by Raymond Vernon. The economic projection to 1958, *Projection of a Metropolis*, 1960, by Barbara R. Berman, Benjamin Chinitz and Edgar M. Hoover, was published as a techical supplement. M. Ostow and A. B. Dutka, *Work and Welfare in New York City*, Baltimore, 1975, is a useful recent account.

Other important sources from the Regional Plan Association are *Goals for the Region Project*, New York, 1963, a series of five booklets summarising present trends and planning choices; *Hub-Bound Travel in the Tri-State New York Metropolitan Region*, Bulletin No. 99, New York, 1961; *Spread City: Projections of Development Trends and the Issues they pose: the Tri-State New York Metropolitan Region, 1960–1985*, Bulletin No. 100, New York, 1962; *The Region's Growth*, New York, 1967; *Jamaica Center*, New York, 1968; *The Second Regional Plan: A Draft for Discussion*, New York, 1969; *Urban Design Manhattan*, New York, 1969; *The Office Industry*, New York, 1972 and *The State of the Region*, New York, 1975.

These should be supplemented by the massive five-volume Plan for New York City by the City Planning Commission, New York, 1969, which is usefully summarised in *Plan for New York City 1969: A Proposal*, New York, 1969; and by the important review by the First National City Bank (introduced by Nathan Glazer), *Profile of a City*, New York, 1972.

The Tri-State Transportation Commission have published a series of major reports including *An Interim Plan*, New York, 1966. *Regional Development Alternatives*, New York, 1967, *Measure of a Region*, New York, 1967, and *Regional Forecast 1985*, New York, 1967.

On transportation planning an important source is: Port of New York Authority, Comprehensive Planning Office, *Metropolitan Transportation 1980: A Framework for the long-range planning of transportation facilities to serve the New York–New Jersey Metropolitan Region*, New York, 1963.

On government, Victor Jones, 'Local Government Organisation in Metropolitan Areas: its relation to Urban Redevelopment', in Coleman Woodbury (ed.), *The Future of Cities and Urban Redevelopment*, Chicago, 1953, and Luther Gulick, *Metro: Changing Problems and Lines of Attack*, Government Affairs Institute, Washington DC, 1957.

A useful historical account of New York is Alan Nevins and John A. Krout (edd.), *The Greater City: New York, 1898–1948*, New York, 1948.

For the concept of Megalopolis, see Jean Gottmann, *Megalopolis: The urbanized northeastern seaboard of the United States*, Twentieth Century Fund, New York, 1961. Chapter 8 on urban land uses is especially pertinent, as also chapters 9–12 on the economy. It should be supplemented by Irene B. and Conrad Taeuber, 'The Great Concentration: S.M.S.A.'s from Boston to Washington', *Population Index*, 30, 3–29, Princeton, 1964, Regional Plan Association, *The Region's Growth* (above), and Marion Clawson, *Suburban Land Conversion in the United States: An Economic and Governmental Process*, Baltimore, 1971.

On the New York City fiscal crisis, see Congressional Budget Office, 'The Causes of New York's Fiscal Crisis', *Political Science Quarterly*, 90, 1974, and the special issues of the journals *Dissent* (23/1 of 1975, with articles by Bensman and Muchnick), *Society* (13/4 of 1976, with articles by Fainstein and Fainstein, Sternlieb and Hughes, and Gerad and Starr) and *Liberation* (19/8 and 9, 1976, with contributions from Zevin, Charlop and Piven).

8 Tokyo

The economic development of Japan from early times up to 1960 is comprehensively treated by G.C.Allen, *A Short Economic History of Modern Japan*, revised edition, London, 1962. For the modern period it may be usefully supplemented by Maurice Moreau, *L'Economie du Japon*, Paris, 1959, and by P.Schöller, 'Wandlungen der Industriestruktur Japans', in W.Hartke and F.Wilhelm (edd.), *Deutscher Geographentag Köln 1961: Tagungsbericht und Wissenschaftliche Abhandlungen*, Wiesbaden, 1961. Basic geographical accounts are: Ryuziro Isida, *Geography of Japan*, Tokyo, 1961; Shinzo Kiuchi, *A Brief Survey of Japanese Geography*, Tokyo, 1964; Teizo Murata and Shinzo Kiuchi (edd.), *Reconnaissance Geography of Tokyo*, Tokyo, 1957; and Shinzo Kiuchi, 'Tokio als Weltstadt', in Joachim

H. Schultze (ed.), *Zum Problem der Weltstadt* (Festschrift zum 32. Deutschen Geographentag in Berlin 1959), pages 112–26, Berlin, 1959. On current planning problems, there are three important information pamphlets by the Tokyo Metropolitan Government: *An Administrative Perspective of Tokyo* (revised annually); *City Planning, Tokyo*, 1962; and *An Outline of the Ten-year Plan for Government of Tokyo*, 1963. More recently the excellent *Tokyo Municipal Library* of the TMG has included No. 4 on *Pollution* (1971), No. 5 on *Housing* (1972), No. 6 on *Renewal* (1972), No. 7 on *Finance* (1972), No. 9 on *Social Welfare* (1974), No. 11 on *New Revenue Sources* (1976) and No. 12 on *Land* (1976). Important recent official reports include: *Report on Tokyo Metropolitan Government* by Professor William A. Robson, Tokyo, 1967, and *Second Report on Tokyo Metropolitan Government*, by Professor William A. Robson, Tokyo, 1969; *Master Plan for the National Capital Region*, by the National Capital Planning Region Development Corporation, Tokyo, 1966; *Sizing up Tokyo: A report on Tokyo under the Administration of Governor Ryokichi Minobi*, Tokyo, 1969 and TMG, *Planning of Tokyo 1975*, Tokyo, 1975. The monthly *Tokyo Municipal News*, from the TMG, is another rich information source in English. The most important single source for 1960s planning problems is a series of ten articles by Gyo Hani, 'The City in Crisis', *Japan Times*, Tokyo, 4, 5, 9, 10, 12, 14, 16, 17, 19 and 23 March 1962. Some material from these articles is quoted in a useful summary of the problems, by John Barr, 'Chaos in Tokyo', *New Society*, 1, No. 15, 12–15, London, 1962–3. Also very useful is City Planning Association of Japan, *Giant City: Tokyo*, Tokyo, 1963.

9 The future metropolis

On the growth of the suburbs, particularly clear evidence is available from the United States: Donald J. Bogue, 'Urbanism in the United States, 1950', *American Journal of Sociology*, 60, 471–86, Chicago, 1954–5; Amos K. Hawley, *The Changing Shape of Metropolitan America: Deconcentration since 1920*, Glencoe, 1956; and G. A. Wissink, *American Cities in Perspective: with Special Reference to the Development of their Fringe Areas*, Assen, Netherlands, 1962, with a comprehensive bibliography. International statistics are assembled in International Urban Research (Director, Kingsley Davis), *The World's Metropolitan Areas*, Berkeley and Los Angeles, 1959. The relation between transportation techniques and city growth is documented in Harlan W. Gilmore, *Transportation and the Growth of Cities*, Glencoe, 1953 and Colin Clark, 'Transport – Maker and Breaker of Cities', *Town Planning Review*, 28, 237–50, Liverpool, 1957–8. For the functions of the central city, see Robert M. Haig, 'Toward an Understanding of the Metropolis', *Quarterly Journal of Economics*, 40, 179–208 and 402–34, Cambridge, Mass., 1925–6'; P. Sargant Florence, 'Economic efficiency in the metropolis', in R. M. Fisher (ed.), *The Metropolis in Modern Life*, pages

85–124, New York, 1955; Raymond Vernon, 'Production and Distribution in the large Metropolis', *Annals of the American Academy of Political and Social Science*, 314 15–29, Philadelphia, 1957, *The Changing Economic Function of the Central City*, Committee for Economic Development, New York, 1961, and Peter Cowan et al, *The Office: A Facet of Urban Growth*, London, 1969. For the role of communications see Richard L. Meier, *A Communications Theory of Urban Growth*, Cambridge, Mass., 1962; Aaron Fleischer, 'The Influence of Technology on Urban Forms', *Daedalus*, 90, 48–60, Cambridge, Mass., 1961; Karl W. Deutsch, 'On social Communication and the Metropolis', *ibid.*, 99–100; Bertil Thorngren, 'How do contact systems affect regional development?', *Environment and Planning*, 2, 409–429, 1970; John Goddard, *Office Linkages and Location: a Study of Communications and Spatial Patterns in Central London*, Oxford, 1973, and Alex Reid, 'What Telecommunication Implies', *New Society*, 1284–1286, 1971. For theories of future development: Kevin Lynch, 'The Pattern of the Metropolis', *ibid.*, 79–98; Melvin M. Webber, 'Order in Diversity: Community without Propinquity', in Lowdon Wingo, Jr. (ed.), *Cities and Space: The Future Use of Urban Land*, Resources for the Future, pages 23–54, Baltimore, 1963; and 'The Urban Place and the Nonplace Urban Realm', in Webber, *et al., Explorations into Urban Structure*, pages 79–153, Philadelphia, 1964. For the 'concentric' theory of urban growth, see Ernest W. Burgess, 'The Growth of the City: an Introduction to a Research Project', in Robert E. Park, Ernest W. Burgess and Roderick D. McKenzie, *The City*, pages 47–62, Chicago, 1925; for the 'sector' theory, see Homer Hoyt, *The Structure and Growth of residential Neighbourhoods in American Cities*, Washington, 1939. On the role of models, see Britton Harris, 'Some Problems in the Theory of Intra-urban-Location', *Operations Research*, 9, 695–721, Baltimore, 1961. Ursula Hicks, *The Large City: A World Problem*, London 1970, is a useful comparative introduction to urban fiscal problems.

Index

Catalog

If you are interested in a list of fine Paperback
books, covering a wide range of subjects
and interests, send your name and address,
requesting your free catalog, to:

McGraw-Hill Paperbacks
1221 Avenue of Americas
New York, N.Y. 10020